Praise for

THE CULT OF THE LUXURY BRAND

"In this superb book, through a series of case studies and insightful analyses, Chadha and Husband highlight new marketing tools that companies are successfully implementing to create and build the luxury cult. This is a must-read book for executives who want to build their luxury brands in the booming Asian markets."
Sunil Gupta, Professor of Marketing, Harvard Business School

"Fascinating. Full of insight and vital source material for anyone interested in understanding modern Asians."
Miles Young, Chairman of Ogilvy & Mather Asia Pacific

"Painstakingly researched and easy to read, an amazing look inside the luxury brand trade."
Ambar Brahmachary, President of JWT Japan

"Excellent and timely. Chadha and Husband have got the story. It's 'hands-on', accessible, informative, professional and lively."
Dr Kaori O'Connor, University College London and author of The Way We Wear

"There is no other place in the world where luxury is the currency of power than Asia, where what you wear speaks volumes about who you are. Fascinating and informative, *The Cult of the Luxury Brand* is a must-read for anyone who is looking to enter the retail development market in Asia, an invaluable tool in understanding the psychology of the Asian consumer."
Bertrand Pellegrin, Marketing Director of Lane Crawford

THE CULT OF THE LUXURY BRAND

INSIDE ASIA'S LOVE AFFAIR
WITH LUXURY

Radha Chadha & Paul Husband

NICHOLAS BREALEY
PUBLISHING

London • Boston

To the best home team an author can hope for: My husband, Sanjeev, who commented on every draft; my son, Kabir, who pulled those pesky endnotes together; my daughter, Noor, who visualized diagrams and double-checked facts. This book is as much yours as mine.

Radha

To my wife Nancy whose interest and passion for the world's best brands made this such an enjoyable journey.

Paul

First published by
Nicholas Brealey International in 2006
Reprinted 2007 (three times), 2008, 2011

3–5 Spafield Street
Clerkenwell, London
EC1R 4QB, UK
Tel: +44 (0)20 7239 0360
Fax: +44 (0)20 7239 0370

20 Park Plaza, Suite 1115A
Boston
MA 02116, USA
Tel: (888) BREALEY
Fax: (617) 523 3708

www.nicholasbrealey.com
www.cultoftheluxurybrand.com

ISBN: 978-1-904838-05-0

British Library Cataloguing in Publication Data
A catalogue record for this book is available from the British Library.

Library of Congress Cataloging-in-Publication Data
Chadha, Radha.
        The cult of the luxury brand : inside Asia's love affair with luxury /
Radha Chadha & Paul Husband.
                p. cm.
        Includes index.
        ISBN-13: 978-1-904838-05-0
        ISBN-10: 1-904838-05-7
        1. Brand name products--Social aspects--Asia. 2. Luxuries--Social aspects.
3. Brand name products--Asia--Marketing. 4. Social status--Asia. 5. Social
classes--Asia. I. Husband, Paul. II. Title. III. Title: Inside Asia's love affair with luxury.
HD69.B7C467 2006
306.3'4--dc22

                                                                                                2006015486

Printed in India by Gopsons Papers Ltd., Noida.

CONTENTS

Luxury bag in hand, Asia's on the move!

INTRODUCTION: WEAR YOUR SUCCESS

"You never really understand a person until you consider things from his point of view... until you climb into his skin and walk around in it."

Harper Lee, To Kill a Mocking Bird[1]

You'd think it was a rock concert, not a store opening, the way thousands queue up days in advance to get a toe in on Day One at yet another mega-sized luxury brand store. When they've left, the store has been stripped clean, as if by locusts, with hardly a handbag, wallet, or key ring left on the shelves. Hermès in Ginza, Louis Vuitton in Omotesando, Coach in Shibuya, Prada in Aoyama – just put up a megastore in Tokyo and the queues start forming. Japan may have been in on–off recession for a decade, but Japanese consumers – like others in Asia – carry on their obsessive love affair with luxe. A staggering 94 percent of Tokyo women in their 20s own a Louis Vuitton piece. (Some own dozens, but that's another story.) Other brands don't do too badly either – 92 percent own Gucci, 57 percent own Prada, 51 percent own Chanel, and so the list goes on.[2] Welcome to luxury brands in twenty-first-century Asia.

This book is about the cult that is sweeping Asia, a phenomenon so powerful that the continent is now the biggest market in the world for Western luxury brands. It's about stepping into the skins of millions of Asians to understand why they are snapping up Louis Vuitton bags and Rolex watches and Armani suits as if their lives depended on it. It's about how a keen understanding of the Asian psyche has helped the luxury industry create this cult, which, needless to say, has proved immensely profitable. It's about invaluable business insights into how to make money and call the shots in a world where most other product categories face thinning margins and increasing retailer dominance.

So far the nerve center of this cult has been Japan, the Japanese people's passion for luxury brands so huge that they account for over 40 percent of worldwide sales for most major luxury brands. For Louis Vuitton, the undisputed leader of the cult, it's possibly a case of too much love – at one point an estimated 88 percent of Vuitton's global sales came from Japanese consumers (38 percent purchased in Japan, 50 percent bought by Japanese tourists),[3] forcing the company to aggressively grow other markets.

Now the rest of Asia is showing the same passion for brands. Hong Kong, South Korea, Taiwan, Singapore, Malaysia, Thailand – the cult is fast gathering momentum everywhere. China, just out of Mao suits, has rushed headlong into Zegna, Dunhill, and Burberry, displaying such a strong luxe tooth that Chinese consumers – shopping at home and abroad – already account for 10 percent of global luxury brand sales, a figure growing rapidly as we speak. Then there's the other billionaire, India, its full-throttle economy creating new money, its people awakening to luxury.

At first flush, this isn't an easy phenomenon to understand. Why are millions of Asians, not all of them rich, rushing to buy outrageously expensive designer-label bags, shoes, clothes, watches, jewelry, and other accessories? Why do they queue for hours outside stores in Paris, often putting up with humiliating treatment, all for the sake of a logo-splashed canvas bag? Why is it normal for Hong Kong people, whether wealthy tycoons or your average Joe, to own several expensive Swiss watches? Why do South Korean office ladies purchase Ferragamo shoes on installment plans? Why do junior executives in Shanghai happily shell out their entire month's salary for a Gucci purse? Why do some Japanese teenagers even sleep with middle-aged salarymen just to get money together for that all-essential luxe bag?

The answer lies in the massive changes – political, social, and above all economic – that have steadily transformed Asia, in the process dismantling centuries-old ways of denoting who you are and your place in society. From rigid social orders defined by birth, caste, family position, or profession, you suddenly have a free-for-all where how much money you have is the key classifying criterion. Never mind which social class you were born into, make enough money and you can climb up the ladder.

But how do you turn a sizable bank balance into commensurate social esteem? Into this situation of social flux walked Western luxury brands with their loud logos and unmistakable sign language, providing a handy tool for letting the world know your financial prowess. Carry a US$500 Louis Vuitton handbag and you signal that you are from a family of decent means. Flaunt a US$10,000 Hermès Birkin and you are clearly several notches higher. What is amazing is that many Asians of moderate means are simply spending their way up the social hierarchy, often in amounts totally out of whack with their real income.

In today's Asia you are what you *wear*. Those Gucci bags and Ferragamo shoes aren't merely girlish indulgences – neither are the Armani suits and Rolex watches just male vanity at work – they are part of a new social protocol where your identity and self-worth are determined by the visible brands on your body. A new luxury-brand-defined social order is replacing old ways of marking status. A different class system is being created where your spot on the social totem pole is marked by your Chanel suit and your Cartier watch. That's the central thesis of our book:

Luxury brands are a modern set of symbols that Asians are wearing to redefine their identity and social position.

This book is about how and why that came to be. Why a hard-working, essentially frugal people changed into liberal spenders. Why a proud, often fiercely nationalistic society happily submitted to the charms of Western brands. Why nation after Asian nation has followed the same inevitable path, eventually falling under the luxe spell.

A word about how we have defined luxury brands in this book. While everything from caviar to champagne, luxury spas to cruise liners, high-end condominiums to sports cars would qualify, we have limited ourselves to "luxury brands on your person." The reason is simple. A secretary with a Burberry purse isn't going to see the inside of a high-end condominium for quite some time, neither is she hankering after luxurious spa treatments – but sure as night follows day, she is going to buy another designer-label bag, shoe, or watch next season. Large homes with private swimming pools aren't an option even for most millionaires in cramped Asian metropolises like Hong Kong, Tokyo, or Mumbai. Lavish holidays in exotic locations appeal only to a select few, most Asians preferring to go on group tours, often scrimping on hotel accommodation but spending liberally on luxe shopping. The face you show to the world counts more than how you live. The phenomenon that is sweeping Asia isn't one of luxurious living – although that too will come in time – it is one of wearing luxury brands on your person. When we say luxury brands, or simply luxe, we mean Louis Vuitton bags, Gucci shoes, Prada clothes, Tiffany jewelry, Cartier watches, and items from the umpteen other brands that occupy the luxury-on-your-person category.

This book is divided into three parts. Part One is about how and why the luxury brand cult took root and then exploded in Asia. We trace the spread of luxe from Europe, bringing what was once the preserve of the European upper crust into the enthusiastic hands of the mass market in Asia, in the process changing the very shape and structure of the industry. The rise of brands in Asia is of course linked to the rise of Asia itself, and we develop a powerful conceptual framework – the five-stage Spread of Luxury model – that explains the cult in developed Asian markets like Japan and Hong Kong, and predicts the course that emerging powerhouses like China and India will take.

Part Two takes you straight into the key luxury markets – Japan, Hong Kong, South Korea, China, India, Singapore, and the other Southeast Asian countries – which serve as case studies to illustrate the phenomenon at close quarters. We analyze the cultural forces that shaped the development of the luxe habit in these markets; visit the thriving retail scene, from glorious flagship stores in Tokyo to bustling local markets in Seoul; and meet distinct consumer segments, presenting their obsession with luxury brands and the inner motives that drive them.

Part Three takes you behind the scenes to examine how the luxury industry has created this cult. Our Luxeplosion model cracks the code, letting you in on the specialized *cult tools* and *cult catalysts* that are deployed in a heady cocktail of celebrities and parties, of high society and the media, of showbiz and buzz creation – a tried-and-tested approach to creating an explosive following for your brand, which will be of interest to businesses relying on traditional marketing levers. The luxe cult has spawned an unfortunate twin, fakes – we consider the phenomenon of "genuine fakes," impossible to tell from the original, which hit at the very root of the legitimate industry. We end the book with a look at five major future trends that will yet again reshape the market in the coming decade and take the cult of the luxury brand to the next level.

Luxury consumption in the West has been widely studied, from Thorstein Veblen's delightful 1899 classic *The Theory of the Leisure Class* to a more recent spate of titles like *Luxury Fever* and *Trading Up: The New American Luxury*. But when it comes to Asia, while there are news reports, magazine articles, and financial analysts' reports – a barrage of them, such is the interest level – beyond some academic papers there have been few structured attempts to study the subject from a sociological or business point of view. This is the *first* book on Asia's love affair with luxury brands, particularly apposite given the growing importance of the Asian consumer to the world economy.

We traveled to each of the Asian markets and conducted over 150 interviews with people who run businesses in the industry, from global heads of major luxury brands to country managers, from local marketing teams to salespeople at the stores. We talked to specialists who have been observing and participating in this phenomenon – fashion magazine editors, consumer behavior specialists, advertising agencies, research companies, equity research analysts. We observed consumers in action. We posed as shoppers ourselves, checking out the store experience and service standards in each country. We have drawn extensively on our collective professional experience in Asia – over 40 years between us – in consumer insights, marketing, and luxury retailing. And of course, we have often succumbed and shopped, just like the rest of Asia.

But finally, it was meeting ordinary consumers and climbing into their shoes that gave us our most significant insights, and the realization that behind each of those designer-clad luxe lovers was a story of personal struggle and triumph, of rising from a modest background to considerable financial means, and of quite literally wearing their success.

Luxury brands are a US$80-billion global industry. More than half that business already comes from Asians, and the way the cult is snowballing – and Asian incomes rising – luxe is in for some hearty growth. The cult of the luxury brand represents both an intriguing social reality and a profitable business phenomenon in the region. For anyone with an interest in luxury or premium brands – marketers, retailers, shopping center operators, educators, and most importantly consumers – pick up your Gucci and enjoy the ride!

PART ONE

HOW AND WHY

An example of the many elaborate luxury brand cathedrals springing up across Asia – the futuristic Prada Epicenter in Tokyo, with its distinctive diamond grid exterior and space-age interiors.

1
A LOVE AFFAIR WITH LUXE

"How come you don't have the muffler with checks, the one that the Premier wears?" The person asking the question is Jiang Zemin, until recently President of China, the Premier he refers to is none other than the man credited with reforming China's economy, the dynamic Zhu Rongji, and the checked piece of neck accessory in question is the rather contagious Burberry muffler, which also counts thousands of young Japanese women among its willing victims.

The setting of this true-life shopping drama is the Scitech department store in Beijing, not exactly a hot spot for luxury brands in the first place, and certainly not used to having presidents dropping by unannounced. Jiang reportedly makes it to the third-floor men's section unrecognized, before panic ensues and people realize that it's the President himself *sans* security entourage. The managing director of the store rushes down to meet Jiang, who is increasingly impatient to see the checked muffler he has heard so much about. Unfortunately, the store does not carry Burberry. No, heads don't roll, but the next day the local Burberry management is summoned for talks. Pick any spot you like, the department store offers, just put up a Burberry store as fast as possible. A videoconference is hurriedly arranged with chief executive Rosemary Bravo in London, who, tickled by the story, gives the go-ahead. An accessories corner is set up at a prime location in the store, and now Burberry mufflers are readily available, just in case President Jiang does one of his spot checks again.

From presidents to office ladies, from captains of industry to university students, from well-heeled socialites to housewives buying fish in the local wet markets – in Japan, even the fishmongers tuck away their cash receipts in Louis Vuitton bags – every section of society, every country in Asia, is falling under the spell of Western luxury brands. Stroll down the busy streets of Tokyo today, and a barrage of Louis Vuitton handbags come at you on the arms of middle-class women. Settle down for a drink at one of Shanghai's hip nightclubs, and pick out the Chanel, Dior, and Prada bags among the designer-clad crowd. Ride the subway in Seoul and most women are hanging firmly onto their Louis Vuittons and Guccis. Drop off your child at an upscale kindergarten in Hong Kong and a quick glance at the other mums should bring you up to date on this season's new arrivals. Meeting a government official in Beijing? Chances are the suit is Zegna, and that flash of gold beneath the sleeve is a Cartier watch.

It's hard to imagine that luxury brands were once the preserve of the European aristocracy, that a mere hundred years ago these beautifully crafted pieces of clothing and accessories were solely for the pleasure and adornment of a wealthy élite. Now famed luxury houses like Louis Vuitton, Hermès, Chanel, Cartier, and innumerable others serve the consumers of Asia, and, in a strange turn of events, it is the populous markets of this region that are central to their success. Asia has grown into the world's largest market for Western luxury brands, and between the brand-obsessed Japanese on the one hand and China and India's rising new money on the other, the present and future of luxe lie squarely in Asia.

How did the luxury brand culture spread from Europe's élite to Asia's *hoi polloi*? Fickle as fashion is, its business history contains enduring lessons for all marketers, explaining the strategies that changed small family businesses into highly profitable global empires. Importantly, it sheds light on something every marketer dreams of – the seeming paradox of charging high prices based on exclusivity while selling your product to every Tomoko, Sadako, and Yoshiko. The luxury brand industry has managed to do just that; in fact, the fine art of having your cake while eating it too is its core business philosophy today.

THE GENESIS

The forces that created Asia's cult of the luxury brand were set in motion around 100 years ago.

In the early 1900s, while the Belle Epoque unfolded in Europe[1] – a heady period of progress and prosperity, when wealth was shamelessly flaunted and elaborate women's dresses were a prime method of showing family status – a trickle of imported luxury products had already begun to flow into Asia, although they touched only a small wealthy élite. Japan had emerged from its long Edo-period isolation, and had begun trading with Britain and Europe, including jewelry and other luxury goods. A fine crystal vase by Baccarat was said to cost more than the average Japanese home of the time. Burberry set up shop in Tokyo in the 1920s through a local importing company.

In China, Shanghai was living its own version of the Belle Epoque as the Paris of the East in the giddy, hedonistic 1920s and 1930s. While high-society women stuck to the graceful cheongsam for public occasions, men wore fine French suits, and Swiss watches such as those made by Omega – which entered China in 1895 – were prized items.

Royal families in India had a natural affinity for European luxury brands, shopping on trips to London and Paris, or simply commissioning pieces from the likes of Vuitton and Cartier. The famed Patiala necklace was made by Jacques Cartier for the Maharaja of Patiala in 1928 – it's a showstopper with 2,930 diamonds totaling 1,000 carats, including the 234-carat De Beers diamond, the seventh largest in the world.

Then came the crunch in one way or another for all the Asian nations. The Second World War knocked the breath out of Japan. In newly independent India, it became more chic to wear *khadi* – a handspun cotton cloth sported by adherents of the freedom movement – than luxuries imported from Western countries. In Communist China, you risked your neck if you deviated from clearly laid-out style codes, and any expensive items your family might have possessed were confiscated. Independence struggles in Southeast Asia led to the Americans leaving the Philippines in 1946, the Dutch departing Indonesia in 1949, and the British quitting Malaysia and Singapore in the late 1950s,[2] but a combination of patriotism and poverty meant there was very little place for imported luxe. In many Asian countries protectionist policies limited trade, and the import of luxury items was punished with hefty taxes, if they were allowed in at all. Harsh postliberation economic realities meant that people toiled to rebuild their country and themselves; making ends meet and saving for their children's future were the

A century of world fashion as seen through the Chinese cheongsam

Even a century ago, Asia was taking its fashion cues from the West. Here we trace the impact of European designers and Hollywood divas on the cheongsam – the graceful, body-skimming Chinese dress with side slits – that evolved in tandem with international fashion trends. Shanghai, China's style capital in the first half of the twentieth century, dictated the look, passing the mantle on to Hong Kong after the Communists took over.

1920s – The cheongsam was slimmer, "the silhouette was slinkier, copying the bias cuts of Chanel; the sleeves got shorter, the slit higher. Hair was straight and bobbed, skin was pale and lips, red." Think Garçonne.

1930s – The cheongsam was ankle length, the feel was lighter, "sleeves were cut to reveal the underarm. Hair was permed, eyebrows drawn thin and arched like Greta Garbo's."

1940s – The cheongsam was worn with "jackets with padded shoulders and platform shoes like Joan Crawford's."

1950s – The body was "more structured, a Chinese hourglass," *à la* Christian Dior's New Look. "Hair was brushed into sleek rolls," strong eyebrows, smoldering eyes like Ava Gardner's.

1960s – The cheongsam was "shorter and more boxy," "patterns and prints were much bolder." Hair was "teased up" bird's-nest style. Think Yves Saint Laurent or Pierre Cardin.

1970s – The cheongsam was "paired as a tunic with bell bottoms." Psychedelic prints reflected the swinging seventies.

1980s – A "power cheongsam with a more padded shoulder." Very Giorgio Armani.

Today – The cheongsam disappears from daily life, only to be reincarnated as fashionable eveningwear by Chinese design houses such as Shanghai Tang.

Adapted from Hong Kong-born fashion designer Vivienne Tam's book *China Chic* (New York: ReganBooks, 2000, pp 270–74).

Photos courtesy of Valery Garrett, Kareem Jalal, Elizabeth Chung, and Shanghai Tang.

priorities. For all practical purposes, imported luxury brands went into hibernation in Asia for several decades, only slowly reappearing in the 1970s.

In the meantime, there was plenty of action on the couture front in Europe in the first half of the century, creating many of the fashion houses that Asia loves today. The elaborate dresses that had women trussed up in corsets gave way to more comfortable clothing thanks as much to the world wars – which forced women to work in practical out-fits – as to the imagination of designers like Coco Chanel, who pro-moted the Garçonne look. After the Second World War Christian Dior brought back the stars in women's eyes with his extravagant New Look, waists nipped in to create an hourglass figure. It was a time of dramatic upheavals in Europe – war, occupation, liberation, economic scarcity – but despite ups and downs, Paris retained its sense of style and remained the world's fashion capital, thanks to designers like Jeanne Lanvin and Pierre Balmain, who incidentally counted the Queen of Thailand among his loyal customers.[3]

The US, where the upper crust had relied on Paris for imported cou-ture, slowly started coming into its own with the emergence of local designers like Claire McCardell and Hattie Carnegie. Paris was still the mother ship – McCardell studied fashion there, Carnegie retailed French labels – but both were designing for American sensibilities. Wallis Simpson chose American-born designer Mainbocher, then based in Paris, to design her wedding dress. (Incidentally her husband, the ex-king of England, had his trousers tailored in New York, preferring the more advanced American-style belts and zips to braces and buttons – Savile Row at that time considered belts and zipped flies to be vulgar.[4])

US designers continued to rise in the 1970s – Calvin Klein and Ralph Lauren among them – defining a more leisure-oriented casual ele-gance as the American style. They added a completely new dimension to the fashion equation – savvy marketing. The likes of Brooke Shields advertising "Nothing comes between me and my Calvins" and the uproar that accompanied it showed the Europeans the power of brand-ing unleashed through the mass media. It was a turning point in the his-tory of fashion: Suddenly it wasn't just the design or product that was critical, it was the image and lifestyle that the brand projected. Ralph Lauren created an empire through marketing a lifestyle – British landed gentry reinterpreted for modern America – starting with Polo menswear and extending to women, children, home, formals, casuals, and just about everything else. The era of mass marketing of luxury had begun, a force that would be adopted relentlessly by the French in the 1990s as they set about targeting a wider consumer base.

The period after the Second World War also saw Italy emerge as a serious supplier of fine clothing and accessories for European ready-to-wear labels – a bit like China's position today – and it was only a matter of time before the nation emerged as a major stylesetter. The ingredients were always there: a tradition of fine craftsmanship with leather products and tailored men's suits, an abundance of excellent-quality materials, modern production technology, and, most importantly, a passion for *la dolce vita*. If France was about luxurious couture and America was about casual elegance, Italian design combined both – it gave the feel of pure luxury in ready-to-wear clothes. Think Armani suit, exquisite fabric, stylishly cut, immaculately executed, engineered for comfort, the work of a master designer at a price that wasn't totally out of reach – a powerful package in furthering the spread of luxe.

At the same time, the Italians showed that they had what it took to do couture – Valentino was among the early designers, his sumptuous creations finding favor with glamorous women of the time, including Jackie Kennedy who chose a Valentino dress for her wedding to Aristotle Onassis. While the Americans were master marketers, the Italians excelled at creating the right kind of buzz, another powerful tool in spreading the luxe culture. It came naturally to them, with flamboyant figures like Gianni Versace creating as much news as his clientele of princesses, stars, and high-society women. Italy rose rapidly and today Milan is as much a fashion center as Paris.

ASIA'S TORRID AFFAIR WITH LUXE

Back in Asia, it was time for Japan to rise and it did so on two fronts. It produced a daring bunch of designers who sprang onto the international scene in the 1970s and early 1980s – Kenzo Takada, Kansai Yamamoto, Issey Miyake, Yohji Yamamoto, and Rei Kawakubo. The last two in particular had the fashion world gasping with shock and delight, their creations of tattered rags a complete departure from anything Paris had seen before. On the second front, Japan produced an enthusiastic consumer base that has grown to be the backbone of the global luxury industry. Japan's economic rise in the 1970s and the heady years of the 1980s brought huge buying power to its people, and they took to European luxury like a fish to water. Luxe became the national obsession – by the 1990s every third woman in Japan owned a piece of it. With luxury goods being purchased on such a scale, soon the top brands were counting the Japanese as their single largest consumer segment.

Japanese tourist-shoppers first became a noticeable phenomenon in the 1970s and their numbers ballooned to gigantic proportions in the 1980s and 1990s. Europe's luxury houses sat up and took notice, and started setting up shop in Japan – Gucci opened its first store in Tokyo in 1972 in response to unprecedented demand from Japanese tourists in Europe; ditto for Louis Vuitton, which entered Japan in 1978. Soon the Japanese were not only turning in huge sales at home, but also shopping so maniacally in Europe that they were almost single-handedly supporting sales of luxury goods. (JP Morgan estimates that tourists represent more than 80 percent of Louis Vuitton's Champs Elysées store sales.[5]) The wider Japanese tourists traveled, the more brand stores were opened at all their favorite destinations; even remote islands like Guam had well-stocked larders of luxe. They jump-started luxury retail all over Asia – Hong Kong sales skyrocketed in the 1980s thanks to them, duty-free sales in Seoul and Taiwan took off with their blessing, and even just-emerging markets like Bangkok reported hearty sales to the Japanese. Stores the world over geared up to cater to them, price tags and labels were rendered in Japanese, and sales staff were trained to speak their language. (One of our more endearing sights was on Rome's luxury store-studded Via Condotti, witnessing a svelte Italian salesgirl serving a demure Japanese woman, the whole transaction conducted in fluent Japanese with plenty of bowing on both sides.[6])

The development of every successive luxury brand market in Asia has followed a similar pattern of growing economic prosperity and the government's willingness to be kinder on policies toward such goods. After Japan came Hong Kong, which experienced its own heady rise in the 1980s and 1990s, with much money being made by enterprising locals on the stock market and property speculation. Sure enough, along with money came a robust appetite for luxe. Today, Hong Kong has developed into a luxury-shopping Mecca, offering the best selection in Asia (outside of Japan), at the best prices in Asia, attracting a large number of tourist-shoppers. Major brands have six or seven large stores in the city, far more than they have in Paris, London, or New York.[7] Armani has its global flagship in Hong Kong, a feast of eight outlets spread over 34,000 square feet on three floors of Chater House in Central: Giorgio Armani, Emporio Armani, Giorgio Armani Cosmetics, Armani Casa, Armani Fiori, Armani Libri, Armani Dolci, and a huge Armani Bar – in concept, scale, and style, this collection of stores is cutting-edge retail.

South Korea and Taiwan's luxury markets began growing in the 1990s after their governments dropped import duties and loosened controls. South Korea boasts its own Rodeo Street, with swank flagships and extremely well-stocked department stores. More importantly, the South Korean consumers have gone label crazy – as many as 50 percent of Seoul women reportedly own a Louis Vuitton bag, although no one knows for sure how many of those are fake. Forget keeping up with the Joneses, here it is all about outdoing the Kims and Chungs. The story in Taiwan follows identical lines.

That brings us to China. Everyone waits with bated breath and towering expectations as China takes its first wobbly steps in Manolo Blahniks, teetering headlong into the world of branded luxury. The Chinese people have taken Deng Xiaoping's exhortation "To get rich is glorious" to heart, and indeed many are getting seriously wealthy. What puzzles many people, however, is how a country with per capita GDP of less than US$2,000 can be a significant luxury brand market. The answer lies in uneven development: Selected cities and regions are emerging as pockets of wealth, and the ones with money are in a hurry to spend it. It's as if a dam has burst and, with no checks in place, China's growing ranks of nouveaux riches are gorging themselves on newfound goodies. Conspicuous consumption is the name of the game in today's China – and every major luxury brand is already there to play along.

Reminiscent of the Japanese in the 1980s, the Chinese tourist-shopper is making heads turn and jaws drop in the 2000s. The mainland tourist has rapidly become the mainstay of Hong Kong's luxury retail sector, some stores reporting as much as 70 percent of their sales to this segment. With visa restrictions being relaxed and many Western countries giving group tourist visas, the number of Chinese tourists to Europe, the US, Australia, and indeed the rest of Asia is rising steadily. This new class of tourist is acquiring a reputation for spending generously, routinely picking up luxury brands as gifts for friends and family back home. Members of a small élite segment have started flying to Paris and Milan to refresh their wardrobes every season.

And now the slumbering giant, India, is finally awakening – its economy sizzling at a more than 7 percent growth rate – and is showing all the signs of falling under the spell of luxury brands. India always had a thin upper crust of old money that discreetly shopped in London and New York for luxury essentials. Now clanking new money is joining the spending spree. These are early days, with only a handful of luxury brands dropping anchor, and admittedly there's a lot of spadework to be done in terms of developing a retail infrastructure and building brand awareness. But these are exciting times when fundamental social changes are sweeping a once-conservative country. The spurt in IT and outsourcing businesses is putting substantial money in young hands. The media explosion is bringing in global values. Splurging on credit is replacing Gandhian frugality. Bollywood, which has a stranglehold on the nation's collective psyche, is depicting extremely liberal fashions in its films. Midnight's children are giving way to liberalization's offspring – fertile ground indeed for luxury brands to take root and prosper.

DEMOCRATIZATION OF LUXURY IN THE 1990S

What caused the explosion of luxury brands in Asia? A fortuitous alignment of the stars, you might call it. In the 1990s the European luxury industry was going through a major change, shedding its traditional family-business mindset and reinventing itself as a lean, mean corporate machine with global retailing ambitions. For senior management, changing hemlines became a lesser priority than growing toplines and fattening bottomlines. Spunky new creative blood was installed to energize aging luxury houses, and more affordable ready-to-wear and accessories were used to woo younger and more mainstream consumers. "Democratization" was the buzzword, throwing the doors of exclusivity open to ordinary people. At the same time the economies of Asia were booming and a freshly prosperous generation was raring to acquire the new-fangled symbols of wealth. The frugal living ethic of their hard-working parents slowly evaporated – money made easily was spent just as easily, and the cult of luxury went from mild infatuation to manic obsession in the space of a few quick years.

Haute couture finally ran out of commercial steam in the 1970s, with the number of clients said to have dwindled to 3,000,[8] not enough to keep an industry going. The role of haute couture shifted from main course to appetizer – big runway shows used to spin out marketing propaganda, on the back of which ran the real money-making business of ready-to-wear and accessories, a practice that continues today. The new clients were younger and they neither had the big bucks needed for serious haute couture, nor was it their style to be tied down by elaborate outfits in the free-spirited 1970s. Ready-to-wear and accessories were also the ideal vehicle for expanding into new markets, which became a necessity as luxury houses searched for fresh avenues for growth. Designers like Yves Saint Laurent opened boutiques worldwide. Licensing became a common method for entering new markets, and its master practitioner, Pierre Cardin, built an empire lending his name to a growing and at times bizarre list of products, including chocolate bars and frying pans; today Pierre Cardin has 900 license holders in 140 countries, 27 in China alone.[9] Franchising was also a popular distribution method for European brands to extend their reach.

However, many licensees took a great deal of license with the brands under their care, the product often being cheap and damaging to the brand name, completely disastrous in the luxury context. Many Asian franchisees, on the other hand, may have stuck to the brief in terms of how the brand operation was run, but they had a tendency to milk it dry, always reluctant to invest in the marketing expenditure so necessary to build and sustain a name. As a consequence, many brands underperformed. Luxury companies awoke to the need for control and stepped into the retailing arena themselves. They bought back licenses en masse – for example, YSL had bought back 152 licenses by 2001.[10] They centralized production and integrated vertically, backwards and forwards – the luxury companies simply took charge of the whole show from design, production, and marketing to retailing. Cost control became a major priority. Profits were in fashion again, and rapid growth was the new muse. From being privately owned, many companies also now answered to the stock market, a more demanding mistress than any fashionista they had ever served.

Over the 1990s, luxury companies adopted a series of strategies to spread their gospel.

First, the strategy of distribution control evolved into more and more elaborate free-standing stores, the most dizzying examples in Tokyo where brand cathedrals have sprung up, rising several floors. For example, the Prada Epicenter in Aoyama, Tokyo is a futuristic six-story glass confection with cave-like tubes that serve as an intimate retail setting. The quality of execution at these new stores is outstanding all over Asia, and in Tokyo some are so beautiful you feel the urge to kneel and worship – and of course, walk out blessed with a piece of luxe. Their role in bringing the brand alive and offering the consumer an intimate 3D experience has made these flagships yet another marketing tool in the luxury arsenal.

Secondly, brands like Christian Dior reincarnated themselves, virtually abandoning their old avatar for a younger, sexier one, which struck home with Asia's relatively younger consumers. In most Asian markets the biggest spenders on luxury brands are young women between the ages of 20 and 30. Appealing to these young women meant recalibrating a brand's "cool quotient," that slippery intangible that defines how "in" the brand is among their peer group, how well they relate to it, how relevant it is to their lifestyle. It entailed shedding the brand's staid old image for a youthful one, or widening its appeal by adding trendier products – like a denim handbag – to the classic repertoire, as Louis Vuitton did.

Thirdly, the luxury industry played its master move, the "logo-fication" of the handbag, plastering instantly recognizable symbols in a continuous pattern all over the bag. For Asian consumers this was a godsend: It did the job of letting people know you were of a certain class and standing in society. We examine the status-defining role of luxury brands in greater depth in the next chapter, but here we emphasize that the logo-fication of bags was the single most important factor in spreading the luxury brand mania in Asia. Luxury companies cottoned on to the simple truth that the LV monogram and the Gucci Gs were what Asian consumers were after, and soon every other brand from

Coach to Dior, Fendi to Ferragamo was doing its take on the monogram. It is a lesson that marketers of other consumer goods can learn – logo lines have grown so fast that they account for up to 80 percent of sales for some brands.[11] Asia was in the bag, so to speak.

Fourthly, luxury brands s-t-r-e-t-c-h-e-d – they sliced and diced a person's life and offered a product to fit every aspect of it, inside out, 24/7, wherever he is, whatever activity she is engaged in. A brand might have started life in couture, its strength might lie in handcrafted leather goods, or it might have built a reputation for fine jewelry – but now it is extending its equity over a spectrum of products. Every brand seems to be firmly headed down the path of providing a full suite of products and that suite itself gets redefined and enlarged each day. Going for a holiday on the beach? Try a Prada bikini and D&G flip-flops. Skiing? Chanel has a range of glamour skiwear. Riding? How about a saddle from Hermès? Going to the office? May we suggest a Dunhill briefcase designed to cradle a laptop? Want the time? Check out Louis Vuitton's latest line of watches. Something for baby? Hermès has a range for newborns. A diaper bag for mommy? Baby Dior has the look. An iPod case? Try Gucci. Lounging at home? Versace sofa. Going to sleep? Ralph Lauren bedsheets. Decorating the Christmas tree? Armani Casa has modern baubles. This invasion of designer brands into every detail has taken the cult to another level, and by increasing the catchment area, luxing up every aspect of life, companies are raking in even larger revenues.

Luxury hasn't just been democratized, it's become inescapable.

THE MALLING OF ASIA

Hand in hand with the economic boom and urbanization in Asia came an explosion in retail development, thereby providing the necessary infrastructure for luxury brand stores. It started with department store chains in Japan, such as Mitsukoshi, Sogo, Isetan, Seibu, and Daimaru. Soon the Japanese became so good at setting up department stores that they were doing it in other Asian markets like Hong Kong, Taiwan, and South Korea. Elsewhere in Asia's megacities shopping malls started springing up in the 1980s, a trend that accelerated in the 1990s. They offered a merry mix of retail, food, and entertainment, a one-stop leisure destination that pulled in the crowds. In cities like Manila and Bangkok, malls also played a very basic role in providing a chilled atmosphere – rather than frying in the hot sun outside, lounge around in the cooler climes of an air-conditioned mall, even if you only window-shop.

The malling of Asia – and here we use the term in a broad sense to include the variety of retail-center formats that dot the urban landscape – has played midwife to the birth of the cult, making available upscale retail space, the ambience and atmospherics consistent with the high-end image that luxury brands need. In fact, in many up-and-coming Asian cities the lack of suitable retail space has slowed down the march of luxury, forcing friends Louis Vuitton, Gucci, Prada, *et al.* to spend the first few years in improvised stores in the lobbies of five-star hotels until the retail infrastructure catches up.

More importantly, the malling of Asia has provided a real-life setting for consumers to learn about luxury brands and the lifestyle they denote. This is the theme that sociologist Ken Young amplifies when he calls shopping malls "open access academies of social distinction."[12] As people wander through a mall, looking at shop windows, trying out products, observing other shoppers, they are taking in important lessons in consumption behavior. What is more, they are learning to slot brands into status hierarchies, picking up cues from the store settings and location. Often the cheap and cheerful brands are on the lower floors, and as you rise higher so does the caliber of the brand and, needless to say, the price. How do you want to package and present yourself? Over time, and a process of hit and miss, you learn the right brands and products to help you create the identity you desire.

THE WORLD'S BIGGEST MARKET TODAY: ASIA

The Asian luxury goods market constitutes 37 percent of the global market of US$80 billion (Figure 1.1). The actual size of Asian spending is higher because of the Asian penchant for shopping abroad, ably led by the Japanese and Chinese, easily adding another 15–20 percent to the continent's share. By conservative estimates, it would be fair to say that Asians consume half the world's luxury brands (Figure 1.2).

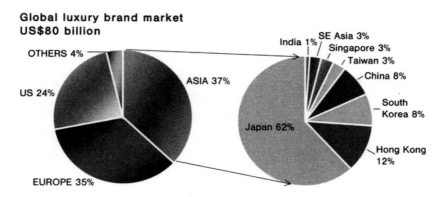

Figure 1.1 Asia is the world's #1 luxury market: Geographic breakdown
Source: Authors' analysis.

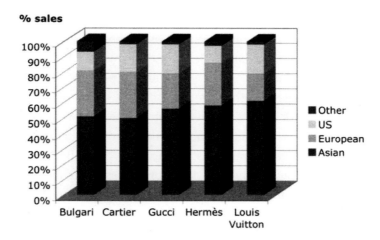

Figure 1.2 Major brands earn more than half their revenue from Asian consumers.
Source: JP Morgan, *European Luxury Goods Sector*, 2 November 2005.

Within Asia, Japan dominates with a sumo-sized 62 percent share. Hong Kong has always been the second biggest – currently a 12 percent share – but that's a position it will soon have to cede to China, which is growing by leaps and bounds. South Korea is the next substantial market with an 8 percent share. Taiwan and Singapore contribute 2–3 percent each. Other Southeast Asian countries – Thailand, the Philippines, Indonesia, and Malaysia – are still relatively small luxe markets, but there is a select group of extremely wealthy business families, mostly of Chinese origin, who regularly shop abroad, either in Hong Kong, Singapore, or Europe.

Let's look at things from a brand's perspective. If yours is a major brand, expect to get a third to half of your sales from Asia (plus lots more from Asian tourists flocking to your stores in Europe and the US). Of course, the Japanese consumer would be your darling, a luxe glutton, gorging heartily at home and then feasting abundantly abroad. If you removed the Japanese consumer momentarily from the equation – a feat that could only be accomplished by dragging her screaming and shouting in a most un-Japanese manner – then your sales would simply take a nose dive. That is the degree of luxe brands' dependence on Japan.

How deeply entrenched is the luxe habit in Asia? In Japan, an estimated 25 percent of the adult population owns a luxury product. For other Asian countries the penetration of luxe is about half of Japan's. A survey by market research firm Synovate, covering Hong Kong, South Korea, and Singapore, found that between 12 and 15 percent of Asians had purchased a luxury brand in the last six months.[13] The same survey validated what is abundantly clear on the streets – Asia's love for the designer bag. In Hong Kong, a whopping 64 percent of luxe shoppers surveyed had bought leather goods in the past six months.

What are Asia's favorite brands? Asians make no bones about the fact that they are after "famous brands" – the term for "luxury brands" in several Asian countries translates into just that. So while Asia is a highly competitive market with over 100 companies slugging it out, consumers are more interested in the winners. Based on sales figures and brand image indicators, we have compiled Asia's Top Ten (Table 1.1). It confirms what every luxe-loving Asian already knows: There is nothing to beat the charms of Louis Vuitton and Rolex.

Where will future growth come from? The answer is the same as for every product category in the world: China and India, the twin engines of growth in the twenty-first century, China offering the more immediate opportunity, India the longer-term play. Bernard Arnault, chairman and CEO, LVMH Group, remarked in the company's annual report that geographical growth opportunities are "mainly to be found in Asia, most notably China, a market that is awakening to luxury products."[14] He should know: Louis Vuitton has seen its business grow by close to 50 percent every year since it entered China in 1992, and it was profitable from year one. Needless to say, Arnault sees India as another "promising territory for the future."[15]

Table 1.1 Louis Vuitton is Asia's #1 favorite
ASIA'S TOP TEN LUXE BRANDS

1	Louis Vuitton
2	Rolex
3	Cartier
4	Gucci
5	Burberry
6	Hermès
7	Chanel
8	Prada
9	Tiffany
10	Armani

Source: Authors' analysis, based on sales performance and brand image scores.

Given China's gung-ho growth trajectory, the question is when its luxury market will surpass Japan's. The general expectation is around 2014, about the same time that China's economy is expected to overtake Japan's, but it may well happen sooner for several qualitative reasons. The delicate Japanese culture allows for only subtle displays of wealth, but in China it is all about blatancy – you win respect and admiration for achieving success. The Japanese are diligent employees who toil hard in big corporations for fixed salaries; the Chinese are a nation of aggressive entrepreneurs intent on making it rich. Japanese men allow their wives to shop for their clothes; Chinese men have led the fashion movement in China, and the men's market is bigger than the women's even today. Japanese women tend to be followers: They all rush into the same shops, buying up the same products. Of course, fashion by definition has to have a popular following, but the fact that Chinese women are motivated by the need to stand out as against merge into a Louis Vuitton-carrying crowd means that there is more room for a vibrant fashion scene to emerge. And then there's the Chinese trump card, the Shanghainese woman, born with in-built fashion antennae and a tankful of sass and spunk. She'll make sure that the Paris of the East regains its rightful place.

Is China the new Japan for luxury brands? Only insofar as it presents an untapped potential for massive long-term growth. For the most part, China is simply the new China. It offers its own set of opportunities and challenges. There is plenty of legwork still to do and robust profitability is down the line. Ian Hawksworth, executive director of Hong Kong Land, which holds the most prestigious retail property portfolio in Hong Kong, comments:

It's not a profitable market domestically in the next three to five years because of the cost of doing business there – the establishment of new stores, the establishment of distribution channels, the taxation position on luxury goods. As WTO bites, the margins will become easier to achieve in China.[16]

THE RISE OF SHOWBUZZ

Two major forces fueled the spread of luxury: the conglomeration of the luxe business, and the emergence of a new kind of marketing, part showbiz, part professional buzz – we call it "showbuzz" marketing.

Conglomeration of Luxury[17]

In the good old days the designer *was* the brand. Jeanne Lanvin started the house of Lanvin, Gabrielle Chanel was the force behind the House of Chanel, Christian Dior, Hubert de Givenchy, Yves Saint Laurent – they all brought their own talent, personality, and mystique to bear in creating a couture house in their name. They may have been apprenticed under an established name before venturing out on their own, as Yves Saint Laurent was under Dior, or they may have taken the helping hand of a savvy business partner to bankroll them. Or it may have been a family affair: Aldo Gucci carrying on what dad Guccio had started, or Georges Vuitton building on the fine tradition of parent Louis. The name on the business was the name of the designer; their vision led the future of their design house. They may have flogged the name, as Pierre Cardin and Yves Saint Laurent did using licensing arrangements to spread their wings to far-flung places, squeezing as much profit as possible in one lifetime; but at least it was their own name they sold. The designer was integral to the brand, and the business model was simple: the designer, their name, their business.

All that changed with one man, Bernard Arnault. So far the French had excelled at designing fashion, but this Frenchman took a giant leap outside the box and set about designing the *business* of fashion. Arnault didn't see the point of limiting the scope of a company by running it like a mom-and-pop store, albeit a high-fashion one, when there was the possibility of conquering the world and raking in higher sales and higher profits. And he didn't see the point of following rules. In his vision everything was interchangeable, designers could be hired and fired, brands could be bought and sold, management changed, and companies restructured. Big, that's what Arnault was after, a big conglomerate of brands with big revenues and big profits. Like a game of luxe monopoly, he set about buying prestigious brands and building them into larger profit-generating machines. With one brand you had only so much reach, financial muscle, and negotiating power; with a stable of brands you called the shots.

Arnault set the trend, and other luxe-monopoly players followed. This pursuit of greater size and greater profits helped the luxury culture spread like wildfire. The formula of the 1990s consisted of finding new brands (even if they were a century old) to buy, finding a hot new designer to breathe life into them and a hot new management to match, finding new products to stamp those brands on, finding large new consumer segments to buy them, and finding new markets all over the world to sell them in – all the time exercising control on costs, control on production, control on distribution, control on brand expression. Control freaks with expansionist tendencies, you might call these luxury conglomerates, just the sort of companies that stock markets love, so of course going public became the mode, listing on both sides of the Atlantic, bringing in cash to finance all the expansion activity.

The conglomeration of the luxury business began in earnest when Arnault took over Christian Dior in the mid-1980s, buying its holding company, a bankrupt textile firm called Boussac. He followed that with a rather acrimonious takeover of Louis Vuitton Moët Hennessy in 1989, and he's been shopping aggressively ever since.[18] The result: an empire of over 50 brands – which brought in €13.9 billion in revenues in 2005[19] – that will keep you covered in luxury from head to toe and in fine spirits too. Arnault has fashion and leather goods brands such as Givenchy, Loewe, Celine, Kenzo, Marc Jacobs, Fendi, Donna Karan, and more. He has picked up an equally impressive portfolio of cosmetic and perfume brands, Parfums Christian Dior and Guerlain among them. He has bought watch brands like TAG Heuer, Ebel, Zenith, and Chaumet, and has now extended the Louis Vuitton name into watches. He's got top-quality wines and spirits: Moët & Chandon, Dom Perignon, and Veuve Cliquot, which is apparently the beverage of choice at the famed Louis Vuitton store-opening parties. He's also into retailing with designer cosmetics at Sephora and selling luxury to travelers at DFS. The jewel in the crown, however, remains Louis Vuitton, its mono-grammed wares spreading like an unstoppable epidemic.

If Louis Vuitton is the bread, butter, and jam for the world's biggest lux-ury group, the French brand Cartier plays the same role for the second-largest group, Switzerland's Richemont, started by South African billionaire Anton Rupert in 1988 and later run by son Johann. Richemont is another well-spread conglomerate with a major interest in watches and jewelry, which accounts for two-thirds of its business.[20] It has a drawer full of top-drawer watches: Piaget, Baume & Mercier, Vacheron Constantin, IWC, Jaeger-LeCoultre, and Lange & Söhne among them. There's Van Cleef & Arpels. There's Mont Blanc. There's Alfred Dunhill. In other words, there's a collection of brands that Asia loves, especially China, where people buy Cartier watches by the dozen as gifts, as well as enough blazers and brief-cases to keep Dunhill's retail network of 50-plus points of sale ticking away. In terms of sales, the Richemont Group has about a third of LVMH's.

The third significant luxe conglomerate is the Gucci Group. Its busi-ness history reads like a Hollywood thriller: A near-insolvent feuding family business becomes the most talked-about turnaround, then the subject of a fierce takeover battle by two of the most headstrong French men in the luxury business – LVMH's Arnault, and François Pinault, who heads the French retail conglomerate PPR (previously Pinault-Printemps-Redoute) – then transforms itself into a major luxury group and goes shopping for brands itself. In the late 1980s Gucci was gasp-ing for breath and Domenico de Sole as CEO and Tom Ford as creative director were brought in to resurrect it, which they did so successfully that every brand since dreams of "doing a Gucci." Ford's sexy designs and savvy advertising campaigns – not to mention his own movie-star

Table 1.2 The conglomerates behind some of Asia's favorite brands

LVMH	RICHEMONT	GUCCI
Louis Vuitton	Cartier	Gucci
Christian Dior	Dunhill	Yves Saint Laurent
Fendi	Mont Blanc	Boucheron
Celine	Van Cleef & Arpels	Bottega Veneta
Loewe	Piaget	Sergio Rossi
Donna Karan	Baume & Mercier	Alexander McQueen
Kenzo	Vacheron Constantin	Stella McCartney
Tag Heuer	Chloé	Balenciaga
Marc Jacobs	Shanghai Tang	
Givenchy	Panerai	

Source: Company websites, selected list only

looks and irresistible charm – had women drooling in the newly revamped chain of Gucci boutiques around the world. Gucci shook Asia, it became the brand to die for, and even today, although Louis Vuitton outstrips it in sales, for many Asians Gucci is the first brand that comes to mind, and the one they would love to buy.

In 1999 Arnault mounted a takeover attempt on Gucci, but his bid was foiled by Pinault, who purchased a 42 percent stake. It was corporate warfare, gloves off, with plenty of lawsuits and controversial press. The boardroom action became as interesting as the show on the catwalks. Pinault won the day. He also subsequently bought another company that Arnault was after, Sanofi Beauté, which owns YSL.

Gucci Group has since acquired Sergio Rossi, Bottega Veneta, Boucheron, and Balenciaga, besides luxury watches, cosmetics, and perfumes. In yet another twist to the Gucci saga, Ford and de Sole left the empire they helped create when their contracts expired in 2004 – reportedly, they couldn't see eye to eye with Pinault on their degree of autonomy in running the business[21] – to be replaced by Robert Polet, former head of Unilever's ice-cream unit. Pinault finally owns the whole show – PPR bought back minority shares – and the Gucci Group was delisted from the Amsterdam and New York stock exchanges.

The forces of conglomeration influenced smaller luxury houses as well. Prada went on a shopping spree, buying Jil Sander, Helmut Lang, and Church & Co. Hermès acquired a 35 percent stake in Jean Paul Gaultier.

Part of the conglomeration strategy is to infuse fresh life into acquired brands – to do a Gucci, so to speak. To do a Gucci you need a Tom Ford, and while there is just one of him, there's a fair supply of exciting new designers with plenty of artistic talent. The search for gutsy designers to give a modern twist to aging brands has resulted in an interesting game of musical chairs. Ironically, vintage French and Italian brands are being entrusted to young American and British designers.

Arnault is the acknowledged master at conducting twenty-first-century surgery on nineteenth-century brands, finding the right balance between life-giving innovation and the brand's traditional core. American Marc Jacobs is the designer behind the updated image of Louis Vuitton, wittily adding a touch of pop and kitsch. Fellow American Michael Kors, known for his minimalist approach, was the man Arnault chose to revive Celine. For Christian Dior, Arnault first hired Gianfranco Ferre in 1989, then replaced him with Spanish (but raised in the UK) John Galliano from house brand Givenchy. British designer Alexander McQueen filled Galliano's spot at Givenchy, before defecting to rival Gucci Group and setting up his own label. In the meantime, Galliano continues to shock and delight with a young, brash, urban sexiness that is the "new new look," miles away from the ladylike glamorous New Look that Christian Dior created in 1947.

At Richemont's fashion house Chloé, Stella McCartney (daughter of ex-Beatle Paul McCartney) succeeded the legendary Karl Lagerfeld in 1997, making waves with her first collection, which combined vintage touches with modern tailoring. McCartney did a McQueen, forming her own label under the Gucci Group. Her assistant and good friend Phoebe Philo, also from Britain, took over at Chloé (until she also left in 2006), with such success rumors swirled that Philo was doing the designing all along.

It's not just American designers who are lending a hand in the rejuvenation of European brands: American managers are pitching in too, bringing a much-needed professional touch. Rosemary Bravo's turnaround of the very British label Burberry is a shining example. She arrived in 1997 and, with the help of Italian designer Roberto

Manichetti and an advertising campaign by master photographer Mario Testino, teleported Burberry into modern times, showing supermodel Kate Moss in a skimpy bikini made of the ancient Burberry tartan. Michael Burke, another American, has been with Arnault right from the start of his LVMH empire-building foray (it shows in Burke's faultless French accent and effortless shoulder shrugging), played a significant role in the group's success and the turnaround of Christian Dior, and is applying his touch to group brand Fendi.

The Emergence of Showbuzz Marketing

With the luxury business itself changing – massive scale, global coverage, professional management – the marketing and promotion of that business took on similar characteristics. Whereas the likes of Coco Chanel and Christian Dior presented their collections in a small salon, today's fashion shows are nothing short of showbiz. Whereas earlier a few influential magazine editors dictated the dissemination of fashion information, now huge media empires with global coverage carpet bomb the planet with up-to-the-minute fashion intelligence. The creation of buzz – getting your brand talked about, making sure it stays in the news – has gone professional too, deploying a range of PR techniques to make a splash, including hired celebrities and over-the-top events. It's the new showbuzz marketing, combining the principles of *showbiz* and below-the-line *buzz* generation.

The need for this new kind of marketing was clear. The earlier concept of luxury goods based on skilled craftsmanship, exclusivity, and longevity became increasingly irrelevant within a machine-made, technology-enabled production process, with batches farmed out to factories sometimes continents away from the home of the brand. Today, it's the aura and image that you build around the logo, the intangible come-hither appeal that you embed in its leather, or the cool quotient that you imbue into the luxe-consuming public's mind – that's what consumers buy as much as they buy the bag. From the product and its inherent quality, the focus has shifted to the brand and its image. Grant McCracken in *Culture and Consumption* calls this the process of "meaning manufacture," where thanks to advertising and the fashion system, culturally significant meaning is "moved" into consumer goods.[22]

As far as luxeland is concerned showbuzz marketing boils down to creating the right kind of buzz, packaging it neatly, and selling it at the store. Well before the consumer reaches that store, there's a whole army of images and words assaulting her, created by a media and marketing juggernaut working at full blast on behalf of the brand. By the time she tries on a dress from the latest collection, or considers the purchase of a new bag in the store window, she already has definite perceptions about the brand and the particular piece in question. And if she is Japanese, she could effortlessly write a 2,000-word paper on it, full of exquisite details about the designer, the theme of his latest collection, how it links back to his earlier work, the model who walked down the catwalk wearing it, the big names in the audience, the international celebrities who are sporting it currently, and the local ones to boot. *Today's luxe consumer consumes the buzz as much as she does the product*, and she spends time discussing it with her pals. Latest brand arrivals are a legitimate topic of conversation, and what you have on and what you plan to purchase are interesting facilitators of social interaction in Asia.

The mass mesmerization with fashion on a season-by-season basis is a direct result of the industry taking on characteristics of showbiz. The same human fascination with glamour and celebrities that draws adoring crowds to Hollywood movies and all the peripheral action and gossip also draws them to the fashion world. Catwalk shows in Paris and Milan have become extravagant productions staged with theatrical expertise. Theme, venue, music, lights, sets, choreography, styling – everything is managed to create a big-bang, visual impact. It's pure entertainment, audacious clothes, glamorous models, and plenty of leg, breast, and more on display. And the shows are staged as much for the live audience of A-list head-turners sitting around the catwalk as they are for the global press that beams them instantaneously to the world.

There are television channels devoted to fashion, leave alone numerous websites. Images from the shows are carried by fashion and lifestyle glossies, international titles like *Elle*, *Vogue*, and *Cosmopolitan*, as well as a slew of local magazines that dish out fashion advice. In China alone, some 200 *new* fashion and lifestyle magazines have sprung up in the last five years. Japanese fashion glossies have become so good that they are sought after in markets like Taiwan, where the current generation can't even read Japanese. But that's the point: This

From the cosy calm of the early salon showings to the razzle-dazzle of today's runway acts, fashion shows have transformed into showbiz. Left, a model poses in an early Christian Dior dress in a rather sedate setting; below, a model struts down the ramp in a dazzler from John Galliano's collection for Dior.

Photo left by Henri Cartier Bresson, courtesy of Magnum. Photo below courtesy of Dior.

visual culture is universally understood, it does not need to be translated into any written language.

Women in Asia are known to tear out pictures from magazines, shots
straight from the ramps, and walk into stores seeking the entire look,
head to toe. The rich and famous go a step further and take the lead
from the richer and more famous – for example Halle Berry's Elie Saab-
designed Oscar dress, a sheer sheath with strategically placed flowers,
was sported by Hong Kong socialite Olivia Davies, who has topped local
best-dressed lists. Lesser mortals have a virtual relationship with designers, much like a fan of Jennifer Lopez would with the singer. If you hear
the intimacy with which a Japanese woman talks about Marc Jacobs,
you are convinced that he is indeed designing those exquisite outfits
and accessories just for her, one on one.

So what is the role of advertising in this showbuzz marketing era? It's
alive and well, but its role has evolved. Advertising creates awareness, it
defines the brand's image, but today's skeptical consumer pays more
heed to what magazine editorials are saying. Many Asian consumers
don't even bother with the inherent image of a brand. Try explaining the
fact that the favorite brand of Japanese teenagers is the decidedly mature
woman's Hermès – they are only interested in how "in" the brand is
among their peers. For that kind of information, it is far more useful to
check out who is wearing what in the company of whom at which
event; back to good old buzz consumption. That's where advertisements
come in extremely handy – after all, which editor is going to treat a big
advertiser unkindly in their editorial content? If you're a conglomerate
your stable of brands puts you in an enviable position – besides excellent advertising rates, you are likely to get excellent editorial coverage.

"Brand parties" are the rage these days, with the local who's who in
attendance – these can range from cozy little affairs to mammoth extrav-
aganzas, especially in China. They ensure that brand names fill the society pages and gossip columns in local newspapers and magazines. Inane
controversies are created. For example, a Hong Kong actress was
accused of "hijacking" the Fendi showing of its autumn–winter fur collection by arriving in a Louis Vuitton dress with a neckline that "didn't
just plunge, it bungeed." As a result, the actress and her assets got more
press coverage than the Fendi models.[23] Celebrities are increasingly
being hired as brand ambassadors, with the specific purpose of appear-

ing at events wearing a particular brand, resulting in reams of news coverage.

Sometimes the brands don't even have to try to be in the news. The luxury culture has not only spread to Asia, it has seeped in so deep that it wells up on its own, without any effort by the brand at all. Showbuzz on autopilot. In the 2003 Sudden Acute Respiratory Syndrome (SARS) epidemic that swept through Hong Kong, residents rushed to buy virus-protective masks. Rumors spread that Gucci and Louis Vuitton had put designer masks on the market, the Louis Vuitton one apparently made of super-soft leather with a monogrammed sterling silver clasp. This led to a deluge of calls at the company's stores and offices. It turned out to be a hoax, but many wished it had been true. After all, a girl needs a good-looking mask to go with her Gucci and Chanel outfits.[24]

F A S H I O N

1837 | 1837 Louis Vuitton starts making trunks at the court of Empress Eugenie and goes on to open his first store in Paris in 1854. A century and a half later, his brand conquers the hearts of the Japanese and its brown monogram bags become de rigueur for Asia's nouveaux riches.

1837 1837 Thierry Hermès starts a saddlery company, which is modernized a century later by his grandson Emile. Its famed Birkin bags at jaw-dropping prices have made it the most desired status symbol in Asia.

1895 1895 Thomas Burberry creates the trenchcoat. First worn by British officers during the Boer War, it is now so well entrenched in Asia that "Burberry" is the Korean word for raincoat.

1913 1913 Coco Chanel opens her first store in Paris, and goes on to shake the city with her breaking-the-mold fashion statements, as well as her unconventional lifestyle. Today, her signature style has found a wide following in Asia, from Japanese teenagers to Korean bar hostesses.

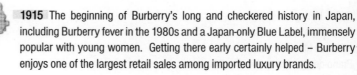

1915 1915 The beginning of Burberry's long and checkered history in Japan, including Burberry fever in the 1980s and a Japan-only Blue Label, immensely popular with young women. Getting there early certainly helped – Burberry enjoys one of the largest retail sales among imported luxury brands.

1932 1932 Guccio Gucci designs the classic Gucci loafers, a symbol for the wealthy. A year later his son, Aldo, creates the interlocking double G logo (after his father's initials), which half a century later becomes the rage all over Asia.

1935 1935 Salvatore Ferragamo sets up his workshop in Florence. He was dubbed "shoemaker to the stars" and his shoes are a must-have item for every South Korean woman today.

1947 1947 Christian Dior's New Look collection creates a stir in Paris, reshaping the female form into an elegant hourglass. Half a century later, John Galliano's outrageous designs cause a similar stir among Asia's A list.

1956 1956 Hermès names Grace Kelly's much-loved bag after her on her marriage to Prince Rainier of Monaco. Waiting lists for this to-die-for bag, costing US$5–10,000, are indefinitely closed in Asia.

TIMELINE[25]

1978 Miuccia Prada inherits her grandfather's business. Her use of innovative fabrics and her minimalist designs make the triangular Prada symbol one of the hottest in Asia.

 1978

1983 Karl Lagerfeld, new design director at Chanel, reinvents the original spirit of Coco in a modern métier. This is the first of what soon becomes a brand-rejuvenation trend among luxury brands.

1983

1986 Imelda Marcos's famed 3,000-strong shoe collection comes to light after the People Power movement overthrows the Marcos government.

1986

1990 Tom Ford joins Gucci as creative director and, together with Dominic de Sole, revives the company to amazing heights of success.

GUCCI

1990

1999 Burberry's signature checks on a bikini worn by Kate Moss transform the 100-year-old label into a modern-day brand. Asia is soon awash in Burberry checks, some with a little help from the fertile counterfeit market.

1999

2001 Hermès's 11-story glass-brick retail extravaganza opens in Ginza, Tokyo, creating hysteria among women who queue up several days in advance to buy the limited-edition bags promised on opening day. The Renzo Piano-designed flagship store sets a high note for the mega-sized flagship store trend that catches on in Japan.

2001

2001 Plaza 66, a state-of-the-art luxury mall, opens on Shanghai's famed shopping street Nanjing Lu, pushing the city's retail to world-class levels in one stroke.

2001

2002 Queues build up three days in advance for the opening of Louis Vuitton's six-floor flagship store in Omotesando, Tokyo, an appropriate retail temple for the luxury brand most revered by the Japanese.

2002

2006 The likes of Armani and Chanel stage haute couture shows in Hong Kong, signaling the opening up of a lucrative ultra-high-end segment in Asia.

2006

2007 India enters a new phase of luxury retailing with the launch of DLF Emporio in New Delhi, the country's first luxury mall with a "who's who" roster of top brands.

2007

The "logo-fication" of bags accelerated the spread of luxe mania across the continent.

Photos courtesy of Coach and Fendi Asia Pacific.

Ever heard of a three-year waiting list... which you can no longer get on to... for a *bag*?!
The culprits: Birkin and Kelly bags by Hermès.

Photos courtesy of Hermès.

2
FINDING MEANING
IN AN LV BAG

"Expenditure on dress has this advantage over most other methods, that our apparel is always in evidence and affords an indication of our pecuniary standing to all observers at the first glance."

Thorstein Veblen, The Theory of the Leisure Class, 1899[1]

"This is what I find remarkable about Americans – they believe that if you buy the right clothes you will be accepted by the right people, regardless of where you come from. It's quite touching, really. I don't know if I believe that. But I suppose it's a good thing because it keeps the fashion business going."

Suzy Menkes, leading fashion commentator,
in the New Yorker, 2003[2]

Thorstein Veblen may have been describing the practices of the leisure class in nineteenth-century America, Suzy Menkes the behavior of today's upwardly mobile Americans, but although a century apart – and a continent away – they could just as well have been describing Asia's avid luxury-consuming class. The right clothes paired with the right Louis Vuitton, Gucci, Chanel, or Hermès bag would certainly put your pecuniary standing in evidence right away in any Asian country today, and forget being *accepted* by the right people, you *are* the right people, and you have the right designer logo to prove it.

In the previous chapter we saw what the global luxe industry did to spread the luxury culture; in this chapter we study what Asia's consumers did to meet it halfway. What is it about Western luxury brands that has Asians following en masse, spellbound behind a modern-day Pied Piper? As we meet important segments of luxury consumers and come to understand recurring patterns of behavior across the diverse countries and cultures of Asia, we find it is not so much what the luxury brands have, as what Asians themselves feel they lack. The world around them has changed dramatically in the last 50 years and somewhere along the line their own sense of identity has been displaced.

NEW MONEY, NEW RULE BOOK

Whereas the developed nations of the West took a century or two doing their developing, Asia's economies have packed it all into a few swift decades, and many are now shoulder to shoulder with Western nations. Japan started rising in the 1960s and 1970s and its per capita GDP already exceeds that of the US; Hong Kong and Singapore's growth started in the 1970s and 1980s and their per capita GDP is on a par with the likes of the UK, France, and Germany; South Korea and Taiwan's rise was largely in the 1980s and 1990s and per capita GDP is more than halfway to that of the developed countries (Figure 2.1). China is off to a flying start and serious wealth is flowing into selected segments of society; India is following suit.

The upshot: Asia is almost entirely about new money. There simply hasn't been the time for the money to sit in oak barrels and mature into fine old wealth, suitably smooth on the palate. There are also few family inheritances coming down the generations to support a life of leisure. Sure, there is a long line of royalty in some countries extending to the present day – the emperor in Japan, the king in Thailand – but for the most part twentieth-century history was harsh, people have been poor, and pockets of old wealth have been small at best, and in countries like China almost completely purged. This is Asia's first and second generation of wealth. This is also Asia's first and second generation of middle-class people with significant spending power. This is also Asia's first and second generation of working women with financial independence.

The change in economic status came so quickly that the rules of consumption and the canons of taste have been fluid and loosely defined. That threw up a rare and powerful opportunity for luxury brands: to write the rule book. Whereas old money is set in its ways and fusses about the accepted way of doing things, new money is extremely open

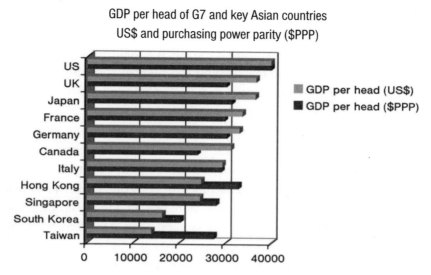

GDP per head of G7 and key Asian countries
US$ and purchasing power parity ($PPP)

Figure 2.1 Asian economies are rapidly catching up with developed markets
Source: CIA, The World Factbook 2006.

to ideas. With few benchmarks to follow, it is, in fact, groping for direction. Luxury brands have been only too happy to oblige, sowing the seeds of a multibillion-dollar market in the process.

Serge Brunschwig, until recently managing director, Louis Vuitton (Worldwide), and now president and CEO of Celine, comments:

We establish very well in a developing economy. In the developed world habits are made a very long time ago. There is a certain way to spend and that has been established, including real estate, expensive holidays, yachts, whatever, and then luxury goods like ourselves must find a spot into it.

On the other hand, consumption patterns in the developing world are "free," allowing companies like Louis Vuitton to be involved from the beginning.

We become part of the landscape very soon. That's what happened in Japan, probably that's what is happening in China now, in Russia, and in India.[3]

The interesting insight for marketers is just how fast the rule book can be written in an emerging market. Louis Vuitton entered Japan in 1978 and was pretty much established within a decade, and as Vuitton's enviable position in that country today proves, once your brand is the rule, it's hard to displace. Vuitton has made it a point to be the pioneer in market after Asian market, shaping the rules of consumption right from the first stirrings of wealth. It has even set up shop in countries like Vietnam, biding its time while the economy ripens.

As Asia's economies develop, other consumption norms are being established. Some norms can be fairly bizarre, for example in Southern China the consumption of exotic animals – civet cats and raccoons included – is considered a status symbol, besides providing "medicinal benefits." Other norms are thankfully more benign, for example a Swiss watch has become an accepted status symbol in Asia, much to the delight of Switzerland's watch industry. Asia is of course the world's largest importer of Swiss watches, with tiny Hong Kong alone comparable with the US, while Japan, Singapore, China, Taiwan, and Thailand are all solid tickers.[4] Another well-accepted symbol is a luxury car – Hong Kong takes the lead again with the highest per capita ownership of Rolls-Royces and Mercedes-Benzes, as well as sports cars like Ferraris and Porsches.[5]

Caroline Roberts of Dolce & Gabbana Far East explains:

It is the Chinese mentality. You don't have to live very well, but you must have a nice car and a nice watch.[6]

The Chinese consumption rule book at work. Given that the Chinese are not just in China, Taiwan, and Hong Kong, but spread all over Asia, controlling major business interests in Singapore, Malaysia, Thailand, the Philippines, and Indonesia, that's a lot of nice cars and nice watches being snapped up.

Since Asia's nations are at different levels of economic development, ranging from the super-rich Japanese to the just-emerging Chinese and Indians, let's look at how the luxury culture spreads within an Asian country with growing prosperity.

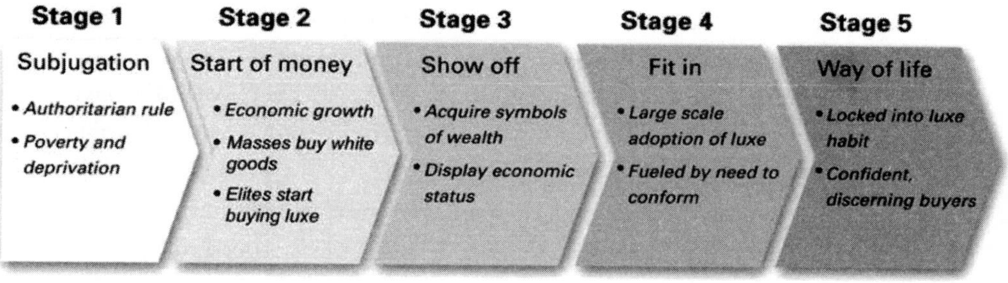

Stage 1	Stage 2	Stage 3	Stage 4	Stage 5
Subjugation	**Start of money**	**Show off**	**Fit in**	**Way of life**
• *Authoritarian rule* • *Poverty and deprivation*	• *Economic growth* • *Masses buy white goods* • *Elites start buying luxe*	• *Acquire symbols of wealth* • *Display economic status*	• *Large scale adoption of luxe* • *Fueled by need to conform*	• *Locked into luxe habit* • *Confident, discerning buyers*

Figure 2.2 The Spread of Luxury model

THE SPREAD OF LUXURY MODEL

The spread of the luxury culture in Asian countries has typically followed a five-stage process (Figure 2.2). Ironically, the first stage is *subjugation*, and every country in Asia has gone through some form of it – Japan was defeated and ruled by the Americans; South Korea had first a Japanese occupation to cope with and then an American presence; Taiwan exchanged Japanese rule for an even tougher time under Chiang Kai Shek and his cronies; China subjugated itself through a series of purgings when the Communists took over; Hong Kong was under the British who only got liberal a few years before it was time to leave; India, Singapore, and Malaysia were under the British too; the Philippines lived under centuries of Spanish subjugation then the American "liberators" became its rulers; and Indonesia had the Dutch to deal with before the Japanese dropped by during the Second World War.[7] Whatever the means of subjugation, it mostly led to a fairly miserable life for the people: hard work, little money, and limited personal dignity.

What deprivation does is build a hunger, a desire, a dream, however distant and unattainable it might be. When you release the pressure, as all these nations eventually did, the desire invariably bursts out and the hunger has to be fed. That's what makes subjugation the essential Stage 1.

Japan was the first to rise from the ashes and we will use it to illustrate the model. Stage 2, the *start of money*, began in earnest. The economy grew and people had money for the first time. Washing machines and television sets became the new luxury goods for the emerging middle class, while a smaller segment of élite consumers were already well versed in Hermès bags and European jewelry. With increasing prosperity came travel and the discovery of Louis Vuitton and Gucci, and soon lots of luxury bags were making the journey from Europe to Tokyo.

Stage 3, the *show off* stage, had been reached. When you first have money you need to announce it. People started acquiring the symbols of wealth and displaying them in earnest. Thorstein Veblen's first rule came into play: No point merely possessing wealth, you have to make sure it is "always in evidence" to gain the esteem of others[8]; albeit in a Japanese variation, far removed from the leisure classes that Veblen sought to explain. With Western brands busy writing the consumption rule book, what was in evidence was a lot of imported luxury goods, clearly branded so everyone could get the message at a glance. It's what marketing speak calls "status markers." The Louis Vuitton or Gucci bag became a status marker: It said that you came from a respectable family of decent means, it signified your membership of a certain stratum of society. Five to ten years into the show-off stage and a market typically reaches tipping point – the crucial point of no return after which the luxury culture spreads rapidly.

In the case of Japan, the 1980s saw a rapid growth in personal income and the emergence of a wealthy middle class. Soon a large enough chunk of the population were carrying their status markers, and now the overriding need was to conform to this new set of rules about how to express your status. This is the stage at which the collectivist nature of Asian cultures kicks in strongly: If the group prescribes that you carry Gucci and Prada, you do exactly that. If you don't carry an appropriate status marker, you run the risk of being considered socially deficient or, worse still, losing face. The fourth stage, *fit in*, took hold in Japan and helped spread the luxury culture even further.

Japan is now in the last stage, where luxury brands have become a *way of life*. The point about luxury goods is that there is no going back – unless of course there is a dramatic drop in financial status and you simply can't afford them any more. Once you get used to the fine quality of Zegna suits and Prada shoes, you find it next to impossible to wear a Marks & Spencer suit or a local brand of shoe. The eye is so well trained, personal standards of quality are set so high, that you are locked into a lifetime of luxe buying. For the Japanese, quality has always been a keen point anyway, and that only reinforces their use of luxury goods. By this stage the cult has become well entrenched and it stays put – the Japanese have continued to buy luxury brands in large quantities despite the recession of the 1990s. They can't help themselves. Besides, luxe goods continue to perform the all-important status marker function.

While we have used Japan to illustrate the stages in the spread of the luxury brand culture – and admittedly Japan's greater personal wealth, acute need to conform, and fixation with quality have accelerated and exaggerated the spread – the basic model holds true for all of Asia. After Japan, Hong Kong was the next to go through all the stages. Much of Hong Kong's population consists of refugees from China escaping its turbulent times. Living in cramped camps, they toiled hard in the 1950s and 1960s, and with the economy taking off in the 1970s and a great deal of money made in stocks and the property boom in the 1980s and 1990s, people had personal wealth to spend. In the early 1990s, when Hong Kong's wealthier women were dressed head to toe in Chanel while others carried their Gucci and Prada bags, they were simply showing off their status. Then it became a social necessity to fit in and the use of luxury goods spread further. Consider the fact that in Hong Kong your *first* car is often a BMW or a Mercedes, and if you can't afford that you may as well not bother; a lower-priced Toyota is worse than no car. Hong Kong is now firmly in the *way of life* stage and a confident and discerning luxe consumer society has emerged.

India is at the *start of money* stage. A large and growing middle class is buying washing machines and mobile phones and reasonably priced cars on installment plans. The next rung is taking budget holidays to Thailand and Singapore. In the meantime, a small élite segment is indulging in luxury brands – a mix of India's established business families and spanking new money. These are the ones keeping the newly opened luxury stores in business.

China is at the *show off* stage. Wealth has arrived to select segments of society, concentrated in the coastal cities, and these people are tripping over each other trying to acquire the symbols of wealth and displaying them in the most conspicuous manner. The rich are going over the top with mansions and cars, sending their children to boarding school abroad, and even the pet dog has designer accessories. Veblen would have been pleased to see his theory revalidated by the emergence of China's new leisure class, never mind what Mao would have thought.

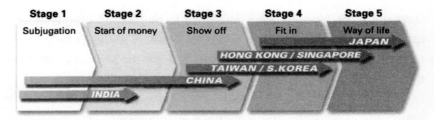

Figure 2.3 Asian countries' stages of luxe evolution

While the leisure class splurges and struts, an up-and-coming segment, and a substantially larger one, is at Stage 2, where modest incomes are allowing people to taste a few luxuries of life – a washing machine, a decent apartment with a toilet of its own, and private tuition for your only child. Sadly, most of the Chinese population is still at Stage 1, subjugation of the economic kind.

The economic boom for South Korea and Taiwan came in the 1980s and 1990s and they have rapidly progressed to the *fit in* stage. South Koreans display a competitive edge to their purchasing behavior – they like to outdo one another – and as a result higher and higher standards of luxe consumption are becoming the norm.

Like Hong Kong, Singapore too is at Stage 5 – luxury brands have become a way of life, but at a more subdued level. The warm weather all year round and the relaxed dress culture mean that Singaporeans will buy more casual brands like Polo Ralph Lauren, pairing them with expensive watches and swank condominiums. Perhaps reflective of the *way of life* stage, local girls only half-jokingly say that when trying to land a good husband check out how well he delivers on the all-essential 5Cs: condominium, car, club, credit card, and carat – needless to say, in the last category a nice big Cartier diamond would help.

Wealth reaches successive layers of society over time, so even within a country different layers of society are at different stages of luxe consumption (see Figure 2.3). As we saw, in China's case it ranges from *subjugation* to *show off*. Similarly, other countries have a range of stages being played out at any given time.

The Spread of Luxury model not only explains the stages that a country has been through, it helps *predict* what is up ahead, thereby assisting companies in planning their next moves. It's neither obvious nor easy to see what's around the corner. For example, in India the prevailing belief is that luxury brands will remain a well-contained élite indulgence, backed by the seemingly irrefutable logic that it is only the élite who are buying luxe today. This is consistent with our model – in the *start of money* stage, only a tiny élite buys luxury brands – but as India's economy develops, the next stages are inevitable and the cult is destined to spread. It would be worthwhile for India to get ready for this, by for example building high-end retail infrastructure, which the country sorely lacks.

The model also highlights the immense potential that Asia holds. While the luxury culture has made great strides, virtually saturating Japan, there is still plenty of growth left in other markets. Can you imagine what it will be like when China progresses to the *way of life* stage? There will be a bountiful feast for luxury brands.

Luxury Gourmands to Luxury Nibblers

There is a straightforward equation: The fatter the bank balance, the greater the luxury consumption. This leads to three distinct categories of luxury consumers:

* At the top end are the *luxury gourmands*, who devour luxury in great big bites, donning designer labels from head to toe, 24/7. Needless to say these are high net worth individuals (HNWI), with upwards of a million dollars in financial assets.
* Next you have the *luxury regulars*, who while not quite in the gourmand league are nevertheless on a staple diet of luxury goods. These are affluent people with financial assets in excess of US$100,000.
* And finally there are the *luxury nibblers*, who partake in a few small bites of luxe every season, a bag here, a watch there, whatever they can afford. They are typically young people with next to no savings in the bank, but with an increasing income-generating capacity thanks to a decent education and a well-paying job.

While all three segments are united by their love for luxury, their behavior and lifestyle are drastically different, and so are the opportunities they present to marketers. Let's take a closer look.

Luxury Gourmands

According to the Merrill Lynch/Cap Gemini's *World Wealth Report*, one in four millionaires resides in Asia.[9] That translates into 2.4 million HNWIs with a combined wealth of US$7.6 trillion – a lot of money, more than the combined GDP of the UK, Germany, and France. What is more, the number of Asia's millionaires and their wealth have been growing steadily over the years and now compare quite well with the developed West – Europe has 2.8 million HNWIs holding US$9.4 trillion; North America has 2.9 million HNWIs with US$10.2 trillion.

These Asian HNWIs (the overwhelming majority of whom are men), their wives, mistresses, sons, and daughters – these are the luxury gourmands. Take Hong Kong. A self-respecting tai-tai – a "lady who lunches," on which more below – could spend US$500,000 a year on her wardrobe. Plenty of women in this league change their wardrobe every season. And it's an open secret that sugar daddies and mistresses account for large chunks of business in this segment, especially jewelry from the likes of Cartier or fur from Fendi.

Understanding the nature of Asia's wealth is instructive. Take China, which has 320,000 HNWIs.[10] Inheritance has played no part in these men's fortunes. The average age of China's richest men is under 47,[11] a lot younger than Europe's wealth, which is quite literally old with an average age of 59–62, while North Americans shave a few years off that, averaging between 55 and 57.[12] The fact that not only is China's money new but its owners are so much younger makes a dramatic difference – the tastes and consumption behavior of a man in his 40s sitting on a pile of money he made yesterday are unlike that of a man in his 60s who has been marinating in the green stuff for many generations.

The implication is that marketing to Asia's luxury gourmands is a very different ball game than marketing to the wealthy in Europe or North America.

Luxury Regulars

The reason the democratization of luxury has worked so well in Asia becomes apparent when you look at the growing number of "mass affluent" Asians, in other words individuals with liquid assets in excess of

US$100,000. As is to be expected, the bulk of these individuals are in Japan, but in recent years their numbers have risen sharply in countries such as China and South Korea. According to Datamonitor's Global Wealth Model, in 2004 there were an estimated 30.3 million such people in just the five Asian markets of Japan, China, Hong Kong, Singapore, and South Korea[13] – naturally, these are the markets that are critical for luxury brands. They are typically professionals such as doctors and lawyers, entrepreneurs running their own businesses, executives in senior and middle management positions, bankers, and consultants.

Again, China presents the most exciting picture. In 2004 there were an estimated 3.3 million individuals in the country with more than US$100,000 in liquid assets, and that's a *lot* of money in China. Go a notch lower and there are another 3 million Chinese with US$50,000–100,000 in liquid assets, and in China that too is a fortune. That's 6.3 million Chinese with over US$50,000 in the bank, a number that's growing by the minute.[14] A mouth-watering target for luxury brand companies.

Luxury Nibblers

The luxury nibblers exemplify the new "asset poor, income rich" mindset that is driving the democratization of luxury. As Michael Burke, former head of Christian Dior and now CEO of Fendi, explains, that's a major difference:

In today's world the luxury goods consumer is characterized not necessarily by high net worth but by high disposable income… So we have people who earn enough money to pay for luxury goods, and they'll buy it, they become our consumers, and that's one reason why the average age of our consumer has dropped so dramatically over the last 20–30 years.[15]

Most of Asia's luxury nibblers – a mix of junior executives, secretaries, and even teenagers – have very little savings if any at all, spending what they earn and not being afraid to use that handy credit card to stretch their capacity. Individually, these shoppers may spend relatively small amounts, US$500–2,000 a year, but there are large numbers of them, small drops forming a substantial ocean of luxury sales. Importantly, many of these nibblers are on career paths that will see them rise quickly. For example, a market research executive in a multinational company in China would start off on a salary of US$5,000 a year; five years later she would be earning US$20,000, thanks to China's acute shortage of trained talent. She might buy a wallet to begin with, but rest assured she will be spending on bags, shoes, and more by year five.

Brands have geared up to service this "mass luxury consumer." In sharp contrast to the personalized, away-from-the-public-glare strategy deployed to service luxury gourmands, this is all about being accessible on two fronts: price and physical location. It entails having a strategy of lower price points, making part of the range accessible to the nibblers. The omnipresent Louis Vuitton monogram bag, for instance, starts at US$700; the LV wallet would be US$200–250 – not exactly loose change, but the nibbler sees it as a good investment. She might have to wait for Prince Charming to get a nice big Tiffany diamond, but the company's silver jewelry line is well within reach, starting at US$200. Cosmetics and perfumes perform the same function, putting luxury brands in nibblers' hands for US$20–50. Another strategy is to create diffusion brands to reach out to a wider consumer base. For example, Armani has created a ladder of brands at different price points: Giorgio Armani is top of the rung, Emporio Armani is a step lower, whereas Armani Exchange and Armani Jeans are accessibly priced – you can get a trendy shirt for under US$100.

Increasingly, stores are being designed to show off the lower-priced items up front, smack as you walk into the shop. Even the choice of store locations has been influenced, putting them in busy shopping centers. Ian Hawksworth, executive director of Hongkong Land, explains:

Ten years ago they [luxury brands] wanted no traffic, quiet environment, and exclusivity. Today, they'll still tell you they want that, but frankly what they want is traffic.[16]

A whole network of save-a-buck-on-luxury retail options have sprung up to cater to the nibbler segment. There are parallel import shops that offer the latest range of products at prices 15–25 percent lower than local stores. There are secondhand outlets, even chain stores like Milan Station in Hong Kong, which are making the selling and buying of secondhand luxury systematic and simple. There are even rent-a-bag services. And there are the usual warehouse outlets selling discounted merchandise, mostly the previous season's. Luxury on a shoestring is eminently possible.

TAI-TAIS TO TRENDY TEENS

Stretching across the spectrum from luxury gourmands to luxury nibblers, we see six distinct consumer segments emerging across Asia:

* Celebrity set
* Tai-tais
* Mistresses and junior wives
* Corporate climbers
* Office ladies
* Trendy teens

There are country-by-country differences, and we will highlight these as we delve into individual countries in subsequent chapters, but here we present the common ground that defines these segments.

Celebrity Set

If being in the media limelight is your *raison d'être* then dressing for the cameras comes with the terrain, and that means plenty of Gucci, Prada, Dior, *et al*. Asia's celebrity set consists a colorful cast drawn from the world of entertainment, fashion, business, and politics, as well as high-profile socialites. They enjoy a certain cachet and media-pulling ability in their own nation and a few are able to stretch their appeal across several countries – for example South Korean star Bae Yong Jun draws a crowd in Japan, China, Hong Kong, and Taiwan.

There is a symbiotic relationship and a happy convergence of interests between celebrities and luxury houses, both tied by the pursuit of media publicity. Parties thrown by luxury brands have become a potent image-building tool for both. Innovative themes, creative locations, fashion shows, and mingling with the beautiful people – all the ingredients are there for a great evening and, more importantly, conspicuous coverage in the society pages the morning after. The glamorous evening dresses and other accessories that celebrities wear are singled out and commented on by the media.

Just how sought after these parties have become is illustrated by the case of Hong Kong beauty queen turned actor Candy Chiu Ching Yee. She was so upset at not being invited to Louis Vuitton's global store-opening party in Hong Kong, despite her repeated requests, that she promptly made a press statement announcing her intention to get rid of her entire collection of more than 500 Louis Vuitton items.[17] At a conservative estimate, that's half a million dollars dumped.

The media in turn has a symbiotic though tumultuous relationship with celebrities. After all, you can't become famous without media coverage, and there's nothing like a saucy story to push newspaper/magazine sales. Taiwan's local media is notorious for its vicious tabloid-style coverage, but despite complaints and the occasional lawsuit threat, the love–hate relationship carries on.

Tai-tais

The term tai-tai literally means "wife" in Chinese, but locals use it to refer to the rich "ladies who lunch" set. They are both envied and giggled at in the same breath. With a seemingly bottomless bank account at their disposal, the wives of tycoons, typically in their 40s or 50s, lead a life of beauty treatments, shopping expeditions, and lunches with the girls at trendy restaurants, followed by leisurely afternoon teas, with possibly a manicure squeezed in between. There is a healthy rivalry between these women and that translates into outdoing each other on the shopping front. Furs, diamonds, jewelry, watches, designer outfits, hairdos – you can immediately tell a tai-tai when you see one, whether you are in Taipei, Seoul, Bangkok, or Hong Kong.

There is of course an element of vicarious consumption – the wife encouraged to spend her husband's big bucks so as to reflect the man's high status – but today's tai-tai takes this a bit more personally. She is furiously charging her husband's credit card as much for her own glory as for her man's, and she certainly needs no encouragement. She's a feisty soul, who in many cases has chosen to marry the bank account rather than the man – she knows, in the Asian context, that chances are she will eventually have to share her man with a series of mistresses and junior wives – and she crafts what she considers a meaningful life using unabashed materialism as her tool. While the rest of the world works hard to afford the luxuries of life, spend time with friends, and perhaps do some good for the world, the tai-tai simply eliminates work from the equation and does the luxury and friends bits. Neither is she a slacker when it comes to conspicuous charity engagements, fund-raising through magnificent charity balls being her forte.

The "intelligent tai-tai" is a growing sub-breed within this category. A rich husband, time for lunching with the girls, lots of luxe shopping, she fulfills all the requirements to be part of the tai-tai club. The only difference is that she also works, at least part of the time. She might start a business, a boutique, a spa, or a club, or she may work for a company, even a luxury house.

The tai-tai typically has a wide repertoire of luxury brands – you would too if you shopped as frequently as she does – but some of her favorites are Chanel, Hermès, and Cartier.

Mistresses and Junior Wives

Mistresses exist the world over; the only difference in Asia is that having a mistress is institutionalized. As far as luxury brands are concerned, mistresses form a very significant chunk of their business. Then there is the uniquely Asian concept of a junior wife. In the olden days, Chinese men would take a second or third wife – different from a concubine, who was just a mistress – and the practice continues in modern form. For example, Hong Kong's Stanley Ho is well known for his gambling empire in nearby Macau and equally well known for his four wives, each in a separate mansion. *Legal* matrimony may apply only to the first wife, but Ho has remained loyal to all four, as well as supporting the children that have come from these alliances. What makes such women extremely important to luxury brands is the fact that all the wives, senior and junior, have an annual shopping budget, and when you are married to a Forbes 500 billionaire like Ho with a personal fortune of US$6.5 billion, that budget can be substantial.[18] Of course, it isn't easy for luxury houses to handle multiple clashing egos married to the same man and many tricky situations arise – if you have a hot new item, which wife do you call first?

In South Korea, Taiwan, and Japan, the bar hostess market is also very significant for luxury brands. Businessmen in Asia frequent hostess bars, taking important clients and settling business deals over a few drinks, preferably Hennessy cognac or Absolut vodka. These are expensive affairs – an evening of drinking alone could cost US$1,000 a head. Many bars cater to traveling Japanese businessmen, who are known to be lavish spenders. While pouring drinks and chatting with the men is the hostess's official job definition, judging by the amount of luxury shopping these girls do that definition is often stretched. *Mama-sans*, the mother figures who run the show, are extremely well dressed.

In South Korea, the bar hostesses favor Chanel suits – they feel that it helps them project an intellectual look, important since their clients are typically from the top echelons of the corporate world. Thankfully, they are also known to buy glamorous evening gowns, Christian Lacroix among the designers. In Taiwan, Chanel has become so associated with the bar hostess scene that some working women in senior corporate positions are wary of using the brand.

Interestingly enough, the "other woman," whether bar hostess or mistress, has historically played an important role in the spread of fashion in Europe too.[19] It was the *demimondaine*, with her innate sense of style and daring, who first donned the latest fashion creations, happily willing to give risky ensembles a go. She was in that line of business anyway. She played the crucial role of trendsetter, while "ladies of refinement" followed at a safe distance. Our Chinese concubine, Korean bar hostess, Hong Kong junior wife, Taiwanese mistress – these lovely ladies are simply doing for fashion what the French *demimondaine* did a century ago.

Corporate Climbers

Call it the luxing of working clothes. People in managerial positions at all levels, men and women, treat the suit as a corporate uniform, and therefore form a large and regular clientele for luxury brands.

In Hong Kong, Tokyo, Seoul, even Beijing and Shanghai, the dress code for men in multinational companies, law firms, banks, financial organizations, and consultancies is a business suit, and this being Asia that invariably translates into a designer suit. Senior managers prefer Zegna, Lanvin, and Giorgio Armani, expensive pieces that start at US$2,000. The younger men typically have a small collection of designer suits, reserving them for important client meetings – their preferred brands are Hugo Boss and Emporio Armani, the more fashion conscious among them venturing into Prada or Gucci, if they have what it takes to carry off the slim-cut look. In trendier professions such as advertising, PR, fashion, and retailing – especially of luxury brands – the bar is set higher and creativity and personal style are taken far more seriously. A female advertising executive in Tokyo told us:

If you walk down the office, turning up the jacket collars to check the label, I bet 90 percent of the guys in client servicing will be in Armani suits.

How does she know? "You hear the men talk about it in the office," she explains.

Professional women are even more important customers, as besides suits and other clothes they are big accessories shoppers, snapping up Manolo Blahniks and Jimmy Choos while building up an extensive collection of high-end bags. This is a brand-savvy segment with perhaps the widest repertoire – ranging from expensive Hermès cashmere suits and Chanel jewelry to fashionable pieces from Narciso Rodriguez and Marc Jacobs. They know what they want and they have the money to buy it. Little wonder, then, that in advanced markets such as Hong Kong, this segment accounts for almost 50 percent of luxury brand sales.

The reason is simple to understand. This is the first generation of women in Asia who are climbing higher in the corporate world – admittedly not quite in the league of their counterparts in the UK and US, but nevertheless significant in number. Many of them are in top and middle management, armed with a higher education and making it further in what is no longer a man's world, although Japan remains the one big exception to this. At the same time, many are delaying marriage and continuing to live with their parents; and others who are married are putting off having children. As a result, their focus is squarely on them-selves and their money isn't sucked away into childcare and mortgages. It can be spent on luxury goods.

Asia's women have traditionally put their families above themselves, and while family remains extremely important, for the first time work-ing women are thinking of themselves and saying hey, it's OK to indulge myself. They take pride in their achievements and reward themselves, often with a piece of branded luxury. One young marketing executive in Hong Kong told us she pats herself on the back every year with a glam-orous Valentino suit. Businesswomen in China are doing the same – success is a new feeling and they are rewarding themselves with Dior boots and Chanel bags.

The ability to afford these luxury goods further bolsters their sense of achievement – not only have they acquired the symbols of success, they have done it with their own money.

Office Ladies

In secretarial and junior administrative positions, the "OLs" are big on accessories, especially bags – you could justifiably call them designer bag ladies. Their greatest importance as a segment is in Japan, where they are a consumer force to be reckoned with. Trapped in mindless jobs with no prospects of rising up the corporate ladder, the Japanese office ladies live it up once they step outside the office: eating out, enter-tainment, holidaying abroad, and plenty of luxury brand shopping.

In other Asian countries OLs splurge selectively – they look for value for money and almost always seem to find it in designer bags and other accessories. Outside Japan these women earn modest salaries, so when it comes to clothes they may well settle for mid-market and cheaper brands, but they go out of their way to acquire a few well-branded designer accessories, even if these are just wallets.

Trendy Teens

Mostly girls in high school and college, this is a segment that has no business buying luxury goods, but consists of surprisingly keen shop-pers. Japan takes the lead here, its trendy teens being big enthusiasts when it comes to designer bags, as well as wallets and smaller accessories. In Thailand, one comes across the incongruous sight of school girls in uniform, clutching books in one hand and swinging a Fendi bag in the other, strolling through high-end department stores presumably looking for more.

The designer bug (and bag) has somehow crept into the teenage culture and young girls find it hard to resist peer pressure – it's pretty much a case of "buy the designer item currently in favor or be the odd one out." The older generation's materialistic culture has seeped into the teen world. They watch their idols, pop stars and actors, donning designer labels, they read magazines that promote luxury brands, and they follow the lead, adapting a designer piece to their teen dress code – for example stressed denims, colored hair, cute t-shirts, and a designer bag.

Getting the money to finance this expensive habit is another story altogether, and sadly some of them resort to extreme behavior, as we shall see in the next section.

Five Themes that Bind Asia

The markets of Asia are at different stages of development, ranging from China, still at the gleeful show-off-my-goodies stage, to Japan, a full-blown case of luxe addiction. Each country has its own endearing eccentricities that make it unique. But sift through the patterns of behavior, dig into the reasons behind them, and five themes emerge that stretch across all the markets. These are Asian truths, if you like, that bind these seemingly diverse people, speaking of a common set of deeply held beliefs that result in remarkably similar behavior.

The Phenomenon of Compulsory Brands

Louis Vuitton and Gucci have become "compulsory brands" – junior office ladies to society high priestesses, everyone's got to have them, whether it's one odd wallet or a Candy Chui-sized collection. Even those who might not want them still buy them. A senior Japanese executive told us his wife had sworn off Louis Vuitton because it's so "common," but, zombie-like, she ended up buying one this season anyway.

While Louis Vuitton and Gucci are across-the-board winners, there are other brands that rule smaller terrains – a country, a consumer segment, a product category. Ferragamo is a compulsory brand in South Korea: Without a pair of these magic shoes you are like Cinderella well past midnight. In China, Zegna and Dunhill are must-haves for men who walk the corridors of power. Hermès has a stranglehold on the affections of upper-crust women from Thailand to South Korea. Chanel has ruled steadfastly among the ladies-of-the-night segment; in what could be interpreted as a fight to get back their men, some wives of rich businessmen are also keen Chanel shoppers. Rolex and Cartier are sure shots if you are looking for expensive watches. As for pens, you can't possibly go wrong with a Mont Blanc – from directors in the boardroom to recently hired management trainees, everyone's writing with one.

It is remarkable that a handful of brands have managed to stand out in what is clearly a very crowded arena, with over 100 companies milling around a dozen product categories. What propels Asians to flock to this small set of power names? The answer lies in the simple fact that Asians are looking for status markers (a concept we looked at earlier), therefore head for the brands, and more specifically products within a brand, that do an excellent job of marking status.

You speak, others understand – that's what makes a successful status marker. Want to ensure your brand is compulsory? Develop a symbolic language and invest in making it universally understood. That's what the logo-fication of bags was all about, creating a luxury brand Esperanto, spoken globally. While logo patterns are arguably the loudest and clearest, companies are also investing in other visual idioms. Chanel has the gold chains, the quilted leather, the signature flower. Ferragamo shoes have the snaffle bits that give them away. Burberry you can check out from a mile away. Mont Blanc's white symbol is unmistakable at close quarters. Of course, it needs years of steady and massive investment in highly visible publicity campaigns to make these symbols instantly recognizable, to turn your brand into one of the *ming pai* or famous brands that Asian consumers want.

Why not start teaching the luxe lingo to newborns? Reflective of the times, Singapore mother Amy Allen has written *This Little Piggy Went to Prada*, tongue-in-cheek versions of popular nursery rhymes that the designer-nappy-bag generation of mums can relate to, and presumably sing to their gurgling babies. A sample:

There was a young woman who lived in her Choos,
Though she once had a house in a smart Chelsea Mews.
So much on Jimmy,
The house had to go,
And with it, her Amex and husband in tow![20]

If you are seeking a status marker, the price of a product acquires a great deal of significance, as your standing is being gauged by the amount of money you are seen to be spending. Like the symbol, the price needs to be universally known, and thanks to the popularity of these compulsory brands – even if you aren't buying them, you're window-shopping and studying your copies of *Vogue* and *Cosmo* – everyone seems to have a fair idea of the ballpark range. That helps slot people into various levels by simply looking them up and down. She is carrying a Bottega Veneta bag, she must have spent a cool US$5,000 on it, she is obviously loaded – simple deductive consumer logic.

Caviar and popcorn

The coat is a US$1,000 Burberry, the black t-shirt underneath a US$20 Esprit. The US$700 bag is from Gucci, but the stressed denim embroidered jeans are from a bustling street market for US$25. The suit is Armani, US$1,500, the Rolex is fake, US$15. There's a move toward mixing the highly expensive with the barely expensive all over Asia. Caviar with popcorn, so to speak.

What's the logic behind this trend of combining the cheap with the pricey? For the rich, it's an entertaining game whereby you extend an already extensive wardrobe – a bit of naughty fun, announcing casually that the diamond bracelet is Van Cleef & Arpels and the Cartier watch is Shenzhen, China.

For the not so rich, it's about saving on the basic elements, the t-shirts and trousers, to be able to indulge on the statement-making pieces. Maximize status on a budget. Buy the shirts, blouses, trousers – blacks and whites, the building blocks of a wardrobe – from Giordano, Bossini,

Esprit, and other Gap-like brands, preferably on sale. Pick up a few snazzy jeans, scarves, mufflers, trinkets, and baubles, colorful touches that spice up your wardrobe, all from local night markets and fashion streets that brim over with cheap finds. And then you add a few final touches of luxury goods to complete the look. A Gucci watch, a signature piece from Tiffany, sunglasses from Christian Dior – all excellent investments that add instant class. You could substitute one or two of the designer pieces with cheaper fakes, but it's a tricky tightrope in this segment of society. The rich can buy fakes with relative impunity as people assume they are real, but the not so rich have to be careful – if you are in search of social kudos, you have to have enough genuine designer pieces to earn it.

The caviar-and-popcorn logic applies equally to men. The head of a Hong Kong-based company – a natty dresser and self-confessed luxe addict – told us he had traded down from US$3,000 Armani suits to US$125 suits by local brand G2000. However, he accessorizes them with a Gucci belt, an Armani tie, Prada shoes, a Bulgari watch, finishing off with a bag from his favorite brand, Louis Vuitton, of which he has a 20-strong collection. His view: No point wasting money on an expensive suit, people think it is a designer brand because everything else is.

Ironically, mixing cheap with designer chic has acquired a certain street cachet of its own: The cleverness with which you put together a look is in itself considered worthy of respect. But make no mistake, *savoir faire* will get you only so far. You need the force of Louis Vuitton or Gucci, Chanel or Dior, to hit the home run.

This behavior underlines the importance that Asians place on *publicly* visible symbols over for-my-eyes-only products – public flash versus private pleasure. The insight for marketers: Consumers spend what it takes on visible symbols, but tighten their belts on invisible products. If your brand is an excellent status marker you can command a fat premium, but the market for even very high-quality privately consumed products is much smaller by comparison. For example in China, the leading brands of mobile phones in Beijing, Shanghai, and Guangzhou are imported ones like Nokia and Motorola, which cost twice as much as local ones. As Tom Doctoroff, CEO, JWT Greater China points out, cellphones are a "powerfully public means of projecting individual identity," so consumers pay up. When it comes to home appliances, it's a different story — lower-priced *local* brands like TCL, Haier, and Konka dominate. "Sony, Panasonic, and other Japanese trademarks drip prestige but few consumers (other than upscale yuppies) buy them. They are not displayed; only the family uses them."[21]

Sacrifice at the Altar of Luxe

Youngsters in Seoul survive on cup noodles to put together enough money for a pair of Ferragamo shoes. Young working women in Taipei prefer to travel in crowded buses so they can save enough for a Burberry bag. University students in Thailand may acquire a sugar daddy to finance their luxe craze. Japanese teenage girls, some as young as 14, may even turn to part-time prostitution, using mobile phones to find partners for what is euphemistically called "paid dating." Many South Koreans have overspent liberally on luxe, stretching their credit cards to snapping point, and in a few tragic cases this has led to suicide.

The degree and extent vary from country to country, but the phenomenon of sacrifice for the sake of acquiring branded luxe beyond one's financial means is there in each and every country, affecting most acutely the young. How do you explain the intense hankering for designer labels that calls for such excessive measures? It is not as if these are necessities of life like food, shelter, or the wellbeing of your family — circumstances that might justify such behavior. Bags with logos could easily be substituted with cheaper bags, one would think. Clearly not. Herein lies the most potent evidence, sad and sobering as it might be, that in Asia branded luxury goods aren't fripperies you can dispense with, they have become essential items, without which you are seen to be a lesser person in the eyes of other people and yourself. You have to have them to maintain your self-esteem, even if doing so calls for self-sacrifice.

At the heart of this phenomenon is the fact that luxury brands have entered teen culture in a big way. Nicole Fall, Tokyo correspondent for online trend-analysis service WGSN, did a feature titled "What's in your bag?" for which she stopped teenagers on the street and had them empty out their bags. She found between three and seven designer pieces in the typical teenager's bag: a Gucci wallet, an LV key chain holder, a Prada make-up bag, a Chanel lipstick, all housed in a Prada rucksack or a Louis Vuitton bag.[22] It's pretty much the law of the jungle: If you don't have the luxury items that others in the group have, then they will ostracize you and your so-called friends may not talk to you. Barbaric and incomprehensible as it sounds, this is the reality for many Japanese teens, and to varying degrees in other Asian countries.

Teenagers and young adults are most vulnerable to this sacrifice phenomenon, as their financial means are insignificant and high-priced luxury brands are furthest from their reach. Their backgrounds are not necessarily poor; more often than not these teenagers come from families with decent incomes. It's not the lack of money, rather it's the lack of understanding, as many parents don't see the point in spending US$500 on a bag for a teenager.

The Magalogue Diet

Staying ahead of the curve wins you greater kudos. That means you can't wait till goods are in store windows, or look around and see what's hot – you've got to proactively seek out advance information and act on it. Call it just-in-time fashion, when you hit the store as soon as the new arrivals do. Sometimes you hit the store *before* the goods arrive, patiently queuing up for a day or two for highly sought-after limited editions. Of course, it helps if you figure on stores' VIP lists, then your advance information system comes into play and store managers call you up to give you first rights on scarce and precious items even before they're put on the shelves. The rest of us flip through fashion magazines – youngsters study them like they're revising for an exam. Knowledge is key.

A whole slew of magazines dole out advice, analyze trends, point out what's hot, show who's wearing what, present the right look. There are local editions of the international biggies like *Elle*, *Vogue*, *Marie Claire*, and *Cosmopolitan*; even the international editions from London and New York have a certain following. Then there are a vast number of local magazines, especially in Japan where the magazine stands offer a feast of titles, each a weighty volume, a cross between a magazine and a catalogue – a "magalogue."

These magazines play the role of perpetrators and saviors at the same time. It's their high-decibel declarations of what's hot that set trends, their do-it-yourself guidance on shopping, mixing, and matching that has girls rushing to the stores and copying looks. In Japan people talk about fashion magazine editors with hushed respect – they're very powerful creatures indeed, changing the fortunes of brands they choose to smile on, shaping consumer perceptions through sure-footed editorial pronouncements. On the other hand, if you're a consumer struggling to keep up with ever-changing trends, these fashion bibles are a godsend: at least you know what to do. Magazines provide the fuel on which the complex fashion machinery runs, linking the catwalks of Paris and Milan, the global and local celebrity scene, and the retail scene with its store openings and product launches, depositing images and actionable information on consumers' radar screens. They imbue brands with social meaning – one more "meaning manufacturing" agent – wear this hot look, carry this hot bag, and you will be hot yourself.

The implication for marketers is interesting. As consumers rely on fashion intelligence from magazine articles, you have to do what it takes to be part of these write-ups. Traditional advertising gets you noticed, but to create a full-blooded trend your products have to be recommended by the fashion glossies.

Cleavage in a Gucci Bag

Look at Milan and Paris catwalks and the message is clearly sexy. Forget cleavage, the whole breast is exposed through sheer fabric. There's also plenty of leg, waist, shoulder, back, and bottom on display – the art of fashion is as much about what you cover as what you show. Clothes are cut to emphasize sexuality; even a full-body ski suit has built-in oomph. Gucci, Prada, Dior – most brands' advertising campaigns present a raw sensuality. Dior even posted a nude on Hong Kong billboards, causing a furore in the city. All through the history of fashion sex has been integral to the look, whether it was the early corseted dresses with a flattened bosom spilling gently upwards, showing an expanse of creamy flesh, or today's sexually aggressive clothes, not just on the runways but also on the streets.

Except in Asia. Asian women buy all the sexy designer labels, but they dress and present themselves with nearly nun-like primness. Smart, chic, classy, pretty, feminine, ladylike – yes. Sexy – no. Asia may be very permissive when it comes to designer-label consumption, but it's conservative when it comes to sexual expression. Japanese and South Korean women go for the suit look: skirts and jackets; Hong Kong's "women in black" have a great sense of style: skirt suits, trouser suits, skillfully mix-and-match looks; Taiwan's women are the opposite, preferring colorful casual. But rarely is there a sexy edge. Teenagers and youngsters may dress in outlandish outfits, but not often will there be the level of overt sexiness that one finds in young people's clothing elsewhere in the world. Cute, punky, even surreal in Japan, but seldom provocative. In South Korea, the fashionable *pin-jok* look that swept through youngsters had them dressed in neat skirt suits and low-heeled shoes, the focus on a diamante hairpin after which the look was named. The movie-star and celebrity crowd is arguably more forward, but even they seem tame compared to Hollywood standards of anatomy display. Ask a Hong Kong fashionista who her style icon is and chances are she'll say Audrey Hepburn.

The underlying belief is that decent girls don't show flesh, even if it is just a flash of cleavage. In Japan, the excessive bowing culture means that necklines have to be cut appropriately so that bosoms are not inadvertently revealed while bowing. In Beijing, a luxury brand store manager told us it was very hard to sell the more blatant outfits in a season's collection. Dior's sexy advertising and in-store merchandising, far tamer than the aforementioned Hong Kong nude, caused a stir in Shanghai. Even if a woman personally wants to add oomph to her style, she has her relatives to think of – Asians set a lot of store by their family's face, and the last thing she'd want to do is embarrass them by dressing inappropriately. (Singapore is the one exception, where the warm weather has added a Mediterranean touch to dressing – skimpy tank tops and shorts, for example – and a lot more skin is visible here.)

With sexuality ruled out, the ways in which a woman can express herself are narrowed down. Hong Kong-based psychologist Jean Nicol explains that a Gucci bag is a safe choice in a society that rules out other options.[23] A Gucci bag is a permissible indulgence. It does not send out a sexual message, but at the same time it cues money and prestige, which, of course, is highly valued. What is more, Gucci uses sexuality in its communication and its clothes, so you are in fact buying a provocative brand, but the safe part of it. A Gucci bag instead of a low-cut dress – an acceptable message of high status instead of an unacceptable message of "I am sexy."

A New Class System Is Born

For the most part, the brands Asians choose are European. French ones like Louis Vuitton, Hermès, Chanel, and Cartier. Italian ones like Gucci, Prada, Armani, and Zegna. British ones like Burberry and Dunhill. Swiss ones like Rolex and Bally. American brands have had limited influence on the Asian scene so far, the one big exception being Tiffany, and of late Coach has found a large following in Japan on its "accessible luxury" platform and its new logo-pattern look.

Whatever the brands, the more pertinent question is why Asians have taken to Western luxury brands en masse and with such passion – cutting across countries, slicing across segments of society, willingly making sacrifices where necessary.

The starting point is the fact that the twentieth century was a time of massive change in Asia, upheavals on the political, economic, and social front. The result: Old ways of defining who you are and your place in the world around you were systematically dismantled. Look back in time and you find a well-defined social order in all Asian societies. The Japanese had the Samurai–Farmer–Craftsman–Merchant system with the Shogun as ruler. The Indians had the Brahmins–Kshatriyas–Vaishyas–Shudras caste system. (The Brahmins were priests and scholars, Kshatriyas warriors and princely rulers, Vaishyas merchants, farmers, and artisans, and the lowly Shudras were laborers.) Koreans and Chinese had similar social classes. In all the systems the common thread was a division of society by profession, or membership of a certain class determined by birth, and movement along social classes was rarely allowed. There was a clear-cut pecking order, with the higher classes commanding more respect, and the clout of a religion such as Confucianism or Hinduism legitimized and enforced the whole system. People's identity was defined by the social class they were born into. And whether they liked it or not, there wasn't a great deal they could do about it, except perhaps hope for a higher birth in the next life. (China was the one exception where the system of Imperial Examination allowed common people to enter the bureaucracy, and thereby raise their social status.)

The interesting, and somewhat irrational, point to note in all these systems is that the guys who made money, the merchants and craftsmen, actually came pretty low down the social hierarchy. The Japanese relegated them to the lowest spot. The Indians placed the merchant class just one notch above the laborer class, and certain kinds of labor (such as making shoes) rendered you physically untouchable, unfit even to draw water from the village well. (Sweet irony there: Today's Indian élite would not only happily pay top dollar for Manolo Blahniks or Jimmy Choos, they would vie to have the designers as dinner guests.) Michael Pinches calls the downgrading of such people "cultural antithesis,"[24] in that direct engagement in economic pursuits or mundane material production only served to exclude you from the world of the socially privileged class. The obvious pursuit of money was dirty; unless of course you were born into it, ruling aristocrats or wealthy landlords collecting rent and taxes – that was worthy of respect. Better still if you were a scholar or warrior, then you enjoyed high social status. Even the era of Western colonization of various Asian countries did not significantly change the local social order, except to add a substantial middle-class bureaucracy that helped foreign rulers administer the occupied countries.[25]

In contrast, professors (the current equivalent of Brahmins) or army officers (modern-day Samurais, if you will) aren't likely to turn many heads in today's Asia. In all likelihood, they make a modest amount of money and are accorded a modest amount of respect. The new math is pretty straightforward: The more money you make, the higher your social status. Admittedly, your family credentials still count, but they have been superseded by the new religion of money. And it doesn't matter *how* you make your money – it's perfectly OK to engage in the once lowly acts of manufacturing and trading. Suddenly, the merchant class has been propelled to the top of the social pyramid, successful entrepreneurs are the new nobility, and professionally trained managers who run corporate businesses have become highly paid hotshots.

How did this turning of the tables come about? After the colonial powers left, the main focus of independent Asian governments was national development, the task of building essentially poor countries into powerful economies. Though many experimented with various forms of communism and socialism (which limit the role of the entrepreneur), by the late 1970s and 1980s the mantra changed to liberalization, at least on the economic front. Suddenly the patriotic thing to do was to be a successful entrepreneur. Not only were you getting rich yourself, you were building companies, providing employment, building the nation. Your wealth was your achievement, worthy of celebration and respect.

Take the example of Anil Ambani, who heads Reliance Group offshoot Anil Dhirubhai Ambani Enterprises. He has a personal net worth of US$5.5 billion and was voted MTV Youth Icon in 2003. His father Dhirubhai, with just a high-school education, started life as a small-time trader and built up Reliance from scratch – family credentials that would have been sneered at a few decades ago. On receiving the MTV Award the younger Ambani said:

I think wealth creation is no longer a bad word and enterprise is valued by youngsters today much more than in the past.[26]

Liberalization also let in foreign investment, seen as a necessary route to national development. Soon multinational companies were trooping in, offering hefty salaries to professional managers. Work for Goldman Sachs or Morgan Stanley and with a bit of luck you'll be taking home a million dollars a year by the time you're 40. You don't have to be an entrepreneur risking your capital, you can strike it unbelievably rich just being employed by one of these companies. Suddenly getting a professional education, preferably a Western one, becomes your ticket to corporate employment and financial success. An MBA from Harvard, Stanford, or Wharton also functions as a status marker.

But making money is only one part of the equation. To gain social stature you have to let the world know you've got it. We are back to Veblen, having to find a way to translate a sizeable bank balance into sizeable social esteem, and no reliable status-marking system in sight. Enter Western luxury brands, with their whole meaning-manufacturing machinery in tow. Air meets vacuum. Knife meets butter. Gucci meets tai-tai. A brand new and much-needed system of marking your place in the current fluid social order takes root. Luxury brands have become the lingua franca of status. Don Hèrmes, Chanel, and Cartier, throw in a Mercedes or Ferrari for good measure, and you're immediately cueing membership of the upper classes. One of the regular-issue Louis Vuitton monogram bags says you come from a family of decent financial standing, at least enough to cough up US$500–1,000 on that bag.

Many people take matters into their own hands and dress their way up the social ladder, hence the disproportionately high spending on luxury goods by segments of society who should know better. Out go Scholar–Warrior–Artisan–Merchant; in come Vuitton–Gucci–Rolex–Tiffany. From that follows the central thesis of our book:

Luxury brands are a modern set of symbols that Asians are wearing to redefine their identity and social position.

The intriguing question is what makes this particular Western luxury brand-defined system stick in Asia. Why don't people smart enough to achieve significant financial success, many extremely well educated, make choices based on their own individual preferences, instead of blindly following the luxury brand-dictated norm?

That's just it. To understand what makes the luxe code tick and stick in Asia, one has to appreciate the differences between the collectivist societies generally found in Asia and the more individualist ones of the West. Cross-cultural anthropologist Geert Hofstede has mapped geographic distribution on a collectivist–individualist scale. As would be expected, Japan, South Korea, Hong Kong, Taiwan, Singapore, and other Southeast Asian countries are staunch collectivists, while the US, UK, and Australia are three of the most individualist countries in the world.[27] While the West celebrates individual differences – setting much store by personal preferences and their expression, defining your identity in terms of what's unique about you – the Asian way is almost diametrically opposite. Asians' membership of a collective shapes their identity, and as a result they emphasize the views and goals of the groups they belong to.[28] Whereas individualism believes in self-realization even in the face of social pressure to conform, collectivism believes that conforming to the norms set by your groups is the proper way to behave, even if they are opinions you do not personally share. If luxury brands become the norm, then it makes perfect sense to buy them.

To this predisposition to conform add the Confucian idea of "face." The concept is of Chinese origin, but has wide applicability across Asia. There are two distinct aspects of face: *mien-tzu* and *lien*.[29] Both pertain to a person's reputation. *Mien-tzu* refers to material prestige, being successful, and displaying wealth through ostentation; *lien*, on the other hand, refers to one's moral standing, the loss of which would make it very hard to function in Chinese society. *Mien-tzu* plays a crucial role in enforcing the luxury brand norm. It is, in fact, very similar to Veblen's concept of conspicuous consumption in the pursuit of social esteem – the only difference is that the robber barons he referred to did it of their own free will, whereas *mien-tzu* pretty much prescribes the socially appropriate thing to do. A sophisticated high-society woman in Bangkok told us that face was a major motivator in her use of luxury brands – her husband's face, her family's face. You have to look good to make your family look good.

The contrast in cultures leads to interesting interpretations, especially in cross-cultural situations. For example, an American woman we spoke with was critical of her new Asian sister-in-law because she's "into all this brand-name stuff like Gucci." On the other hand, another American woman, who by marriage has landed in an élite South Korean family, says her in-laws in Seoul started treating her better when she bought her first pair of Ferragamo shoes.

This brings us to the final question: Why has a set of Western brands been chosen to form this Asian status-marking system? There are two reasons. First, Asian luxury goods of such stature and universal meaning do not exist. Secondly, in the age of globalization, international symbols are the ones that Asians value – it's not so much the fact that they're Western that beckons, but the fact that they're international and they stand for the best, in terms of both quality of product and quality of image. At the moment European luxury goods rank the highest on that score, and therefore are the most sought after. That could change, however – well-developed US designer brands have a great opportunity, especially in emerging markets where the association between luxury brands and Europe is not yet deeply entrenched. For example, premium US brand Tommy Hilfiger hit it off in India from day one.

Ironically, the use of Western brands brings on its own anxieties. It is one thing to graduate from bamboo chopsticks to silver-capped ones, but it is altogether another matter to deal with salad forks and fish forks, or to tell a French Bordeaux from a Californian Merlot. Equally, it isn't easy to learn to mix Prada trousers with Dior jackets, Armani jeans with Dolce & Gabbana shirts, and who knows what is the proper way to wear a Hermès scarf, leave alone pronounce the company's name. Not much point asking mother, who in all likelihood wore a kimono, cheongsam, sari, or Mao suit. Luxury brands are still unfamiliar turf and it's going to take time – a generation or two – before *savoir faire* comes naturally.

In the meantime, Asians flock to safe bets, the compulsory brands, using luxe's status-marking prowess to define their identity and their place in the topsy-turvy world around them. You can't possibly go wrong with Louis Vuitton – as we shall see in the next chapter, on Japan.

PART TWO

WHAT AND WHERE

"Louis Vuitton is like the measles... everyone has to get it eventually."

Photo courtesy of Jeff Laitila (www.sushicam.com).

3

JAPAN: AN INSATIABLE YEN FOR LUXURY

"Now that we are very big in Japan, there is a risk that people consider us as a Japanese brand."

Kyojiro Hata, President of Louis Vuitton Japan[1]

The queue started three days before the opening of Louis Vuitton's six-story $100 million flagship store in Omotesando – Tokyo's up-and-coming version of Fifth Avenue – and swelled to 1,400 hopefuls including mothers camping with young children, ending in a record-breaking first-day bonanza of ¥125 million. Forget the 30°C stifling heat, forget that 30 million Japanese already own a Louis Vuitton piece, forget that prices in Japan are a steep 40 percent higher than in Europe. A girl needs her luxury fix, it's as simple as that, and there's nothing like the high of a limited-edition specially designed opening-day bag, the reigning craze in Japan.

Luxaholic Japanese consumers are in a league of their own. Their appetite is boundless, not just for Louis Vuitton but for a variety of imported brands. Almost every known luxury name is present here. Sales within Japan itself account for nearly a quarter of the global luxe market. Add on the Japanese tourist-shopper's binges abroad and you are looking at over 40 percent of world sales coming from Japanese pockets.[2]

Japan's rise from zero to luxe gluttony in two decades flat – from the mid-1970s when the craze began to the mid-1990s when the market peaked – is a startling case study of what could happen in other emerging Asian markets. The country's climb from emerging market to wealthy nation saw the luxury market rise in tandem, and the mad bubble years in particular saw frenzied growth, with brands like Louis Vuitton posting 40–50 percent growth rates,[3] creating a nation of luxury gourmands. The habit set so deep and spread so wide that even after the bubble burst and the country went into years of recession, Japan remained firmly in the *way of life* stage (see Chapter 2). Many brands still saw spectacular growth. Take the case of Coach. It managed to start and develop its business very successfully in the post-bubble years, with growth rates a hearty 30 percent plus, achieving no. 2 spot in 2003 – after Vuitton, of course – in the imported accessories market.

Japan is now a mature market; in fact, the overall imported luxury market has started declining in recent years. Major brands still keep the faith, though: They continue to invest *and* grow. Richard Collasse, head of Chanel in Japan, summed up the industry's sentiments well. At the opening of the brand's 10-floor super-luxurious US$240 million flagship store in Ginza, the costliest yet in Japan, he said: "The future of luxury in Japan is a lot more luxury."[4] Needless to say, that is Chanel's biggest boutique in the world, for what is still the most significant consumer in the world.

Japan is a market like no other in Asia, and in this chapter we analyze the unique psychocultural eccentricities that make the Japanese such voracious consumers of luxe; look at the riotous retail scene that feeds this frenzy; marvel at and unravel the magic formula of the mother of all luxury brands, Louis Vuitton; and finally take home some lessons from this goliath to apply to emerging giants like China and India.

GLOBAL LUXE CHANGES THE FACE OF JAPANESE RETAIL

Just as a fashionista goes on a wardrobe-expanding spree, so has the luxury industry been on an aggressive retail-expansion binge, every now and then putting up stunning architectural masterpieces, against which many cathedrals would pale. In the process, luxury brand companies have taken firmer control of their businesses, gained the upper hand over Japan's once-powerful department stores, and given birth to delightful new shopping districts.

Pull back to the 1970s and 1980s when luxury brands were entering Japan by the boatload. The standard route was to find a distributor

– Hermès used a department store chain as its agent, Loewe did a joint venture with a wholesaler – or a licensing arrangement that gave local partners the right to use the brand name on a variety of products. While that served the companies well enough in Japan's boom years, the usual problems of "one bed, two dreams" emerged. Licensing, in particular, left many brands with one foot in the grave. In the 1990s, in tandem with the worldwide trend toward greater control, most major brands canceled their licenses in Japan and to varying degrees took charge of their distribution.

With the fate of their businesses increasingly in the companies' own hands, aggressive retail expansion became the way to tap into Japan's ever-increasing demand. Luxury brands not only built up extensive networks of stores – the LVMH group of brands had 252 stores by 2004 – they started building larger and lovelier outlets, culminating in enormous flagships of jaw-dropping beauty, with few parallels anywhere in the world.

The mega-flagship trend was started by the $138-million La Maison Hermès in 2001 – a stunning 11-story glass brick store in Ginza, Tokyo's primary shopping district – and more flagships have been popping up ever since like popcorn in a microwave. (For a tour of the Hermès store, see overleaf.) The bar was set so high that soon everyone was calling on top architects, including Japan's finest, to create spectacular monuments that embodied the spirit of their brands. Not far from the Hermès building is Chanel's dazzler on Chuo Dori: Designed by American architect Peter Marino, its glass façade projects Chanel's signature tweed pattern. Louis Vuitton held a design competition and winner Jun Aoki created the "randomly stacked trunks" building on Omotesando.

The flagship trend has been single-handedly responsible for changing the face of retailing in Japan, leading to the development of whole new shopping districts. Omotesando was once a quiet, tree-lined neighborhood, known as an art and culture hotspot; now it's a luxury-lined avenue with an architectural who's who on both sides. Herzog & de Meuron designed Prada's futuristic glass rhomboid structure. Avant-garde Japanese duo Kazuyo Sejima and Ryue Nishizawa created Christian Dior's five-story elegant glass sheath of a building. Tadao Ando's Omotesando Hills – part mall, part residential complex – sports an ingenious spiral slope that encircles the retail atrium.

La Maison Hermès: Bigger Is Better

To understand what the flagship fuss is all about, take a tour of the 11-story Hermès store in Tokyo. Luxury stores don't come much bigger or fancier than this.

Designed by Renzo Piano of Centre Pompidou fame, it's a slim glass-brick tower rising among the tangle of buildings along Ginza's main artery, the Chuo Dori. The entire

range of Hermès products is here: men's and women's ready-to-wear, leather goods, bags, accessories, jewelry, watches, perfume, porcelain, babywear, and riding gear. But more than a store, this is the experience of being momentarily ensconced in the world of Hermès, where beauty and design, tradition and modernity, French products and Japanese service come together, and in the process make the cash registers jangle.

There's an art gallery on the eighth floor, featuring a rotating exhibition by Japanese artists, and a museum on the fifth floor that needs a three-day prior reservation for entry. Hermès graciously waived the three-day rule for us and, donning white coats like doctors, we entered a sterile white environment, part outer space and part science laboratory, with not a soul in sight. Objects on display are from the early days of Hermès, while the high-tech headsets tell you about the love of heritage and history that unites the French and the Japanese.

Five floors are devoted to retail. There's a steady hum of customers, which culminates in frenzied activity on the fourth floor where the much-loved bags are sold. No, you can't get your name onto the Kelly/Birkin waiting list, but we can show you the price list – at which point you think it is just as well the waiting list is closed, as the bag you randomly pick, a 32cm crocodile Kelly, costs a whopping ¥1.75 million (US$17,000).

Gaggles of girls giggle gleefully. While most customers wear a cat's-got-the-cream expression of suppressed delight, we spotted two girls so overcome by emotion that they were sitting clutching one another's hands, Hermès orange shopping bags around their feet, weeping tears of joy in a most un-Japanese display. And you finally understand why thousands of Hermès devotees queued for days for the 2001 opening of La Maison Hermès – it truly is a place of worship where prayers are answered.

A short distance from Omotesando is Aoyama, another quaint, tree-lined area that has grown into a luxury retail district. If Omotesando is about mainstream brands housed in mega-flagships, Aoyama is a feast of connoisseur brands in two- or three-story free-standing stores in a quintessentially Japanese setting. Anna Molinari, Narciso Rodriguez, Alberta Ferretti, Jil Sander, Dries Van Noten, Marc Jacobs, Strenesse, Anteprima – the whole Aoyama area is one giant candy store of luxury brands.

Or go to Roppongi Hills, a swank 29-acre city-within-a-city, built at a cost of US$4 billion, offering an eclectic mix of shopping mall, restaurants, movies, art, a hotel, an office tower, and a residential complex. It has a whole avenue, Keyakizaka Dori, devoted to big-name luxury boutiques. And that's not all, there's the Hillside zone that features designer labels like Anna Sui and Vivienne Tam; or there's the West Walk area with trendy fashion brands such as Anya Hindmarch and Armani Jeans.[5]

THE POWER STRUGGLE WITH DEPARTMENT STORES

With the development of flagships and free-standing stores, luxury brands not only changed the face of retailing in Japan, they also succeeded in altering the power equation in what is essentially a department store-dominated country. Mitsukoshi, Seibu, Isetan, Takashimaya – Japan's department stores are institutions in themselves, huge in size, the leading ones raking in US$2–3 billion in sales from a single location. Their traffic-catching ability is also massive – an estimated 450 million people pass through the top 15 stores annually, thanks in part to their being strategically located on top of train terminals.[6] These mammoth department stores have called the shots, and in the past luxury brands operated within their confines, quite happily given the wide and easy distribution reach they provide.

Traditionally, department stores played a stamp-of-authority role for luxury brands. In the early days Japanese consumers were not really confident of themselves and they didn't know what to make of the influx of imported brands. However, they did have trust in well-established department stores, and figured if they bought at Mitsukoshi or Sogo, they couldn't really go wrong. The department store brand was bigger than the newly arrived luxury brand. But that was in the 1980s and early 1990s. Now, Japanese consumers are themselves a store of brand knowledge, well versed in the latest split-second happenings on the luxury front. And the brands have awoken to the fact that life is possible outside the department store stranglehold, with greater autonomy and greater profitability. They have increasingly moved out and set up their own free-standing stores.

In an ironic reversal of roles, it is now the department stores that need the luxury brands more than vice versa. Japan's department stores have been rattled by financial problems and some have tanked; for example Sogo declared bankruptcy in 2000.[7] The decline of department stores had as much to do with the complacent attitude of the stores themselves as with the troubled state of Japan's economy. Dinosaur-like, they did not bother to remain relevant and dynamic.

Take the upscale Mitsukoshi department store in Ginza. It has a wide selection of imported luxury brands, many beautifully showcased in swank stores-in-store. But when we visited the womenswear floor we found prestigious imported brands presented in a homely setting, rubbing shoulders with lesser-known brands, completely lost in a sea of clothes racks. The store managed to make the sublime look pedestrian.

Faced with declining sales, department stores are fighting back – they are sprucing up their offering, investing in upgrading store interiors, and offering value-added services. Key to their revival strategy is bringing prestigious luxury brands on board, to boost their sagging image as well as to pull in the crowds. Imported luxury brands have become chick magnets, attracting that all-important 20–30-year-old female shopaholic segment, and department stores need their shopping dollars.

Luxury brands now have the upper hand in negotiations and they're using it to corner prime spots in department stores on extremely favorable terms. A whole class of free-standing store look-alikes has emerged, large street-facing shops housed within the department store. For example, the Louis Vuitton outlet in the upscale Matsuya department store in Ginza has enormous interiors and an atmosphere so patently Louis Vuitton that once you step in you forget you are in Matsuya. Just as attractive are the financial terms. Luxury brands are

negotiating down the percentage of sales they typically give department stores, with power brands like Louis Vuitton paying as little as
14–15 percent, while less popular brands pay 30 percent or more.[8]
And as the icing on the cake, department stores often take care of interior decoration and refurbishment costs. Suddenly department stores
are looking attractive again.

For decades, doing business in Japan has come with the caveat that
you play by Japanese rules, which are often inflexible and designed to
keep the outsider at a disadvantage. But by conquering the hearts of the
Japanese consumer in so decisive a manner, imported luxury brands
have shown others how to call the shots, even in Japan.

UNOFFICIAL RETAILING FEEDS THE FRENZY

As if a retail landscape dotted with massive department stores and a
slew of free-standing outlets and gigantic flagships wasn't enough, there
are plenty of unofficial channels to help Japanese consumers get their
luxe fix. There are two factors behind the rise of these unofficial channels: the average 40 percent difference between the price in Japan and
the price in Paris, and the mismatch between the demand and supply of
"hot" items.

Enterprising individuals arbitrage, buying cheap in Europe and selling at a neat profit in Japan, but still well below official store prices.
There's significant money to be made – one parallel importer we heard
about claimed to make US$80,000 in net profits annually, which she
considered "not bad for a one-girl show." The *modus operandi* for getting
the goods in is "organized shopping tours," where a seemingly bona fide
group of tourists buys an agreed amount of luxury goods for a parallel
importer, in exchange for the chance to see Europe for a song. Stores in
Europe are cracking down, with policies limiting sales to one item per
person.

If a red-hot product is stocked out in Japan, chances are it's still available in Paris or Milan. The ultimate item to die for is the Hermès Kelly
or Birkin bag – impossible to get from the official Hermès stores in
Japan, where even the waiting lists are indefinitely closed. Don't despair,
just walk into one of Tokyo's unofficial multibrand stores and take your

pick. We gasped in disbelief as we saw a sight so rare: a whole row of Birkins, in a variety of colors and leathers, sitting quietly on a shelf in a corner store in Aoyama. The products looked genuine enough, the store had a first-class air about it, and the three sales girls provided excellent service. You'd be tempted all right.

While perfectly legal, parallel imports and the subsequent over-supply can prove extremely damaging to a brand. For example, Prada was a raging success, especially its trademark black nylon bag, and Japanese consumers couldn't get enough of it. Parallel importers stepped in and inundated the market. Result: Prada went off the hot list, drowned by the flood. Success has its own pitfalls.

PUTTING JAPAN ON THE COUCH

Understanding Japan's fixation with luxury brands is like trying to put an entire nation on the psychiatrist's couch. The answers are far from obvious, and it requires us to step back and understand the larger social forces that have shaped the collective Japanese psyche. Three such drivers have directly or indirectly led millions of consumers, over and over again, to the doors of Louis Vuitton, Gucci, Chanel, Hermès, *et al*.

The Power of Conforming

Counter-intuitive as it may sound, the driving force behind this rampant, aggressive, and conspicuous consumption is a fairly passive value: the overpowering need to fit into a social circle. Conformity is imprinted into the Japanese psyche from childhood and the entire education system is geared to furthering it. The guiding principle behind conformity is the creation of harmony, entirely noble in itself, but over the years conformity has been taken to extreme lengths.

Alex Kerr, in his provocative book on Japan's problems *Dogs and Demons*, says that the first lesson of Japanese schooling is the "importance of moving in unison." He recounts the experience of writer Peter Hadfield accompanying his daughter Joy to her first day in kindergarten in Japan. With all the children instructed to run counter-clockwise in a

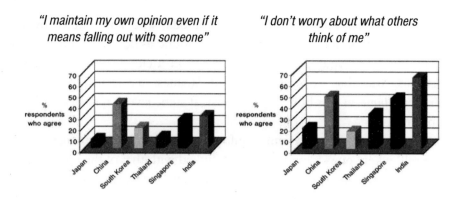

Figure 3.1 The Japanese need to conform is higher than other Asian nations'

Source: Dentsu Institute for Human Studies (March 2001) "Value changes with globalization"

large circle, little Joy chose to run the other way, causing much alarm. Hadfield writes, proud of his daughter's independent stance:

The teachers gently encouraged her to run the "right" way, and silently appealed to me for help. I was proud of my daughter for taking a stand, and proud of her for not just following the crowd. But in the end she has to be part of the system or she will suffer for it. "Turn around, Joy," I said in the end, coaxing her with my hand. "Go the same way as everyone else."[9]

If that's what kindergarten is like, imagine what years of schooling do. By the time the average Japanese graduates from school, they have totally internalized that conforming to the rules of your group is of paramount importance, and that extends to ways of dressing and presenting yourself. As writer Sakamaki Sachiko, quoted in Kerr's book, explains:

An odd nuance of speech or appearance is enough to invite ostracism, and in a society where conformity is everything, no stigma weighs heavier than the curse of being different.[10]

This is what sociologist Harry Triandis calls "tight" collectivism, where the norms are laid out clearly and strict adherence is enforced, often to a tragic extent. In his book *Individualism and Collectivism* he tells the story of 13-year-old schoolboy Yuhei Komoda, who was "bullied by a jeering crowd of schoolmates and shoved around as dozens of other students watched," and eventually suffocated in a closet. One of Yuhei's "crimes" was that he spoke standard Japanese as against the local dialect.[11] *Ijime*, as this bullying is known, at some level has society's tacit approval.

At the heart of this extreme conformity is the collectivist concept of the self, where one's identity is closely linked with that of the group. It's "we", not "me." Edward T. Hall says, "in Japan, one has to 'belong' or he has no identity."[12] *Jibun*, the Japanese word for "self," says it all – it means "one's share of the shared life space."[13] If you derive your identity from that of the group, conforming to its norms is essential.

And this carries over into the world of luxury goods consumption. If Chihiro, Ikuko, and Tomoko have a Louis Vuitton or Gucci bag, it is imperative that you do as well. Otherwise, you face ostracism and ridicule, and indeed you may have difficulty finding any friend at all. This offers a glimpse into the workings of the minds of teenage girls who sleep with salarymen to buy that all-essential bag that membership of their social group demands. What would you do: Face an unbearable life cast out from your circle of friends, or put up with a few sexual encounters with middle-aged men? And in any case, several other teenage girls are doing the same thing at other "love hotels," so there's safety in conforming to yet another trend.

With the immense power of conforming behind it, when a trend catches on in Japan, it spreads like wildfire. Whether it's the blonde-dyed hair that you see on almost every female head in Tokyo (even I, with my naturally black hair, started feeling the pressure), or the fashionable black stockings, fishnets, flowers, and other intriguing patterns that we found on completely sedate women dressed in conservative skirts and jackets – it's all about conforming. Even the rebels, the hordes of Shibuya girls of the late 1990s who dressed in outlandish costumes, were ultimately conforming to the norms of their group. A trend spreads most rapidly among teenage girls, with experts claiming that if you can get 5 percent of girls to buy a particular item, soon almost everyone else will.

The natural corollary to an overemphasis on conforming is that you simply stop thinking for yourself and adopt neatly prepackaged concepts. Take the spread of Western clothes in Japan – as far back as the Meiji Restoration, Japan showed a tendency to adopt prepackaged looks. In 1870, naval academy cadets were ordered into British-style uniforms and army cadets into French ones. (If you've seen the movie *The Last Samurai* you'll know what we mean.) Police, mailmen, government officials, schoolchildren, even conductors on the Tokyo municipal buses, one by one they fell to Western-style uniforms.[14] But it was only after the Second World War that ordinary Japanese women took to Western clothes in a big way, abandoning the beautiful kimono forever. Western brands played it smart: They promoted a prepackaged look, and Japanese consumers simply followed the prescription. Even today, despite all the traveling to and shopping in the clothing capitals of the world, little fashion individuality is in evidence, at least not in mainstream society. It's about doing the done thing, rather than having the nerve to craft a distinct style of your own.

With individual thinking discouraged, the average Japanese relies on a "higher authority" to provide guidance. In the work world the rules of the company and the ways of the boss dictate what you do; in the sartorial world the fashion magazines and fashion editors' word rules. Fashion magazines the world over have considerable sway in building trends and women from Shanghai to San Francisco take their advice, but in Japan these magazines enjoy a different level of power. Their word is law. You don't question it or adapt it, you just follow it.

A plethora of glossies, each a fat tome, dish out fashion intelligence – international titles like *Elle*, *Vogue*, and *Cosmopolitan*; office-lady magazines like *Classy*, *Oggi*, and *Miss*; "rich wife" titles like *Very* and *25 Ans*; teen titles like *JJ*, *Can Can*, and *Vi Vi*. It's the prescriptive tone of these magazines that is remarkable, what anthropologist Keiko Tanaka dubs "blunt and hectoring," reminiscent of the Japanese authoritarian school culture.[15] Magazines tell their readers exactly what to do and what not to do.

Japanese consumers, for their part, are amazingly diligent readers and followers of these magazines. Involvement with particular titles, and the lifestyles they promote, is so strong that their followers are nicknamed after the magazine – NonNo tribe, AnAn tribe (both teen fashion magazines), and so on.[16] As a result, their knowledge about brands is nothing short of encyclopedic, and their thirst for more information mammoth – they've got to make sure all their life-and-death brand decisions are in sync with those of their peers.

Ian Bickley, head of Coach Japan, explains:

Editorial is extremely important in Japan for two reasons – firstly, the Japanese consumer craves information, they like to be very well-informed. Secondly, many of them like to have some back up or security that hey, this thing I'm going to wear is okay, it has the recognition from an authority, and a fashion editor would be considered an authority.[17]

Your Coat Is Your Home

The need to conform to the rules of your social group is no doubt driving and accelerating luxe consumption, but it doesn't explain why Japanese consumers chose luxe as their preferred mode of conforming in the first place. The answer lies in the strange twists and turns Japanese society took as it sped down the path of development – it provided immense economic wealth to the mass of people, but it failed to provide a commensurately high standard of living.

A reality of Japanese life is the tiny size of homes: They've been described as human-sized rabbit hutches, and that's pretty close to the truth. It's not by choice, of course, it's because real estate is so outrageously priced that even fairly well-to-do people are resigned to living in extremely small apartments in distant suburbs. Another reality of Japanese life is dense traffic and tight parking – which means that average folk choose not to drive to work. The net result is this: Whereas in most other countries you express your wealth status through a large home and a sexy car or two, in Tokyo those two options are limited. "Your coat is your home," says the window display at Max & Co. in Omotesando, and it hits the nail on the head. Japanese consumers have only one place to communicate their status, and that's on their body. So they go all out, buying not only Max & Co. coats, but also bags, shoes, watches, jewelry – the luxury goods that catch their fancy. This "instead of" syndrome is the second force leading the Japanese to buy luxury brands in such large quantities.

Ambar Brahmachary, president of JWT, says:

The average Japanese earns as much as the average American's salary, but there are few avenues to show it. It's only through luxury brands that he can express how well he lives.[18]

Commenting on Japan's unique space-poor, money-rich society, Mark Blair, former president of Ogilvy & Mather Japan and now president international clients, Ogilvy & Mather Asia Pacific, says: "They can't buy a fancy car, they can't put a pool in the backyard, they can't buy a big fancy stereo... luxury brands are small and expensive – they fit the physical requirements."[19]

The important distinction about Japanese consumers is that they never show off. It's not an easy concept to understand when you see every Japanese sporting expensive luxe – but that's exactly the point, when everyone has it you are hardly showing off. There's a fine line between expressing your well-to-do status in the midst of other people doing just the same, and blatant exhibitionism. Japan is a very egalitarian society, so there's no question of sticking out. Brahmachary comments: "She wants people to see and comment on her Louis Vuitton bag. But she'll never show it off, or draw attention to it."

Perhaps the only scope for some one-upmanship exists in superior *savoir faire*. Bertrand de Streel of CFN, a Tokyo-based retail consultancy, puts it this way:

Showing off is done in a subtle way. It's through knowledge, it's very sophisticated. For example, ten years ago people bought the most expensive things, now that's not considered trendy, it's too much in your face. Knowledge is the differentiator today – I have money, I also know.[20]

Parasite Singles Lead the Brandwagon

This brings us to the third major social force that has helped spur the luxury brand movement. Japan may be an advanced society on many fronts, but one area where it lags is the relatively low status accorded to women in what is essentially a male-dominated society. But females are finally getting their revenge – they are going shopping. Young working women are not just jumping on but leading the "brandwagon," by accounting for the largest chunk of luxury brand consumption.

The reason for this is the Japanese phenomenon of "parasite singles," a whole generation of young working women in their mid 20s to early 30s who have chosen to give marriage a miss and cling to the comforts of their parental home. The term was coined by Masahiro Yamada, professor at Tokyo Gakaguei University.[21] He estimates there are 8.3 million parasite single women in the 25–34 age bracket.[22] Not that they are on exciting career paths, they're the secretarial and administrative underbelly of the corporate world, while men get the managerial jobs – but even that is better than marriage.

For starters, marriage means giving up your job and doing all the housework, which is a double whammy of reduced spending power and decreasing quality of lifestyle. A night out with office girlfriends in your best Gucci beats changing diapers, cooking and cleaning, and waiting for a husband who isn't going to make it home before 11 pm, and who vanishes bleary-eyed at 7 am. A Cabinet Opinion Survey of 5,000 men and women found that 82.4 percent of Japanese women do housework as opposed to 3.9 percent of Japanese men, and that apparently is an increase for the men over earlier surveys. What is more, 47 percent of respondents agreed that "men should work while women look after the home"; although it's heartening that an equal 47 percent disagreed with that statement.[23]

Japanese women have traded a husband for a Louis Vuitton bag, and seem to be finding that a satisfactory arrangement. Being a parasite single means having your parents take care of your living expenses – the rent and food, and mum very kindly does the cleaning and laundry too – while you get to keep most of your salary and spend it on luxury brands and a lifestyle to match. With salaries in the $30,000 to $40,000 range there's a lot of disposable income to throw down on luxury brands, and that's precisely what these women are doing, aided and abetted by the need to conform with other women in the same boat doing the same boat thing. This is what makes parasite singles the largest consumer segment for luxury in Japan. For the much-loved bag and accessories category, the 20–35 age group of women accounts for 75 percent of the spending.

At some level, luxury goods have become a salve for deep insecurities stemming from women's extremely low status in Japanese society. Female inferiority is so deeply ingrained in the Japanese psyche that there is no escape – women get a full dose of it at work too, doing mind-less jobs with small chance of rising above the clerical level. Disregarded, insignificant, with no voice and no opinion, forced to toe the line and keep their feelings bottled up – as a result women's self-esteem is extremely low. The act of buying luxury goods becomes an affirmation of their existence, of momentary power. As Brahmachary says:

Luxury brands are a counter to low self-esteem. An outlet for repressed feel-ings – it's aggression, it's relief, it's proof that I count.

So what's the ultimate dream of these women? Hold your breath – it's to marry a really rich husband, as in seriously loaded. In Japanese society, and indeed in the minds of these young women too, a career woman is low class and the ultimate aspiration is to become a rich housewife. The lifestyle of that rich housewife, financed generously by not just the hus-band but two sets of doting parents, his and hers, is the most coveted – it's the Japanese equivalent of the ladies-who-lunch set. Ironically, it's the paucity of rich men that is aggravating the parasite singles phenome-non. Young women refuse to settle for less, as that would mean an unac-ceptable decline in lifestyle; instead, they face a never-ending wait to find a rich man. The equation in their head works like this: If they have to give in to a lifetime of subservience to a mostly missing husband, they want it compensated by a hefty bank balance and social glory. Yamada doesn't hold out much hope for men in this regard. "Frankly speaking, it's difficult for poor men to get married," he says.[24]

The power equation between the sexes that keeps Japanese society ticking is this: The Japanese man dominates in every way, at home and at work, but when it comes to spending power the woman holds the purse strings. The man gives his salary to his wife and keeps only a per-sonal spending allowance, leaving the woman to make all the purchas-ing decisions.

Her decision making extends to men's clothing as well. Yukari Kagami, president of Lanvin in Japan – a French brand that carries an expensive range of men's suits – describes the typical decision making process at the Lanvin store:

The women will come a day in advance and choose the products. The man will come in the next day and ask for what his wife has chosen and buy it. Women make 70 percent of the men's clothing decisions – the man knows the rules of the game and follows them. 20 percent of customers come in as couples, but here again it is mostly the woman who decides. Only 10 percent of the men come in and shop on their own.[25]

With their menfolk firmly ensconced in offices and busy with late-night drinking and clubbing, wives are looking to their daughters for friendship and company. As in all things Japanese, this too ends with a trip to the luxury brand store. This generation of Japanese mothers apparently want to be like "close sisters" to their daughters. Even after the daughter is married, she still teams up with mom for shopping trips. No prizes for guessing that mother pulls out her credit card and happily pays for most of the purchases, thereby increasing the daughter's spending power.

It's the combination of these three major social forces that has led to the explosion of luxury brands in Japan: the lack of space resulting in the need for high-value, small-in-size, easily recognizable symbols for expressing one's well-to-do status; the parasite singles phenomenon that has liberated money from mundane household expenditure and reallocated it to luxury goods; and the overpowering pressure to conform that ensures that everyone falls in line, quite literally, at a nearby luxury store.

Consumer Profile
Keiko Okano*: Hermès Kelly Bags as Family Heirlooms

She strips off her gloves, drapes her long black coat on the chair, and settles down for a chat, her eyes sparkling. In her early 30s, Keiko is a secretary at a big international firm. A delightful conversationalist, she speaks excellent English with an American accent, which sounds really cute because her manner is anything but American: "I just swing by Mitsukoshi in my lunchtime, cruise around the brands, and if I like something I buy it."

---

*Name changed.

She is extremely brand literate, talking intimately about designers and models. You instantly fall in love with her, especially when she professes she doesn't really care about brands.

On shopping with Mom
"My mother and I are shopping mates. Whenever she goes shopping I come along, so she can buy something for me, right, as I may not be able to afford certain expensive things on my own salary. Whenever I see stuff that I like and she thinks it's really appropriate for me, she buys it for me."

On their favorite brands
Her mother loves Valentino for suits and casual clothes, and Nina Ricci for evening gowns. She's also on the VIP list at Givenchy, Christian Dior, Ferragamo, Armani, and "little brands" like JP Tod's and Inès de la Fressange.

Keiko loves Cartier watches and "my mother and I both love Hermès so much."

On Hermès
"I love bags and shoes, I do, I do, I do! The expensive Hermès bags, I usually get from my mother. She uses it then passes it on to me, and then maybe I can pass it on to my daughter. It's really good stuff and it really lasts.

"My mother has 10 Kelly bags in different colors, different materials like crocodile, alligator – now these are really expensive, so she hasn't given them to me yet. The first Kelly she gave me was black leather, so I can bring it anywhere.

"For my 30th birthday, my mother gave me a Birkin. They are hard to get here so she bought it in Copenhagen through a friend who works in Hermès there. It wasn't as expensive as Japan – around ¥360,000 (US$3,500) and in Japan she would have paid double."

On gifts
"Whenever my mother goes to a party, she has to prepare a gift. So if it is a young daughter or son, she'll go to Gucci or Prada, buy a bag for the girl or shoes for the boy. They carry nice stuff."

On Louis Vuitton
"I don't really like Louis Vuitton and I think nobody would really value it but for the media, they promote it so much. I remember when I was a little girl, LV was not so popular, but now every single person knows LV.

"People like it because it's not too expensive compared to Hermès. So many people have it, it's like a uniform to them, that's why it's so popular. Also it's such a sure thing. This is such a brand-conscious country, so if you have a LV bag, you won't feel left out. Everybody buys it, even high schoolers."

On teen sex for brands

"It's disgusting but true. Not all the girls are lucky to have the bags, sometimes their parents don't allow them or they don't have the money. Everybody has the LV bag and are talking about it all the time. So the only way to get it is to find a old man and have sex for money.

"Japan is like we all have to do the same thing, we have to look the same, otherwise you feel completely left out and don't have any friends. So the young girls are doing it."

On Western brands

"Japanese women are small. The Italian brands are cut small, the French ones too. The trouser lengths are longer, when you wear them with high heels, they make you look like 'leggy women.' Western brands make women look nicer than Japanese brands."

LOUIS VUITTON: UNSTOPPABLE JUGGERNAUT

"Louis Vuitton is like the measles," says Hiroshi Ogawa, President of Baccarat. "Everyone has to get it eventually."[26] Just look around the streets of Japan and you see a measles epidemic in progress. Stay long enough, and you catch it too.

One of the fascinating and perplexing phenomena in Japan is the ubiquity of the Louis Vuitton brand. While industry experts have a long list of reasons for its abiding success, even they admit it's a case of sheer bag magic. "Control" is a key word in luxury marketing: restricting your brand's availability and presence to maintain its life-giving exclusive image. Prada failed to do that and it hurt. Hermès controls to such an extent that even its waiting lists are closed. On the other hand, there is such large-scale "democratization" of Louis Vuitton that the billion-dollar question is how it withstands the inevitable backlash of ubiquity. Its success has been so remarkable that Kyojiro Hata, who has steered LV Japan from day one, felt compelled to write a book explaining it.

Right from Vuitton's start in Japan, it was evident that here was a company able to think way ahead of the curve. After a brief alliance with local distributors, Louis Vuitton Japan was set up in 1981. It did something path-breaking – a decade before control-your-own-distribution-and-brand came into fashion, Louis Vuitton set up its own distribution subsidiary, giving local distributors a miss. It changed wholesale agreements with department stores to shops-in-shops, so that it had control over its products till they were sold. It trained the department store staff in the Vuitton way. While most other imported brands were left in the foster care of distributors or licensees till the late 1990s, the Louis Vuitton brand was being nurtured and raised by a doting parent.

Having taken control, what did Louis Vuitton do to build such a cult following in Japan? What was its magic formula? We posed exactly that question to Serge Brunschwig, former managing director, Louis Vuitton (Worldwide). "Absolutely no magic," Brunschwig says, attributing Vuitton's success to a "job done right consistently over the years."[27] Consistency is certainly one of the key ingredients, but we believe what sets the company apart is its uncanny ability to combine two seemingly contrary factors and make them work like magic. Nineteenth-century tradition tangos with twenty-first-century smarts. Upper-crust exclusivity sits happily next to office-ladydom. Steep US$1,000 price tags for canvas bags are seen as sheer value for money. And the glue that holds it all together consists in the three magic words: quality, quality, quality.

Let's take a closer look at the LV formula in action. Realizing how important tradition and history were to Japanese consumers, from the early days the company set about promoting those elements, which it had in abundance. Louis Vuitton himself was born in 1811, the son of a carpenter who opened his firm in Paris in 1854. The famous LV monogram was introduced in 1896 and was soon marking out the luggage of aristocrats and royalty.[28] Historical baggage pieces have now become central display features in Vuitton stores. And the brand that has always symbolized privileged travel has become a symbol of privilege for the mass market in Japan.

Keeping one foot firmly in the "tradition and history" mold, Louis Vuitton has nevertheless innovated and experimented to keep its offering relevant and alive to modern consumers. On the one hand LV makes small changes to its existing product range, never straying too far from its basic styles, so that the old faithfuls keep coming back for newer versions. On the other hand it makes a dash to the wilder end of the spectrum – for example the graffiti bag in 2001, or the collaboration with Japanese artist Takashi Murakami in 2003 that produced the cute and colorful "Eye Love Monogram" range. If LV is the mother of all luxury brands, then the monogram is the mother of all LV products – that's what the throngs of consumers are after. Understandably, a great deal of effort has gone into keeping the more than 100-year-old monogram as fresh as a young woman in full bloom. Brunschwig explains:

There is a lot of creativity going into the monogram, a lot of new designs, a lot of new things. Marc Jacobs has played a lot with it as well, so it is something that's truly lively, at the same time rooted in the nineteenth century.

This lively creativity also goes into the company's local promotional efforts. Louis Vuitton has been using younger celebrities from the entertainment and sports world, up-and-coming stars who connect well with the often teenage bag-loving Japanese consumer. LV keeps the excitement coming in regular dollops, whether it is new products, new stores, new celebrities – so that the short-attention-span Japanese consumer doesn't have a chance to get bored and stray. On the global front too its advertising campaigns have plenty of pizzazz. Just look at what it has done with Jennifer Lopez – tightly contained oomph, a predatory look in her eye, she poses with hunky men, only to use them as mere props – and the willowy Uma Thurman, who manages to look vulnerable-and-sexy and glamorous-and-inaccessible at the same time, to be followed by the stunning Brazilian model Gisèle Bündchen, who is striking bold poses for the brand's campaign in 2006. Phew, you want that bag.

Lest all this pandering to the public alienate its top-end customer segment, Louis Vuitton has simultaneously been at pains to ensure its élite image remains untarnished. While the office ladies and their mothers are stocking up on canvas monogram bags, the top customers are buying the more expensive products – trunks, leather bags, clothes, watches, jewelry. The shops recognize and treat high-end customers with appropriately high-end service. There are special VIP lounges, hidden away from the public eye, and there's the opportunity to order customized pieces. It doesn't get more exclusive than that.

Different strokes for different folks, that's the LV magic at work again – the left hand reaches out to the mass market with a trendy image and entry-level priced products; the right hand cradles the élite, giving them exclusive products and service. For his part, Brunschwig does not see scarcity as part of the definition of luxury. "I don't think exclusive people buying the trunk are offended because the office lady has a wallet," he says. Now we know why.

That brings us to quality – something that both Louis Vuitton and Japanese consumers have running deep in their veins. The Japanese obsession with quality stems from a well-trained eye for detail as well as a desire for durability. Recognizing this, LV upped its already high quality-control standards for Japanese consumers and found ways to increase perceptions of durability. For example, it opened repair service centers, promising to mend Louis Vuitton products no matter where they were bought, thereby increasing a bag's life. This emphasis on quality and its maintenance further enhances the value-for-money perception.

Head of Louis Vuitton Japan, Kyojiro Hata, recounts how during the first 10 years products had to be regularly returned to Paris because the Japanese won't accept even the smallest imperfection. Paris was flummoxed. "If we complained the stitches were not straight, they said it was because of the nature of hand stitching and they could sell the products in Paris," he writes. On one occasion he returned all the products, saying "Please sell these in Paris." After years of toing and froing, "the quality control system in Paris was finally reformed."[29]

The concept of quality and consistency extends to all aspects of the company's dealings with customers, making it a reliable, no-nasty-surprises kind of brand. Take its pricing strategy, which is linked to the exchange rate, keeping prices 1.4 times those in France; when the yen gets stronger LV reduces prices and vice versa. Advance notice and full explanations are provided before any price change, so customers know what to expect. Furthermore, there are never any discounts; Louis Vuitton never goes on "sale." It doesn't need to, not with people queuing up to buy. The quality of service was consistently high in the several beautiful stores we visited in Tokyo.

But in the ultimate analysis, Louis Vuitton's magic lies in the eyes of the bag-holder, and what LV has come to signify to the Japanese people. It has become the status marker par excellence, and there are millions of people to vouch for that. Other brands have suffered from ubiquity but not Louis Vuitton. It is well past the stage of a trend, it has become an enduring requirement – like sushi or green tea – essential to the Japanese way of life. With expert marketing tactics, stoking the fire with the right stimuli, the company has taken the trend to conform to its logical end: To be Japanese means to have a Louis Vuitton bag. The brown bag with the original monogram pattern and the pale leather trimmings has come to define the Japanese national identity.

MARKETING TO THE CONVERTED ISN'T EASY

With this huge appetite for imported brands, one would have thought luxury brand marketing would be a cakewalk. Far from it. In fact, the cost of marketing to the extremely sophisticated and brand-savvy Japanese consumer is huge. For starters, building the monumental flagship stores costs monumental amounts – Hermès US$138 million, Louis Vuitton US$100 million, Chanel US$240 million – and with flagship stores becoming par for the course, the bar has been permanently raised. The trend toward directly operated stores also means further investment in Japan's pricey real estate. Other costs are equally high, from retail execution to advertising and promotion. Catering to the peculiarities of the Japanese market means playing a high-stakes game.

You are dealing with the pickiest consumer in the world. Ironically, Japanese consumers have forced luxury brands that pride themselves on infallible quality to upgrade, as we saw with Louis Vuitton. And it's not just product quality, the same spotless expectations extend to every aspect of retail execution – service, merchandising, store design, packaging, the works. For example, Cartier has five decorators checking store displays every day, whereas it makes do with one in France. As a result, it's retail Olympics on a daily basis, with every brand trying to be "faster, higher, stronger" just to live up to Japanese standards. Hard work if you are managing the brand, sheer pleasure if you are a consumer strolling through the stores.

To begin with, the selection of products on display is more extensive and more exciting. With massive stores that run to several floors, it's only to be expected that the range of goods is wider. But beyond that, it's as if the Japanese store buyers have a keener eye, they pick up items that you don't see in London and Hong Kong, and the result is the equivalent of a carefully laid-out gourmet feast.

Merchandising is again in a class of its own – its hallmarks are extreme care combined with a highly refined aesthetic sensibility. Without exception, the windows and in-store displays are superbly rendered. It borders on art – in fact, it *is* art. Take the black Gucci dress with Japanese *obi* sash inspiration, one of Tom Ford's creations in his final years at the company – it was presented like a work of art in a slim glass drawer, discreet spot lighting heightening its solitary splendor. We had the same dress pulled out for us in Shanghai: The salesgirl did it willingly enough, but she wasn't entirely sure how the itsy-bitsy pieces of the garment came together.

Japanese service has to be experienced to be believed – that there can be so much grace, beauty, and kindness in salesgirls who are just doing a job is amazing for a non-Japanese to comprehend. Very knowledgeable and intelligent, they handle nuances and details like no other country's salespeople we have come across. It's like having an enjoyable conversation with a friend, discussing the finer points about a bag or a piece of jewelry – unhurried and sensitive – and a world away from the pressure tactics and bad temper you might encounter elsewhere.

We believe this outstanding level of service is a very strong reason for Japanese women going shopping over and over again. Given the average Japanese woman's place in society, shopping is about the only time she can experience what it's like to be served and pampered. JWT's Brahmachary again:

Women are being repressed from day to night. At home they have to serve their husbands, at work their bosses. The shop is the only place they are being served, a moment of pleasure, a moment when you are respected as a human being. Women go shopping just to experience the pleasure of being served.

Advertising and promotion form the other aspect that is extremely expensive in Japan, but also extremely important. Inundated by an "orgy of overchoice,"[30] as sociologist John Clammer describes shopping in Japan, consumers have a very short attention span, and need constant stimulation. As a result, brands need to be seen to be doing something new all the time in terms of marketing activities, otherwise they run the risk of dropping off the ever-changing retail radar screen. Building a luxury brand in Japan is also critical not only for sales generated there, but for sales generated all over the world by Japanese tourists. The "intention to buy" is created in Japan, although the sale may be consummated in London or Hawaii. A heavier focus on brand building in Japan – and a larger marketing budget – is therefore essential.

Luxury brands have more than risen to the high standards of retailing and promotion that the Japanese market demands, and despite the high costs are also making high profits. In the process, they have acquired expertise and learnt lessons that they could teach the rest of the world.

LESSONS FROM THE MASTER

Japan is a luxury giant in the advanced stages of luxe addiction, but is admittedly different from other Asian countries, and certainly a world apart from its neighbor China. Despite these differences, Japan's importance lies in the fact that it has run the entire spectrum of economic development from abject poverty to extreme wealth, and has played out the accompanying five stages in the spread of luxury model we described in Chapter 2 – from *subjugation*, through *start of money*, *show off*, and *fit in*, to today's *way of life* stage. Japan is a case study of the path that other luxury markets in Asia are likely to walk down.

Commenting on Louis Vuitton's huge dependence on Japan in 2001, head Kyojiro Hata declared:

We need to broaden our business in more markets other than Japan. Therefore, it is the #1 priority for Louis Vuitton to study the factors that brought success in Japan and apply them to other countries.[31]

What are the lessons we can learn from Japan?

Asians Will Always Prefer Western Luxe to Asian Luxe

In our interviews in other Asian markets, when asked why there was this preference for *Western* luxury brands, the oft-repeated answer was: What else is there? While there are Asian designers that enjoy influence in local circles, hardly any have made a significant impact internationally. Japan is the notable exception: Its designers created waves on the world stage as early as the 1970s. It boasts masters like Issey Miyake, Takada Kenzo, Yohji Yamamoto, and Kansai Yamamoto. Here's an Asian country that offers a viable and attractive alternative to Western luxury brands, and yet Western luxury brands reign supreme there. Louis Vuitton, Gucci, Cartier, Hermès, Chanel – these are on a completely different planet of desirability in Japan. The hard truth is that Western is superior to Japanese as far as the luxury brand category is concerned, and European brands in particular are held in higher esteem. The Japan business head of a major luxury house laughed weakly when we asked if there was a potential market for local luxury brands. His view: "It's very hard to sell 'made in Japan' in this category as the consumer prefers imported brands."

This is what is commonly known as the country-of-origin effect, when certain products are strongly associated with certain countries. The Japanese see Europe as the fountainhead of luxury goods expertise since that's where the luxury goods tradition emanated from.

To an extent, local designers have themselves to blame for not making much headway. In the early days of Japan as the master at copying everything, local designers did just that. They picked up fashion styles from Europe and offered imitations on the local market. We're not talking of international designers in the Kenzo and Issey

Miyake league who were making their mark in Paris, but of others who catered largely to the Japanese market. Unfortunately, the copying image stuck. One consumer told us: "Japanese brands are affordable, yes, but it's a bit like buying fake stuff as the designs are not really original."

There are some who disagree. Michael Causton of Japan Consuming, a retail and marketing consultancy that publishes a magazine by the same name, argues:

Western brands are superior is an old view. Young kids don't think that way. The Japanese tend to have a superior/inferior viewpoint on things, but young people are more comfortable with peer-to-peer viewpoint, so they are more likely to see a few Japanese designers as equally good as Western ones."[32]

As evidence, he points to the surge of innovative young local labels like Undercover and Bathing Ape, which attract queues of teens and twenty-somethings at their stores.

Nevertheless, others in the industry feel that while young consumers may be giving local Japanese designers a try, these are emerging trends on the edges of society. The young may rebel for a while with on-the-fringe choices, but once they enter mainstream life they quickly fall into the toeing-the-line pattern. As a result, for mainstream Japan Western luxury brands remain steadfastly at the top of the pyramid. Given that consumers don luxury brands to express their well-to-do status, they will always buy the ones that deliver best on this score. So far there's nothing to beat Western luxury brands, and as long as that remains the real reason for purchase, imported luxury brands will remain undisputed kings in Japan.

As they will in the rest of Asia. The social glory of sporting a Cartier or a Rolex watch will always be more than that of a made-in-China or even a made-in-Japan Seiko or Citizen. Ditto for a Louis Vuitton bag or a Gucci shoe, a Chanel dress or an Armani suit.

If you're a Western luxury brand, go forth and conquer – but just make sure your Westernness is never diluted. You might shift your production facilities to cheaper Asia, but while "made in China" labels may pass for American and European consumers, only "made in France" and "made in Italy" will do for Asians.

Quality and Heritage Are the Nicotine of Luxe

If there's one man who knows what makes a luxury brand tick, it's got to be Bernard Arnault, the man who has been variously referred to as the lord of the logos, the pope of fashion, and the emperor of luxury. He believes that heritage, or a quality of timelessness, is essential for a star brand. "A brand must have heritage; there are no shortcuts," he tells Suzy Wetlaufer in an interview with *Harvard Business Review*. It may take decades to get that quality of timelessness, but you can "create the impression of timelessness sooner rather than later" with "uncompromising quality."[33]

Heritage, quality, craftsmanship, expertise – they all form a close nexus of inter-related values so life giving for a luxury brand. In the Japanese consumer, they have found a match made in heaven: A consumer who places an immense value on heritage meets brands steeped in it and lives happily ever after. What luxury brands have done right in Japan is to showcase their heritage quickly and effectively. For instance, a mid-1990s survey on Louis Vuitton's brand image found that Japanese consumers knew the tradition and history of the brand far better than their American counterparts – amazing when you consider that Vuitton had then been in Japan for barely more than a decade, while it has been in the US since the days of luxury liners.[34]

The rest of Asia isn't half as brand savvy as Japan, and in places like China people are snapping up luxury goods without a clue about their heritage or history. Trends come and go, but quality and heritage endure. The lesson here is that brands that invest in educating the Asian consumer about their history, their skilled craftsmanship, and their uncompromising quality will build an unbeatable advantage going forward, helping keep consumers loyal when the competition heats up.

Impeccable Service Standards Are Key to the Luxury Experience

Some of the luxury brand stores we visited in China, Taiwan, and other Asian markets fall significantly short of Japanese excellence in retail execution and service standards, and again there is an opportunity for luxury companies to transfer their lessons from Japan to other markets.

Even though other Asian consumers may not be as sophisticated or demanding as the Japanese, they are slowly and surely going to develop a keener eye as they spend more time with luxury brands. (Remember that Japan itself stood for trashy quality in the 1950s and 1960s and now its consumers are the fussiest.) Setting the bar high for service standards is best done from the very start, rather than fixing a larger problem later on.

For example, service standards in China are extremely variable – a few luxury stores have got it right, whereas most others are shoddy. Sales staff at one luxury store we visited couldn't be bothered even to show us what we asked for; at another every question was answered with a helpless giggle; and at yet another they couldn't tell the difference between mink, fox, and chinchilla. Similarly in India, the staff of some brands were poorly dressed and the stores felt cheap, which only damaged the brand's image.

Brands have an uphill task finding and training staff in emerging markets, especially providing the knowledgeable and sensitive service that is most needed in these markets where consumers themselves have a steep learning curve ahead of them. But snare consumers with superb service, be their friend in the formative years, and they'll be back for more. Just ask any Japanese shopper.

Globetrotting Shoppers Need Respect

The Japanese single-handedly keep cash registers ringing all over the world. They make gracious consumers, subdued and sensitive, and it's relatively easy to cater to their needs. Nevertheless, there's a great deal of suppressed snickering about their eccentricities and lack of "real" fashion sense from snobbish European sales staff. The Chinese and other Asians are now taking to travel in the same manner, shopping all over the world. Their fashion sense is only just beginning to develop, and gracious, subdued, and sensitive are not the first words that come to mind when describing their culture.

However, if you want the Asian luxe dollars, show genuine respect. In our chats with salesgirls in Rome's Via Condotti, we sensed a sneering attitude toward Chinese, South Koreans, and Taiwanese. They are rude, we were told. They are not like the Japanese, we were told. (The

Japanese are being missed not just for their dollars but also for their fine manners, it seems.) Our advice: Shed that uppity manner and train sales staff to be respectful.

The Japanese have yielded huge sales and huge profits for global luxe. The lessons learned in Japan are invaluable for companies that wish to repeat that feat in China and other Asian markets. And perhaps Japan's outstanding sales staff could teach the world a thing or two about courtesy, kindness, and service.

The luxe shopping arcade at the Peninsula hotel yields some of the highest sales per square foot in Hong Kong.

Photo courtesy of The Peninsula Group.

4
HONG KONG AND TAIWAN: YIN AND YANG

Siblings in a sense, born of the same motherland, Hong Kong and Taiwan have the same passion for luxury brands coursing through their veins. As a result both have blossomed into very substantial markets for luxury brands, but here's the curious aspect: While Hong Kong has developed into an island of high fashion, across the strait Taiwan still struggles to find its style identity.

Given that both are likely precursors of what will transpire in mainland China's luxury market, the question is what turned one into a style maven and the other into a style imitator? And which way is China likely to go?

Nature and nurture have both played a hand. Both places are peopled by Chinese immigrants, but their roots are very different. While wealthy Shanghainese and China's business élite from other coastal cities rushed into Hong Kong, bringing with them elegance and a taste for high living, Taiwan's early settlers were dirt-poor peasants, mostly from Fujian and Guangdong, followed in 1949 by Chiang Kai Shek's nationalist army, mainly soldiers and a smaller percentage of rich people. Shanghai's highly evolved fashion scene was transplanted into Hong Kong with the arrival of skilled Shanghainese tailors who had nothing left to do in Mao's drab one-size-fits-all pajama suit regime. Taiwan's largely peasant stock, on the other hand, set little store by the niceties of life – a good woman was one who cooked and cleaned, and raised a family on a frugal budget, not one who donned figure-hugging silk cheongsams and headed for society soirées. Added to that is the fact that Hong Kong under the British provided a far more open international atmosphere with freer access to global fashion trends, while the Taiwanese were relatively closeted on their island and had limited outside influences.

In his landmark work *Distinction: A Social Critique of the Judgement of Taste*,[1] French sociologist Pierre Bourdieu talks about the concept of "cultural capital" – think of it as a bank of *savoir faire*, an accumulated inventory of refined tastes that have the tacit nod of the cultural élite. He identifies two factors that build up cultural capital: social origin, or a family background that is culturally refined for generations; and formal education, whereby you further develop a mastery of aesthetic codes. While his setting is France, the logic applies equally elsewhere – Hong Kong got an infusion of cultural capital and went on to become a style center, while Taiwanese society was shaped by its hardscrabble roots and needs more time and effort to find its aesthetic moorings.

In this chapter we look at Hong Kong first, analyzing the forces that fashioned it into Asia's biggest luxury market outside Japan and a regional luxe hub to boot, and then compare the situation in Taiwan, where matters of taste have not interfered in an energetic adoption of luxury brands – in fact, they seem to have helped. We end by drawing key business lessons that will guide the way in China.

HONG KONG:
WHERE LUXURIES ARE BARE NECESSITIES

THE TAI-TAI PRAYER
Armani, which Art in Landmark, hallowed be thy shoes.
Thy Prada come, thy shopping done, in Central as it is in Paris.
Give us this day our husband's Visa gold card and have him forgive us our balance, as we forgive those who charge interest against us.
Lead us not into Mitsukoshi and deliver us from Wing On.
For thine is the Chanel, the Gaultier and the Versace.
For Dolce & Gabbana,
Amex.

> David Evans in the popular Lai See column of the
> South China Morning Post[2]

Luxe gluttony. You might see it as one of the seven sins, or you might see it as a twenty-first-century virtue essential for the health of the economy. Hong Kong people see it as neither. Frankly, they don't have the time to bother – they're too busy at a mall nearby.

Shopping is the way of life here, as natural as eating, drinking, sleeping, and breathing – and just as necessary. Devoid of the restraining moral judgments that usually accompany excessive consumption, propelled by a value system that glorifies the acquisition and expenditure of money – even in death, loved ones are armed with spending money in the next world by burning "paper money" on their behalf – and fortified with a fine eye for fashion, this city lives to shop.

A duty-free haven, Hong Kong has blossomed into a US$3.5 billion luxury market, not only catering to a luxury-besotted local market but also attracting shoppers from the rest of Asia. It boasts more big-brand stores than in the West – for example, Gucci has eight stores in Hong Kong, but three in New York and Milan, and six in Paris and London; Hermès has seven stores in Hong Kong, but two in New York, three in Paris, one in Milan, and five in London.[3] Hong Kong has what it takes to support that kind of business volume, offering as it does multiple shopping districts, each catering to a different consumer profile. From local tai-tais to mainland tourists buying their first Rolex, Hong Kong knows how to keep a shopper happily occupied.

Like Japan, Hong Kong is at the *way of life* stage of the Spread of Luxury model. Some 14 percent of the local population between the ages of 15 and 65, irrespective of income levels, admit happily to having purchased some luxury item in the past six months. They spent on average US$1,300 in that time, more than double the spending of Singaporeans, who have a higher per capita income. Hong Kong people tend to buy more expensive items – for example, those who bought luxury watches spent an average US$5,400 per head in the past six months.[4]

FROM FISHING VILLAGE TO ASIA'S STYLE CAPITAL

The growth of Hong Kong's luxury market is of course inextricably linked with the growth and prosperity of the city itself. It might have been a sleepy fishing village on a barren rock when the British wrested it from China, but Hong Kong has shown plenty of spirit and dynamism ever since, with a knack for repeatedly reinventing itself, as much on the business and commerce front as in fashion and lifestyle.

Until the 1960s Hong Kong's luxury market was a barren rock too, the closest thing to luxe being mass-produced American suits and Japanese clothing. Luxury brands as we know them today started trooping in during the 1970s, just as Hong Kong's economy began to take off.

Their first customers came from Hong Kong's "Suzie Wong" segment – a luxe industry veteran (who, not surprisingly, prefers to remain unnamed) estimates that 70 percent of luxury sales in the early days came from nightclub hostesses. He comments:

If they carried Gucci, they were able to charge their customers more. If they carried Pierre Cardin, their rate came down. They needed "packaging" to upgrade their professional image.

Early retailers made adjustments to cater to this segment. Specialty stores like Ding How at Star Ferry stayed open till 11 pm, giving the girls enough time to work on their customers and drag them along for a bout of late-night luxe shopping. The standard practice was to return the goods in "virgin condition" the next morning, and the girls usually pocketed a 70 percent refund. The importance of this group sky-rocketed in the 1980s and 1990s with the advent of outrageously expensive Japanese-style nightclubs like Club BBoss, where Hong Kong's business élite took their clients to talk shop and negotiate deals.[5] The girls made so much money that they were soon paying for designer brands by the bagful themselves. Some struck it lucky and married tycoons. Those heady days are now past for Hong Kong – establish-ments such as the legendary China City Night Club have closed – and the girls have had to tone down their spending. Says the marketing head of a leading luxury company:

Whereas earlier the nightclub girls bought one or two designer bags every month, now they buy one every season.

In 1980s and 1990s Hong Kong, reminiscent of Japan in the bubble days, many instant millionaires were made, raking in the proceeds of the hot stock market and the even hotter property market, Hong Kong's twin hearts that pumped life-giving money into local pockets. During this period a new breed of yuppie emerged, educated at Stanford and Cambridge, drawing fat salaries and fatter bonuses in Hong Kong's financial industry, well traveled and holding an international perspective on life. At the same time, Hong Kong's manufacturing and trading businesses continued to boom thanks to excellent overseas orders. The city had money to burn. The *show off* stage of the luxury cycle had arrived, and the way Hong Kong went about putting its new money in evidence would have exceeded even Veblen's expectations. It bought luxury cars. It bought fancy Swiss watches. It bought Cartier jewelry. The men wore Armani, the women Chanel. With prosperity spreading to successive layers of society, soon everyone was buying Louis Vuitton, Gucci, and Prada, in between rounds of buying HSBC shares, queuing up for IPOs, and cashing in on apartments that had doubled in value.

Into this booming city, like a match to a flambé, came Japanese tourists, group upon group of them, and they started buying up shopfuls of luxury goods. The local luxe retail scene simply took off and hasn't looked back since. Fashion visionary Joyce Ma played a leading role, bringing in Armani, Prada, Gucci, Dolce & Gabbana, and several other brands.

The era of franchising began in earnest. Tai-tais who were used to shopping internationally took the plunge and became agents. Famous Hong Kong retailers – among them Lane Crawford, the main purveyor of fashion and good taste to Hong Kong's élite since the early 1900s – extended into luxury goods. Chinese family-run businesses that were into garment manufacturing, suppliers to some of the brands internationally, decided to move up the value chain and become agents; Swank is one example. Hong Kong's *hongs* got in on the act too, with the likes of Jardine Matheson becoming agents for Dunhill. Cosa Lieberman, a Swiss company, brought in Chanel, Karl Lagerfeld, and Van Cleef & Arpels. Shiamus brought in edgy hot brands, the diffusion lines like D&G. Bluebell brought in Louis Vuitton. Many fortunes were made in luxury retailing. The formula was simple: Become an agent for a European brand, set up shop at one of the prestigious hotels or shopping centers, and then sit back and wait for the trusty Japanese tourists to do their job, ably assisted by a growing group of luxury-loving locals.

In most cases, these agents played a wider pan-Asian role. This was the era of the Asian tiger economies, their growing prosperity readying the ground for the entry of luxury brands. Hong Kong agents typically covered markets outside of Japan; that is, South Korea, China, Taiwan, Singapore, and other Southeast Asian countries. They spread the luxe gospel far and wide, and made a killing in the process. Take Burberry, which appointed a new agent for Asia in the mid-1980s. From 1986 onwards, at least one Burberry store was opened *every* month, building up a portfolio of 200 outlets in Asia (minus Japan) by 1997. Sales grew at a breathtaking 25 percent every year till the Asian crash of 1997–98.

The agent-franchisee era was to end soon, however – as it did elsewhere in the world – and Hong Kong was cast afresh in the role of Asian regional headquarters for luxury brand companies. Ironically, around the same time as China was reclaiming Hong Kong's "franchise" from the UK with the 1997 handover, luxury houses started reclaiming their Asian franchises. They brought in European managers and set up their own offices to manage the Hong Kong business as well as oversee businesses in neighboring countries. Louis Vuitton, Gucci, Prada, and more recently Burberry and Zegna reclaimed their franchises, although a few other brands still remain with agents. Broadly speaking, the major brands have taken charge of their own businesses, while relatively niche brands continue with agents, Joyce and Swank being two of the most prominent (Table 4.1).

SHOPPER'S PARADISE

Like a tree laden with fruit, Hong Kong's luxury retail scene is marked by sheer abundance and infinite variety. Starting with the Shui Hing department store, the first to stock imported luxury brands in the early 1970s, Hong Kong spawned layer upon layer of luxe retail until today the city itself could be described as one big shopping mall interwoven with homes and office buildings.

The first spots for luxury stores were five-star hotels. Joyce Ma started her boutique at the Mandarin Oriental hotel, *the* most prestigious venue on Hong Kong island. Across the harbor in Kowloon, luxury brands zeroed in on the Peninsula hotel, a historic site with a

Table 4.1 Big brands have bought back their franchises, smaller ones continue with agents

SELF-MANAGED BRANDS	AGENT-MANAGED BRANDS	
Alfred Dunhill	*JOYCE*	*SWANK*
Bulgari	Alexander McQueen	Christian Lacroix
Burberry	Balenciaga	Gianfranco Ferre
Celine	Emilio Pucci	Givenchy
Chanel	Jil Sander	Kenzo
Christian Dior	Joseph	Marc Jacobs
Fendi	Stella McCartney	
Giorgio Armani		
Gucci	*FAIRTON*	*BLUEBELL*
Hermès	Bally	Moschino
Loewe	Jean Paul Gaultier	Narciso Rodriguez
Louis Vuitton	Max Mara	Paul Smith
Prada		
Tod's		
YSL Rive Gauche		
Zegna		

Source: Husband Retail Consulting

colonial air and the most sought-after afternoon tea service in Hong Kong, extremely popular with tourists. The Peninsula has an extensive multilevel luxe-shopping arcade even today – anchored by Louis Vuitton, Prada, and Tiffany – and still commands the highest luxe sales per square foot in Hong Kong.

Not far from the Peninsula, in 1966 came the Ocean Terminal, which besides being a boarding spot for ocean liners also housed the first upscale megamall in Hong Kong – think of it as "patient zero" in the malling epidemic that subsequently swept the city. Built initially to tap the booming tourist trade, Ocean Terminal became a window to the world outside, where locals came face to face with the Western world of luxury – even if only to window-shop.

The Landmark, arguably Hong Kong's plushest shopping center, opened in Central in the early 1970s, initially housing banks and airlines before evolving into a full-fledged luxury mall. Other spots sprang up in fast succession. The Central district itself attracted a concentration of luxe as a boutique movement, spearheaded by tai-tai entrepreneurs, took shape in the 1980s. From what was originally an army barracks rose Pacific Place, a massive upscale multi-use complex with office towers, hotels, serviced apartments, cinemas, restaurants, and a 711,000 square foot mall with a large complement of luxury stores. Causeway Bay, a bustling shopping district that caters to all budgets, tourists and locals alike, had Japanese stores like Sogo offering high-end luxury, as well as malls like Times Square anchored by the prestigious Lane Crawford, and toward the end of the 1990s came the Lee Gardens, an exclusive luxury enclave.

The 2000s saw Hong Kong's luxury retail grow *even* bigger and *even* more upscale. The mall at International Finance Center, better known as IFC, went fully functional, offering an enormous luxury-shopping extravaganza and a super-luxurious enclave flanking the Four Seasons hotel. Harvey Nichols made an entry at the Landmark. Lane Crawford upped the game with remodeled cutting-edge stores. A line-up of flagship stores flanked Canton Road near the Peninsula hotel, drawing heavy tourist traffic. Even the Chek Lap Kok international airport, a spectacular Norman Foster glass creation, further beefed up its retail spread with some 25 luxury brand stores.

Testimony to Hong Kong's pulling power is the fact that brands have not only put up stores in each major shopping district, sometimes they have *two*, and they still find enough customers to keep both stores buzzing. For instance, the huge Louis Vuitton flagship on Canton Road is within three minutes' walking distance of the company's other store in the Peninsula hotel, and both stores have a crush of customers, sometimes two and three rows deep, crowded around the monogram bag counters.

Not only are the big-brand stores present in abundance, a robust breadth of labels is available to satisfy every kind of shopper, from the in-your-face "compulsory" brands to the extremely exotic and exclusive ones. Hong Kong's new-money crowd plumps for the unmistakable staples – Louis Vuitton monograms, Gucci logo patterns, and Burberry checks. The small, select old-money set likes things a tad more discreet, brands like Hermès, Valentino, Loewe, and Giorgio Armani. A plethora of names appeal to sophisticated fashionistas – Narciso Rodriguez, Marc Jacobs,

Michael Kors, and Stella McCartney. There's color and attitude with Vivienne Tam and Vivienne Westwood, Anna Sui and Anna Molinari; and there's plenty for shoe lovers – Manolo Blahnik, Jimmy Choo, Sergio Rossi, and whatever else you might fancy. There's a wide selection for men, whether it's suits from Lanvin, Zegna, Gieves & Hawkes, or Canali, or contemporary styles from the likes of Gaultier, Junya Watanabe, Roberto Cavalli, or Dries Van Noten. Quite literally every brand of expensive watch on earth would be represented here, from the Rolexes and Cartiers that are the first symbols of success to complicated ones for the connoisseurs, including a nicely ticking market for antique watches.

Tempt them till they succumb, is the retail motto here. If Adam and Eve had lived in Hong Kong, they certainly wouldn't have bothered with the apple or the snake, but would sensibly have chosen a crocodile-leather Hermès Birkin bag instead and possibly a Bulgari watch with an apple-green snakeskin strap, then headed to the nearby Armani Bar to unwind over a martini.

WHAT MAKES HONG KONG SUCH A RETAIL PARADISE?

It is a bit perplexing how a tiny city-state of about 7 million people can support so much luxury retail. But on a per capita basis Hong Kong *outstrips* Japan – Hong Kong has per capita luxe sales of US$500 to Japan's US$145.[6] Hong Kong's secret, of course, lies in creating the perfect conditions for a strong local market topped off by a tourist market on overdrive. Three factors have helped make Hong Kong the retail paradise it is: its duty-free status, its thriving tourism industry, and the way retail has been integrated into the city's everyday life.

Duty-Free Haven

Every other Asian country, barring Singapore, levies import duties ranging from 12–30 percent, plus a variety of other charges and taxes, giving Hong Kong a distinct edge. What is more, its tax structure is the kindest in the world. There is no sales tax. Corporate income tax is a maximum of 16 percent. You have the perfect conditions to make everybody happy – consumers get the lowest prices in Asia, while luxury companies make more money in Hong Kong than they do elsewhere in the continent, with the possible exception of Japan.

This sets in motion a favorable upward spiral. Lower prices lead to greater volumes. Greater volumes allow brands to offer a wider and more exciting product range – they have the luxury of experimenting with edgy stuff, which, even if it doesn't sell too well, forms only a small part of a large volume. This ups the standard of the retail offering, which again pulls in more customers, as that's what fashion consumers are looking for in the first place – variety and excitement.

Hong Kong's own consumers shop at home to a large degree. They do buy a lot in Europe, where prices are 15–20 percent lower, but at least Hong Kong doesn't lose sales to Asian countries. On the contrary, it draws consumers from neighboring nations thanks to the unbeatable combination of low prices, wide range, and being a short flight away.

The Tourist Catcher

Tourism is Hong Kong's lifeblood and it pulls in more than three times as many tourists as the local population, to the tune of more than 23 million tourists annually and spending of US$12 billion.[7] There is no Eiffel Tower, Statue of Liberty, or Great Wall here, but there is that wonder of the modern world, s-h-o-p-p-i-n-g.

If the 1980s and 1990s were the days of the Japanese tourist-shopper, the 2000s heralded the era of the mainland Chinese shopper, whose numbers have skyrocketed (Figure 4.1), making them the largest tourist group – over 50 percent of all tourists in Hong Kong – with the highest spending of HK$6,018 per head, as compared to the overall average of HK$5,502.[8]

The two tourist segments couldn't be more different. The Japanese were extremely easy to service – they came in busloads, they all bought the same thing, and they formed a polite unobtrusive presence, spending liberally. Paulene Hsia, earlier with distributor Shiamus and currently fashion retailing coordinator at the Hong Kong Polytechnic University, comments:

Sometimes you'd order hundreds or thousands of the same style and color for them. Each tourist would buy 5–6 pieces of the same item – they'd be buying for friends, or gifts for people back home.[9]

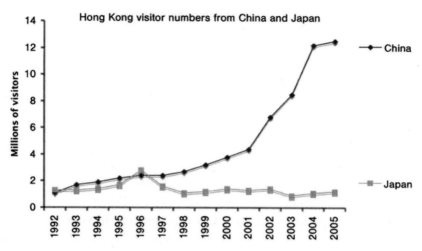

Figure 4.1 Mainland Chinese tourist numbers to Hong Kong have skyrocketed in recent years

Source: Visitor Annual Statistics, Hong Kong Tourist Board.

The mainland Chinese tourist is equally hell bent on buying luxe, often skimping on hotels while splurging on shopping. Although their custom is extremely welcome – life saving actually, given that Japanese tourist numbers have declined – it does pose a piquant challenge for high-end retailers. It's like Julia Roberts in *Pretty Woman*, on Rodeo Drive with a stash of cash. How do you serve a constant flow of mainland Julias without upsetting local customers? The simple truth is that Hong Kong's new money looks down on China's newer money. Ian Hawksworth, executive director of Hongkong Land – landlords to a substantial crème-de-la-crème retail portfolio – comments:

It's a difficult balance they will have to strike in the next five to ten years: How to maintain your brand image but migrate it into China without upsetting the perception of the core customer in Hong Kong.[10]

These problems notwithstanding, many brands are expanding their retail operations in Hong Kong with the specific intent of catching the mainland tourist sales. Hong Kong remains a more profitable and easier place to do business than China, at least for the moment, and brands are targeting marketing campaigns to lure mainland customers. Not that they need much luring, they are rushing in under their own steam,

wads of cash stuffed in a designer bag – or a close copy. No wonder
Hong Kong locals call them "walking ATMs."

Integrating Retail into Everyday Life

Whether you intend to or not, chances are that every single day of your
life in Hong Kong you come face to face with dozens of luxe stores. The
way the abundant retail is physically laid out, woven cleverly into the
fabric of the city's everyday life, ensures just that.

The standard formula is to embed malls in the midst of multi-use complexes. For example, the Landmark is situated among office towers, several
fine restaurants, and the new Mandarin Landmark hotel. Furthermore, it's
in the heart of Central, Hong Kong's prime commercial district where
swank office towers brim over with highly paid professionals, and within
an inescapable web of other shopping centers and high-street stores, all
linked seamlessly through walkways in the sky, sprinkled liberally with
banks, bookstores, hair salons, and doctors' offices. Everything leads to
everything else. Go to the office and you walk past several luxury stores.
Come down to pick up a sandwich and you are just as likely to return with
a pair of Ferragamo shoes. Head home via the underground station and get
waylaid by the latest arrival at Louis Vuitton. It doesn't take long before you
give up resisting and walk in zombie-like to try that new dress in the window – and walk out with it neatly wrapped in a shopping bag.

The formula repeats itself at Pacific Place, Times Square, Lee
Gardens, and so on. The new IFC Mall is located with two office towers
– the 88-floor Two IFC claiming the title of highest building in Hong
Kong – the Airport Express station underneath with in-city check-in
counters, the six-star Four Seasons hotel, a five-theater cinema complex, and several upscale bars and restaurants. As if that weren't enough,
it's linked to the ferry terminal by a skyway, has a bus terminal flanking
it, and the whole IFC development sits on top of the Central MTR
underground station. The only detail missing is a helipad.

Luxe is so constantly in your face that even if you aren't shopping,
you're at the very least being constantly updated on the latest arrivals,
assimilating the season's trends whether you want to or not. Even
diehard luxe naysayers finally surrender to its pleasures. As they say, if
you can't beat 'em, join 'em.

ONLY IN HONG KONG...

The eternal chicken-and-egg question: Is it the 24/7 retail bombard-ment that has made Hong Kong people such luxe gluttons? Or is it the voracious appetite of the inhabitants themselves that has helped spawn a retail paradise? Whatever the answer, the fact is that luxury brands assume a larger-than-life role in most people's existence here, often lead-ing to behavior that other societies might consider excessive or even bizarre. In Hong Kong, no one bats an eyelid.

Only in Hong Kong would it be considered perfectly normal to own a few fur coats, despite the fact that winters are mild and temperatures rarely go below 10°C. But then, who wears fur to keep out the cold?

Only in Hong Kong would it be considered perfectly normal to devise strategies to beat Louis Vuitton's one-bag-per-person edict that applies in its stores in Paris. Tom Hilditch, in the *South China Morning Post*, reports one such case: A party of nine well-known Hong Kongers squeezed 48 handbags out of Louis Vuitton's Champs Elysées branch. "It was easy, we just brought everyone we could from the hotel – driv-ers, maids, valets – and got them to queue up."[11]

Only in Hong Kong would it be considered perfectly normal to line up for the luxuries of life. The mother of all queues is the one for Hermès Kelly and Birkin bags – Hong Kong loves them just as much as Japan. If you're on the list it takes three years to get your bag, and if you're not on it forget it, it's closed in Hong Kong too. Nothing has quite caught the imagination of Hong Kong's Hermès have-nots as these closed queues. One senior professional told us her one wish is to get a Birkin before she dies. Another more practical-minded investment banker had the bag copied in red crocodile leather at one of the shops in the Peninsula hotel for what she considered a steal, a mere US$2,000. Many try their luck on trips to Europe or the US. Mothers only half-jokingly talk about reserving an Hermès for their daughter who is still in diapers.

Only in Hong Kong is there a "label guide" with an accompanying CD, written by socialite Eunice Lam, to reduce the mispronunciation of brand names. At least you should be able to pronounce the name of the Hermès bag you yearn for – keep the *H* silent, Lam advises, adding:

These words are not part of the school syllabus and many people mis-pronounce them. I think that living in a cosmopolitan city, they have to be cor-rected and guided.[12]

This is the straight-thinking, call-a-spade-a-spade – even if mis-pronounced – mentality at work. Lam is right: Consumption is the cen-tral theme of Hong Kong life and perhaps it's time the school syllabus started reflecting it. For example, my daughter was given her first Fendi piece at her ninth birthday party by one of her 9-year-old friends, but, poor dear, it was completely lost on her.

Only in Hong Kong does the save-a-buck-while-spending-a-fortune outlook rule with quite so much force. People routinely carry – and skill-fully deploy – 10 to 20 cards that get them discounts in one form or another at various luxury brand stores. Because 10 percent discounts have become par for the course, it's now about what you can get over and above that; and trust us, there's plenty. There are ongoing promotions linked to various credit cards. There are pre-season discounts, champagne affairs for VIP customers where you get first rights on new arrivals. There are cash coupons. There are gifts. There are special prices for buying through the personal shopper service. Even the genuine "sale" periods start a blink after the new arrivals come on display, and discounts can get really juicy, 30–70 percent. The result: extremely savvy shoppers hooked on discounts.

New Yorker Laura Wenke, who headed marketing and sales at Lane Crawford, says one of the biggest adjustments for her coming into this market was the intense interest in discounts and promotions. She says of Hong Kong shoppers:

They have a matrix of a mind for discounts. I mean the programs and loyalty schemes that are offered up, sometimes I feel I need a software program to go shopping to figure it out.

LUXE: ANTIDOTE TO IDENTITY AMBIGUITY

James Twitchell in *Living it Up: Our Love Affair with Luxury* puts forward the idea that the mass consumption of luxury is actually doing more to promote unity and peace than any religion, culture, political movement, or ideology has done.[13] If Twitchell were looking for a laboratory to prove his theory, he'd find it right here in Hong Kong. In fact, Hong Kong goes one better: It doesn't get into the one-is-doing-more-than-the-other argument, it has simply adopted luxe consumption as its central ideology. Making money and blowing it on the goodies of life – that's the one thing Hong Kong people are clear about. On everything else – politics, patriotism, culture – ambiguity reigns.

Is it simply a case of becoming wealthy and displaying it through consumption? Yes, to a large extent that is true of Hong Kong. The Chinese concept of face works here, especially the aspect of *mien-tzu*, which glorifies both the acquisition of wealth and its ostentatious display. But what is interesting about Hong Kong is not its apparent materialism – that's understandable. Rather, it's the *obsession* with money and materialism to the exclusion of all else. The problem is that "all else" is neither clear nor clearly desirable. Fortunately, money and what it can buy are both.

Gordon Mathews, associate professor at the Chinese University of Hong Kong, has done considerable research on the Hongkongese identity.[14] Mathews suggests one of the reasons for this money-madness is that Hong Kong has no deep-rooted culture of its own. It's a place that people pass through. Immigrants come from China and often migrate to other countries. Others go away to study abroad, work a few years, and then come back, beckoned by Hong Kong's irresistible money-making opportunities. Many hold passports from Canada, the US, the UK, or Australia – as "back-up." In this uncertain and ever-changing world, as one of Mathews' interviewees puts it, "all Hong Kong people can do is earn money, that's all you can count on." The rest may be gone with the wind.

With transience and in-betweenness the hallmarks of their history, even basic stuff like what nation you owe allegiance to becomes a complex question for Hong Kong people. There were certainly no patriotic feelings for Britain, even while the British were the colonial masters. To China then? That Hong Kong is a Chinese city and that its people belong proudly to the Chinese race – about these there is no ambiguity. But the People's Republic of China is another matter. Accept it as political master, yes; proud of its recent progress, yes; see it as a land of economic opportunity, yes. Support the Communist regime, probably no. For instance, every 4 June Hong Kong people still hold candlelit vigils for those who died at Tiananmen Square; crowds of 50,000 or more usually turn up.[15] Like a good Chinese mistress, Hong Kong has given her body to Britain and now China, but neither of them decisively owns her heart or soul.

The question today is: Are you a Chinese or Hong Kong person? This kind of either–or logic only makes sense in Hong Kong – it's the equivalent of asking "Are you American or a New Yorker?" but in that case as strongly as people might identify with their city, they are unlikely to dismiss their nationality. The University of Hong Kong conducts regular polls to measure identity ambiguity. That the question of national identity is far from resolved is clear from the poll results – six years after the handover, 44 percent of those surveyed said they were Chinese while 52 percent said they were Hong Kong people.[16] Another survey, this time of 4,595 secondary students, was blunter – less than half said they love China or are happy about Hong Kong's return to China.[17] More truth from the mouths of babes: Compared to mainland Chinese, Hong Kong people were perceived to be more open-minded, decent, educated, pro-equality, and anti-corruption. Now you know why assuming the Chinese nationality is a complex issue for Hong Kong people.

Thanks to British colonial rule and its *laissez-faire* economic policies, Hong Kong grew into a wealthy metropolis with a distinctly international outlook. And it is this combination of wealth and internationalism that both separates and defines Hong Kong's identity *vis-à-vis* China. That is not to say that Hong Kong people have abandoned their Chineseness – they still very much eat, drink, think, and speak Chinese – but they have added on a layer of well-to-do internationalism. That's what makes them such avid consumers of international products, services, and indeed ideas and cultures. Food, movies, music, art, architecture, schools, colleges, technology – in every sphere of life Hong Kong people partake in what Mathews calls the "global supermarket," and rather liberally in the global luxe supermarket. As Hong Kong-based psychologist Jean Nicol puts it:

A world brand and the price that goes with it define a person as globally significant.[18]

The 24/7 shopping frenzy boils down to this: Thanks to Hong Kong's unique fate of being a modern, prosperous, free-wheeling city of Chinese immigrants, raised by British colonial rulers for 155 years, and then returned to the embrace of Communist China, most Hong Kong people have ambiguous feelings about who they are. Thankfully, there is no ambiguity when it comes to Rolex, Vuitton, and Mercedes – or for that matter Patek Philippe, Hermès, or Ferrari – and the identity that comes from their consumption.

Consumer Profile
Sara Wong*: Made for Luxury

Sara is breathtakingly beautiful, her flawless complexion untouched by make-up, her hair pulled up in a ponytail. She meets us on a Sunday morning, casually dressed in jeans and a jauntily cut t-shirt, walking barefoot as she gives us a tour of her stunning home atop the Peak. There's a Ferrari parked in the driveway, a private pool, roof garden, expansive barbecue area, and a sweeping view of Hong Kong's harbor. At 28, she is half vulnerable girl and half mature woman. She has certainly seen a lot of the world: Born and brought up in mainland China, she now lives in Hong Kong and travels constantly with the man in her life, 50-year-old Hong Kong businessman James.

Sara is unaffected by the wealth that surrounds her, and while she talks knowledgeably about diamond-encrusted Piaget watches and dazzling evening gowns custom-made for her by Italian designers ("I tell them what kind I want"), what really shines is *her*. There is nothing more beautiful than a beautiful heart and there's no luxury greater than the luxury of time – Sara is blessed with both.

We settle down in her spacious walk-in wardrobe for a girly heart-to-heart.

On her favorite brands
"I try *every* brand [she laughs]... these days I like Gucci and Christian Dior for bags and shoes. LV, I don't like their brown bags, but I like the fashion ones. For parties, I buy Armani dresses, Prada dresses, I go to Lane Crawford. I like Dolce & Gabbana, their design is very special, very "for the lady," and they have nice eveningwear."

On her shopping habits
"Every lady in Hong Kong loves to shop [giggles ruefully]. I shop every two to three days... [she doesn't consider herself an ardent shopper]. Sometimes I don't shop for *five* days."

*Name changed.

On how much she spends

"A typical shopping trip would be HK$12,000 [US$1,500]. In a month, maybe HK$50,000. We are not like moviestar people – what they spend on shopping can buy an apartment. Not like the really rich people."

As she talks more and shows what she has bought, you realize she has at best a fleeting idea of what she is spending. There isn't all that much difference in her mind between HK$10,000 and HK$100,000. Her self-perception is that she is spending modestly compared to her friends, and this being Hong Kong, she's probably right.

On shopping abroad

"I spend more when I am in Paris or Rome or Milan. On one trip? Maybe HK$50,000 on clothes in Italy. I get my evening dresses made there." She strokes a rack full of exquisite gowns.

How often does she shop abroad? Last year she went five times to Italy, twice to Paris, and once to London. "We don't go there specifically to shop, you know, but when we are there we shop."

On how long she uses her clothes

"Summer clothes you can only keep for one season, but winter coats you can use longer." She feels she uses her evening dresses quite a lot, "sometimes even two or three times." What does she do with her used clothes? "Sometimes people like them, they buy, or I give to friends. Many evening dresses I just keep, like the winter ones [she tugs at a golden mesh halter], they are quite strong."

On shoes

How many? She honestly doesn't know... she thinks currently it's 60 pairs. Besides her wardrobe where she keeps "active" shoes, she has a storeroom downstairs. How often does she wear a particular pair? On average 10 times perhaps, although some could be worn just once, as they "go out of fashion."

On bags

How many? She doesn't know... [laughs] "perhaps 35."

On watches and jewelry

She shops for watches and jewelry with James. "I can buy small things like earrings [she points to a delicate diamond pair on her ears] and rings on my own, but for serious stuff I go with James."

How often? Watches three or four times a year, jewelry four or five times a year. "It depends, like I bought a lot of Cartier in Italy when the euro exchange rate was good."

On how she organizes her wardrobe

This is a purpose-built room with large pull-out drawers for shoes and bags, hanging sections of varying heights, and rows of shelves. "I put all my bags together... [she pulls out a large drawer with bags stacked neatly in rows, each bag carefully encased in a cloth pouch] like I keep all the Fendis in a row, all the LVs in the next, the Guccis, the Diors, and so on. I separate the shoes by daytime and nighttime..." She pulls out a slimmer shoe drawer with party shoes.

On how she got started on luxury brands

"Five years ago, I didn't care about brands – life was simpler, there weren't so many parties. I used to wear casual clothes, but all my girlfriends would say, 'What's this, Sara? You should wear Gucci and Dior.' So I started buying. Now it's different, there are parties, rich people, I have to wear different dresses every time."

On her plans for the rest of the day

"I'm going to tidy up the house – the two maids are off on Sunday. James is traveling [she wonders if it is New York or London, then gives up] and in the evening, I am meeting my girlfriends for dinner."

MONOGAMY TO MONOGRAMY

Unlike Japan's overpowering emphasis on the parasite singles segment, Hong Kong's luxury consumers are more spread out, falling neatly into three segments based on their luxe appetite.

Top of that list are the famed tai-tais, who might not be huge in number but are huge luxe gourmands. A close cousin of this group are the "faux tai-tais," junior wives and mistresses, who also spend with giddy abandon. Since the fortunes of these women are often interlinked – they share the same man, after all – we club them together in one group. The second group consists of professional women who have tasted success at work and dress accordingly. There numbers are large and their spending, while not in the tai-tai super-league, is substantial – they are luxe regulars, forming a sturdy backbone for the local luxury market. A third group consists of office ladies and junior executives, the luxe nibblers, who may not have a lot of money to begin with but may rise up in life. Hong Kong's men are shaping up into a spirited segment, and we deal with them – and other Asian men – in Chapter 11.

We saw their general characteristics in Chapter 2, now let's take a closer look at Hong Kong's particular set, their distinctive shopping behavior, and their unique motivations.

Tai-tais: Luxury Gourmands to the Core

Hong Kong wouldn't be Hong Kong without its tai-tai brigade. Envy, disdain, curiosity, wonder – they generate a wide variety of emotions among the general public, but as far as luxe retailers are concerned the overpowering emotion is glee. These tycoons' wives have an extremely high spending capacity. There are 50–100 such women in Hong Kong's high society and each of them spends over US$1 million annually on luxe shopping. There are another 300 who lay out between US$500,000 and US$1 million every year on luxe. On top of that they shop abroad, and on average splurge an equal amount overseas.

Typically, these women are given a budget per season by their husbands, and it's this budget that drives their shopping behavior. If they don't use up their entire budget, they run the risk of its being reduced the following season. So they head to their favorite brand, whether that's Chanel or Valentino, and snap up 15–20 outfits, the top customers spending US$150,000–200,000 per season on that brand alone. We asked one tai-tai if it was hard *spending* so much money on one brand. Apparently not – a designer jacket can cost US$2,500, then you need a skirt or a pair of trousers with it, which could set you back another US$1,500; a silk blouse, a handbag, shoes to match, a scarf or a belt, and before you know it just one outfit can cost US$10,000. The typical tai-tai has two or three favorite brands where she focuses her attention and expenditure, and then she shops a tad more modestly at other brands – a piece of accessory that's hot this season, or a dress that catches her fancy.

Some of these tai-tais are wealthy in their own right and have married more wealth. Others entered high society by the trusted route of marrying into it. Naturally their shopping behaviors differ. The former have had plenty of time to refine their senses on Daddy's money, and are well-traveled, overseas-educated, sophisticated women who set their own standards. Caroline Roberts, former Loewe marketing head, counts these among the company's customers.

Loewe is a discreet product, it doesn't have logos everywhere. They are not wearing it to show it off, but to feel luxury on their bodies. They are secure, they know they have made it, they don't have to explain it to anybody.[19]

New money, on the other hand, goes for logos straight away. We asked Bonnie Gokson, former image director of Chanel – and a style icon in her own right – the secret of that brand's amazing success. Her answer is revealing:

Chanel has very good standing as the most luxurious and expensive label. People in Asia love status… they basically like to wear the dollar sign out. For myself, the best is not to have a logo… have the most luxurious fabric, that no one knows, only I feel it. For a lot of women, that's not good – it doesn't have anything – where's the button of the logo, where's this, where's that? They need to show status that proves and upgrades their own status.[20]

Roberts concurs: "Even though some of them develop a quick understanding of luxury, they know quality and workmanship, but they still want to show off."

Whatever the vintage of the money, this high-spending system stays in equilibrium thanks to the roving-eye syndrome that seems to be part and parcel of the wealthy set. It is a well-accepted custom among Hong Kong's successful businessmen to have second wives – in fact, as recently as 1971 it was perfectly legal to do so. Hong Kong historian Jason Wordie argues that many Hong Kong men in their 40s and 50s grew up in "households with plural marital arrangements" and see nothing wrong in following in their father's footsteps.[21] The women walk into the "marriage" with their eyes open, treating it as the equivalent of a well-paid job. And in Hong Kong's money-is-king society, there are few social slights to be suffered or moral frowns cast their way.

But driven by an underlying sense of guilt, these men compensate for their dalliances by giving their wives generous shopping budgets.

First wives are matter-of-fact about this, exacting their revenge through shopping. They trade in monogamy for monogramy. They figure it's better to have a lavish lifestyle and the respectability that comes from being a successful man's wife than to kick up a fuss and lead a lesser life. Luxe shopping takes on yet another role, that of bigamy therapy.

Luxury brands form the central theme in the lives of the second wives as well. In these multiple marriages there's a keen competitive edge and the wives try to outdo each other in spending. The logic: If wife number two spends more than wife number three then it implies that the man loves her more. What might be a tense power struggle among the wives is a heaven-sent bonanza for the brands. Store managers, well versed in their VIP customers' personal tastes, send large selections to their homes, and often the wife simply keeps it all. If she can't wear everything she buys, she gives it to her friends or her maids. Luxury brands are a symbol of power, to be wielded like a remote control on a time-sharing husband.

While this is the life of several super-rich tycoons, men of lesser means simply keep mistresses. They may put the woman up in an apartment and give her a decent allowance, but the commitment is not quite the same as to a junior wife. These women are socially insecure, coming as they tend to do from modest social backgrounds, often from mainland China. In fact, their shopping habits have created what we can call the "Causeway Bay mistress market." These young things are intimidated by the refined air of Central's snooty boutiques, and find the atmosphere of Causeway Bay, with its merry throngs of shoppers, more welcoming. Luxe shopping of course remains central to their existence, quite literally, as the prettier they look the longer they can hang on to their man.

High-Maintenance Professional Women

In step with Hong Kong's evolution from a manufacturing economy in the 1960s and 1970s to today's service-based economy, the situation of working women has changed dramatically. Gone are the days of women laboring in factories, since the factories themselves have moved out of Hong Kong into neighboring China. In have come professional career women to meet the demands of the rapidly expanding service sectors.

This was the best possible scenario not only for the women themselves but, you guessed it, for the luxe industry.

Lawyers, doctors, bankers, brokers, managers in the corporate world, successful entrepreneurs running their own businesses – Hong Kong's enterprising women have gone further in the work arena than females anywhere else in Asia. We are not saying that the glass ceiling has been broken conclusively, but a fair sprinkling of women have made it into senior management, and at middle and junior levels most Hong Kong companies don't bother which gender their managers are, as long as they perform.

The lifestyles of professional working women are extremely fast paced, with hectic workdays followed by an even more hectic social calendar that fills up evenings and weekends, on top of which comes travel, for both work and pleasure, and there may be children and family life to tend to. These are high-maintenance women who need extensive wardrobes to cater to the many roles they undertake.

Take just shoes. Nancy Valiente, managing director of South China Morning Post, a discerning luxe shopper and ardent shoe lover, explains that a girl needs so many shoes because there are so many "variables." First there are four seasons, and clearly a strappy summer sandal won't do for winter; then there are colors: you need a range of colors to match different outfits and just within the color black you need flats, pumps, high heels; then there are shoes you can wear to work, shoes for parties, shoes for weekends; come winter you need boots, and within boots you need a range: party boots, suede boots, and so on; then you need shoes to wear with skirts and shoes to wear with pants. "And just when you get started with pointy shoes, they start going out of fashion," she says ruefully.[22]

With Hong Kong salaries among the highest in the world and maximum income tax a mere 15 percent, these working women have money to burn. On average, they spend US$15,000–50,000 annually on luxury goods. As a group they form the largest segment, accounting for about 50 percent of Hong Kong's luxury market. They shop with great regularity, picking up something every week – in a month they're likely to buy a bag, a pair of shoes, two or three pieces of clothing, and an accessory or two.

Paulene Hsia calls them the "large invisible market." It's not just the famous on the society pages who are big spenders, she says, there are

people from far-off suburbs like Yuen Long and Tsing Yi, and VIP customers who live in 1,200-square-foot apartments in Taikoo Shing. She
says:

*You couldn't run a business on the famous tai-tais alone. There aren't enough
of them.*

Among professional women, there are two distinct categories of shoppers. The first is the mature woman with a sense of style. In her late 40s
or early 50s, she is invariably in the higher echelons of management.
There's an elegant, well-groomed air about her, conservative but stylish,
feminine but firm. The look is best personified by Hong Kong's former
Chief Secretary Anson Chan, a woman with the power to light up a
room with her dimpled smile while administering Hong Kong with a
steely resolve.

These women favor skirt suits at work and have a wide selection of
them – one *amah* (another Hong Kong fixture, *amahs* are imported
maids, the best ones from the Philippines) who had recently cleaned her
boss's wardrobe told us there were 57 black suits alone. Although black
is Hong Kong's all-time favorite, this category of women are also partial
to feminine pinks, pastels, and reds. They favor brands like Chanel,
Hermès, Ferragamo, and Valentino; for jewelry it's chunky Cartier gold,
or Mikimoto pearls, or a Van Cleef & Arpels brooch.

The second kind of shopper is trendy and younger, late 20s to mid-
30s, steadily climbing up the corporate ladder. If she does wear a suit,
it's just as likely to be pants as a skirt. She favors a less formal look even
at work. Instead of a structured suit jacket, she might don a stylish Stella
McCartney one. She pairs a Helmut Lang skirt with a Prada top. The
look is sleek and modern, the silhouette slim and spare – blessed as she
is with a trim figure – the hair is artfully disheveled, the make-up under-
stated. She experiments with a wide swathe of brands, depending on
what's hot and what's not, and what catches her fancy.

She isn't averse to picking up less expensive items and judiciously
blending them in with her pricey designer labels. One of these women
helpfully explained: "A head-to-toe brand look would scare away the
boys. They'll think you are really high maintenance." The fact that she
is high maintenance is, of course, beside the point.

Office Ladies Nibble Away

At the lower end of this spectrum of Hong Kong's luxury consumers are the office ladies, secretaries and junior executives, luxe shoppers on a budget. Unlike Japan's profligate spenders Hong Kong's office ladies are judicious nibblers, although many are known to spend the better part of their month's salary at one go. It's the cost of entering the working girl's club – the sorority of secretaries – and more often than not it's the peer pressure that propels them into their first luxe purchase rather than a personal aspiration for designer brands.

Given that money is a constraint, these women go for maximum effect. The value-for-money principle comes into play and that makes designer bags the first priority – perfect, since a bag is highly visible and can be carried on several occasions, if not every day. A trendy pair of shoes comes second on the list. If there's money to spare they might indulge in a Gucci watch or a Burberry overcoat in winter, but this would be stretching them to her limits. Their luxury shopping is less frequent, once or twice a year for items in the US$500 range, interspersed with smaller purchases. The per head spend in this segment isn't big, it ranges from US$500 to US$2,000 annually, but the number of office ladies out there adds up to a large amount of expenditure.

The office lady goes for brands that aren't coy, and Louis Vuitton, Gucci, and Prada certainly meet her needs. The rest of her clothes may not be luxe brands, but all the same she is trendily turned out, using the extensive spread of reasonably priced local fashion available in Hong Kong. Her spending power comes from the fact that like Japan's parasite singles she lives with her family, thereby cutting down on basic expenses. This generation of young women also don't seem to have a saving habit at all; on the contrary, they are quite happy to flex their credit cards.

TAIWAN: DIAMOND IN THE ROUGH

There are those that will catch public transport, those that will ride a motor scooter, those that will drive a car, those that will have a chauffeur – it goes from top to the bottom, there's something for everyone. It amazes me how a *brand can persuade someone to buy a bag at US$2–3,000 when that's their monthly income.*

Lawrence Elms, former head of Taipei 101[23]

One swallow does not make a summer. Apply the parable to Taipei, and a parallel saying would be: One megastructure does not make a style capital.

Expectations soared higher than Taipei 101 when the upscale shopping mall anchoring the base of the US$1.7 billion skyscraper – the world's tallest to date – opened for business in 2003. Taiwan's leading city at last had a shopping landmark worthy of an island that had transformed itself into a major economic power and a vibrant democracy. Taipei 101 would be a worldwide symbol of Taiwan as a shopping paradise and, by extension, its identity. "Taiwan is in step with the world," President Chen Shui-Bian boasted to the political and business élite gathered for the occasion.

But that rhetoric is still some way from reality. Although 500,000 people are estimated to have swept through the 162-store mall on opening day, Taipei's dreams of becoming a world-class shopping address remain lofty. "It's turning into a tourist spot [for visitors from the south of Taiwan], not so much for shopping," explains a Hong Kong-based fashion retailer with shops in Taipei. In retail speak, the mall has footfall, but healthy conversion rates are still to come for its luxury floors.

Taipei 101's process of evolution could be a metaphor for the pitfalls and promise of business in Taiwan for the luxury brands. The Taiwanese have caught the same fever for designer goods that is sweeping the rest of Asia – and as Elms points out there is demand from every stratum, leading to a US$1 billion luxury market, significant by any standards. Leading brands recorded double- and triple-digit growth during the last decade, and not even the financial crisis of 1997 could hobble the growth of the luxury industry. An extensive portfolio of retail space has emerged with the development of not just Taipei 101, but other malls, department stores, and freestanding flagship stores. Yet Taiwan remains like Cinderella, a fairytale princess among rich countries but missing her glass slippers. The retail scene although abundant is messy, with some locales lacking the necessary class and aesthetic finesse that one associates with luxury. The same holds true for consumers – they wear the finest brands, but the sartorial results are not always the best.

Let's understand why by taking a closer look at Taiwan's luxury retail development and its luxury-loving customers.

LUXURY RETAIL'S MERRY MESS

Luxury retail in Hong Kong is about cutting-edge design and clever planning; in Taipei that is not always the case.

Take the Regent Galleria and its environs, where an upscale shopping precinct has sprung up without any guidelines. The Regent hotel opened in 1991, about the same time as luxury goods were entering Taiwan, and coincidentally the time of the Japanese tourist boom. The Regent put one in touch with the other with two floors of deluxe space – the Galleria with big-brand boutiques and a floor for duty-free shopping. So successful was it that soon space at the Galleria ran out, especially for the superstores that Louis Vuitton or Prada favors. Desperate brands simply put up flagships in the streets and lanes around the hotel, quite haphazardly, so that the height of luxury sat side by side with plebeian scooter parking and chaotic traffic conditions. When we visited the area, cars were being hosed down outside the Regent, the dirty water flowing onto the road. Not that it seemed to matter; the Vuitton flagship had the familiar crush of Japanese tourists.

This is a story that is repeated elsewhere. Taipei, a city of fewer than 3 million people, has more than 20 department stores and shopping malls, with more in the works. But there appears to be little planning, and the result is more madness than method. Take Taipei's other concentration of flagship stores at the Dun Hwa South Road and Ren Ai Road intersection. Luxury flagships are positioned on the streets adjoining a chaotic traffic roundabout. The stores are too far apart for happy shopping, leading to a case of drop before you shop.

Even when retail development is planned, as with shopping malls and department stores, the result can come out short on design, layout, and general aesthetics. The Breeze Center, which opened in 2001, is a circus – when we visited temporary stalls were set up in the corridors selling accessories like Missoni mufflers, and a whole makeshift store, Anya Hindmarch, was plonked smack at the entrance.

Design may also not be the strong point of the Sogo II department store – it has a tight, convoluted layout – but what it does do well is create a classy atmosphere. It is a vertical oasis of concentrated luxe, with the smell of serious money being spent. In contrast to the noisy throngs at the Breeze Center, the Sogo II was quietly humming with tai-tais.

Hope for Taipei's luxe retail lies in the "planned district" of Hsin Yi, with its clean, modern, cheerful, urban feel – a world away from the rest of Taipei. The Taipei 101 mixed-use development looms large over the area. Then there are hotels, office towers, a convention center, and shopping facilities. The Warner Village movie complex and New York New York department store with its designer bridge brands and hip restaurants represent a young and affluent Taipei. A new luxury development, inspired by Milan's Galleria, is underway – with its distinctive Italian architecture and large spaces designed for flagship stores, it should add a touch of class to Taipei's luxury retail. Hopefully, over time, even the mall at Taipei 101 will settle down and turn profitable.

Shopping Order: Who's Who

From the motorcycle pillion rider to the starlet in the leather-bound back seat of a sedan, Taiwanese haven't lived till they have at least one precious set of monogrammed initials. Luxury goods have become the great social leveler, and observers talk about the democratization of the market as though a designer logo is every status-conscious citizen's right.

Although luxury brands entered Taiwan relatively late – 1988 was the turning point when the government eased import policies – with a booming economy pumping money into individual hands the luxe culture snowballed fast and wide. Eva Chang, who manages retail property leasing at Jones Lang LaSalle and has been watching the growth of luxury retail, estimates that ten years ago perhaps one in ten Taipei women had a designer brand bag, five years later the odds had shortened to two in ten, and now it's five in ten.[24] Taiwan has hurtled into Stage 4 – *fit in* – of the Spread of Luxury model, when usage of luxury brands spontaneously brims over to a wide mass of people.

The consumer segments in Taiwan are not unlike Hong Kong's. The apex of the luxury pyramid is formed by families of the millionaire class who made fortunes from land ownership, real estate, manufacturing, and electronics. The sub-sets include tai-tais in their 40s and 50s, scions happy to spend Daddy's cash, and mistresses, who, quaintly enough, tend to pass themselves off as "daughters." Top-to-toe designer attire is just an extension of their lifestyle.

The tip expands into a growing class of executive women and professionals – typically single and living with parents, these 21–35 year olds work hard and play hard, putting in late hours at the office and then meeting friends at trendy bars and restaurants. The accessories market – bags, shoes, and watches – is buoyant on their custom. There's even a small set of creative professionals – architects, designers, advertising/PR professionals, and so on – who are cultivating a local aesthetic.

The base is drawn from across the tiers of Taiwanese society: the office lady tribe, housewives desperate for a bit of glamour, and celebrity-struck youth. The individual spending power of these nibblers may not thrill a salesperson on commission, but their combined numbers make them difficult to ignore.

Consumer Profile
Amy Cheng*: "Once you have one, you have to have more!"

In many ways, Amy exemplifies the new generation of professional women in Taiwan. In her late 20s, supremely confident, international in outlook, and extremely well spoken, she holds a managerial position at a technology company. Previously working in the US, she decided to come back to her roots to be part of the Taiwanese experience.

Amy has an infectious enthusiasm – you feel on a high just being in her presence. She caught the luxe bug in Taiwan, and is now an unabashed lover of luxury brands. "I have to admit when I was in the US, I didn't have a luxury purse," she says. "But now I am here, I have several. It's terrible." We sit down over lunch and talk about her, and Taiwan's, newfound passion for luxury.

On how widespread the luxe culture is
"People I hang out with – professionals, 27 upwards, independent women – almost everyone in my group has some luxury brand. Some have more, some have less, but everyone has something."

---

*Name changed.

On the brands she and her friends love

"Louis Vuitton, they think it's the ultimate brand to have here. Gucci. Fendi. Kate Spade – it has a very distinctive look, beautiful, I like it. Coach. Calvin Klein. People here carry Mont Blanc leather goods – the men carry something weird like a pouch with a loop, a 'male purse.' Armani – younger people who can't afford Armani still have Armani Exchange. I like Jil Sander myself. Prada too, it's special – you see a lot on the street, whether real or not, it copies very well. Burberry is huge here – when you own it everyone knows it's a Burberry. Tiffany. Hermès is pretty big – expensive, but then what isn't?"

On the Taiwanese love for bargains

"We love bargains here, huge bargains. We want to show off, to say that we got this but we got it at half the price. We wait for sales; say Prada has 30 percent off. There is also a trend of selling 'used' items [she laughs]. I bought a Gucci purse for NT$6,000 [US$185] when it would have been NT$10,000."

If you live with your parents, do you spend more on luxury brands?

"No, the parents will watch over you and discourage you to spend on these things. If you live on your own, you control what you spend. Let's say you buy a luxury purse, then you can eat ramen for a week. Nobody can really control you."

On Taiwanese men carrying their girlfriend's handbags

"The women make the guys carry their purses, it's normal. There's an ABC [American-born Chinese] guy who is dating a local woman, and I thought ABC guys wouldn't be wimps like that, but he tells me the women here expect it.

"I went out with this guy who would take my purse, and I'd go 'No!' ... If you want to be a gentleman you can do the door thing, but you cannot touch my purse, it's a personal thing. I find that very odd, but it's a show of affection."

On the custom of second wives

"A lot of Taiwanese men have second wives... here they say Taiwanese men are different before and after marriage. Before they may carry your purse, but afterwards, they'll carry the mistress's purse."

It's About Status, Not Style

Despite the widespread acquisition of designer labels, Taiwan's sartorial scene has yet to gain the critical mass that will turn it into a serious style contender like Hong Kong. There are select pockets that are displaying a sense of style – young professionals like Amy, others who are in artistic or lifestyle fields – but their influence is as yet limited. At the beginning of this chapter we looked at the role played by Taiwan's earthy immigrant roots in shaping current society. Add to that the fact that the country's exposure to luxury brands is relatively recent, it simply has a longer way to go in terms of acquiring *savoir faire* and confidence. As one retailer put it, the Taiwanese customer is a diamond in the rough, who "has to go through the process of refining." In the meantime, the driving motivation behind luxury consumption is solid status, not style. That's why flashy watches and jewelry have boomed, but an avant-garde retailer like Joyce had fewer takers.

Even at the *top* end, a typical customer has cash but not necessarily class, says a high-fashion retailer, citing a 50-something customer who is a pillar of support for every luxury brand in Taipei:

She is extremely wealthy and buys everything. She spends enough that she can even jump a year-long wait list for a hot item.

For the most part Taiwanese women prefer a casual mix-and-match approach, with a partiality for checks (think Daks, Aquascutum, Burberry), multicolored tops, casual jackets, and flat shoes with a sporty look. Even among mistresses, it's the Bollywood kind of sexy siren glamour that you encounter rather than Western chic. For instance, we descended three floors on an escalator behind one such woman, with long straight hair that went into tight curls below her shoulders, dressed in a lacy black inner gown that peeped through another sheer black floor-length dress. The look was half boudoir, half ballroom, an unusual outfit for shopping among the bustling crowds at Breeze Center. At her elbow was a 60-year-old businessman with an indulgent smile, clearly the master to this 35+ glamorous mistress.

With upping status as the prime motivator, shopping itself has become a competitive sport among the élite, cheered on by luxury retailers who cleverly fuel rivalry with their own numbers game. For instance, a brand manager may order four of a much-coveted watch, knowing full well her VIP customers will clamor for it. The next step is to leak the news to those unable to buy – the snubbed shoppers invariably jet off to buy the same watch elsewhere, even if it costs much more.

While Hong Kong has thrived on international influence, Taiwan's recent history and political isolation have made it more inward looking. Even charity balls and gala events, a standard fixture on Hong Kong's social calendar, are rare in Taipei. Sophie Jiang, a public relations honcho with an enviable portfolio of luxury brand accounts, comments:

Our cityscape is dull because for the longest time we were told that localization is good, and everything should be done ourselves. In architecture, art, fashion, and even the social scene, we have had little interaction with foreigners – our taste has been limited until now. We don't have many occasions to dress for.[25]

Many Taiwanese women feel under-confident about their own ability to dress tastefully, and ironically it is this low confidence that is making them go for designer brands. They seek a sense of security in luxury. Tricia Liu, deputy general manager, David Advertising in Taiwan, explains:

If you have taste, if you have the eye, the capability to put a look together yourself, then you don't need to spend so much, you can look good with less. When you don't have taste, then you feel safe with big brands. After all, the designer brands are designed by experts… you are in safe hands.

That the diamond in the rough has begun the process of evolution is evident when one looks at the young generation. Although not luxury customers yet in a significant way, they are dressing with greater flair than their mothers, and experimenting with street fashion. They take their cue from the vibrant pop scene and stars like Jay Chou and Jolin Tsai, among others, who exude an emerging Taiwanese version of cool, which is also finding fans across the strait in mainland China.

What one can say with certainty is that when the diamond finally sparkles it will be a treat: Blessed with slim, tall figures, these young women are among the most attractive in the region.

Style Lessons From the Two Siblings

The contrast between Hong Kong and Taiwan serves to highlight the role of style in the context of luxury brands. How do these "aesthetic codes" – as Bourdieu calls them – emerge in an Asian market that starts using Western luxury brands? Do they depend on a market's stage of development? Does a sense of style really matter for luxury brand sales?

A Market with Style Is More Profitable and Sustainable

Let's put things in the context of the Spread of Luxury model. In the initial stages, when an Asian country starts buying luxury brands the primary reason is to mark status. Style does not enter the equation. If the luxury brand product does a good job of showing off your money, you buy it. End of story. Right up to Stage 4, *fit in* – where Taiwan is currently – it's more about status than style.

The turning point comes with Stage 5. By then consumers have had prolonged contact with luxury, they have tried several brands, they have moved from the initial focus on logo bags and statement watches to buying a wider repertoire of products. They have absorbed the cumulative weight of years of studying fashion glossies. They have evolved. Status doesn't go away, but style is added to the equation. That's what has happened in Hong Kong.

Style brings a higher level of involvement with luxury brands. A keener awareness of seasonal trends. A greater desire to be in tune. A higher propensity to experiment. A growing understanding of what works and doesn't work. Consumers acquire a subliminal grasp of aesthetic codes. Result: Shopping becomes more frequent, acceptable price levels get steadily pushed up in their mind, they spend more than they did before. That's what Hong Kong's professional women are doing, spending US$15,000–50,000 annually on luxury brands, shopping every week or two. They're hooked and they'll keep coming back, forming the base for a sustainable, profitable business.

Fast-Tracking Bourdieu

In Bourdieu's French context, the mastery of aesthetic codes doesn't happen in an instant; rather, the development of good taste is a gradual process taking a few generations. Looking at how Hong Kong has shaped up on the sartorial front in a couple of decades, we believe there is scope to speed things along. We are talking Prada and Chanel anyway, not Mozart and Beethoven.

As a corollary to the first lesson, we are suggesting that luxury brands get involved early on in fast-tracking the development of a sense of style locally. Develop the style, develop the market.

This goes beyond teaching people about your brand – it's about educating people *how to use* your brand's products to maximum effect. It's about spreading know-how. Building an inventory of *savoir faire* in the collective consciousness. Defining what constitutes a stylish look, and showing how you achieve it.

Style schooling can be done in a variety of ways. Fashion magazines, of course, are a tried-and-trusted method. In markets like Taiwan – and indeed China and India – you may need more one-on-one coaching opportunities. For example, as against just salespeople, you might add in-store stylists, trained professionals who can provide advice. The logical conclusion would be to run style schools that impart the art of Western dressing to emerging Asian markets. It could be a profitable side business to boot.

Continual Retail Reinvention

The game changes dramatically once a country is in Stage 5, where increasingly sophisticated consumers need constant stimulation, setting in motion a continuous cycle of newer, bigger, better. Hong Kong's luxury retail scene has been upping its standards on a regular basis. Take the new-look Lane Crawford department stores – they offer highly evolved retail settings that take fashion into the realm of art, a plethora of niche brands for the fashion forward, and a good dose of creativity and humor in their delivery.

Brands too are putting up bigger and more sophisticated stores, such as Louis Vuitton's global store in Central, with features like its suspended Peter Marino staircase and its bag bar. Similarly, Chanel has increased the sophistication stakes with its new store in Central, incorporating Chanel-inspired art installations and extremely high-end jewelry. It's a game of upward and onward.

A sign of the times – Western luxury brands on a charm offensive in China. Wanda Ferragamo, president of Salvatore Ferragamo, meets Zhang Zi Yi, star of Oscar-winning movie *Crouching Tiger, Hidden Dragon*.

Photo courtesy of Ferragamo.

5

CHINA:
FROM MAO SUITS
TO ARMANI

"Bing owns his own business, drives a Mercedes-Benz, wears a Versace shirt and a Rolex watch, and carries a Nokia mobile phone and a Louis Vuitton wallet... 'Do you think that although I didn't go to school in America, I am still on the way to being fully Westernized?' asks Bing."
From *"People's Republic of Desire," a column by Annie Wang,*
writer and social commentator[1]

A celebration of life unfolding at a breathtaking pace – that's China today. After decades of doing without, the floodgates are opening and there's an urgent dash to make up for lost time with newfound wealth. At one level, it's simply a reawakening of the senses, the replacement of drab monotones with loud Versace hues, the exchange of shapeless Mao suits for the fine cut and feel of a Zegna suit, the application of a colorful palette from Estée Lauder and Lancôme to a face untouched by modern make-up. It's the sheen of patent leather on a Chanel bag, the sparkle of diamonds on a Piaget watch, the softness of cashmere on a long Max Mara coat.

But at another level – perhaps the more important one in today's China – luxury brands perform the necessary task of unmistakably marking you out as someone who has made it. You are no longer a faceless statistic, you are an individual with a success story. It doesn't matter that the Dior boots would look better on a taller woman, or that it's time to remove the sleeve label from the Dunhill blazer or learn how to pronounce Louis Vuitton – what counts is the fact that they are easily recognizable symbols that say, baby, I've arrived. This is Veblen's theory in its most direct manifestation, reinterpreted in the Confucian, communist-moving-toward-capitalist, twenty-first-century Chinese context.

It may seem ludicrous to be talking of a growing luxury brand culture in a country where the vast majority of people are poor, but the fact is that China's uneven development has yielded significant pockets of wealth. The cream consists of 400 super-rich with a combined wealth of US$75 billion, equivalent to 7 percent of China's GDP in 2004, according to the *China Rich List* by Rupert Hoogewerf.[2] Not quite in the same league, but millionaires nevertheless, are another 320,000 Chinese estimated by Merrill Lynch's *Wealth Report* to have financial assets in excess of US$1 million, over and above what they may have in hard assets. Needless to say, each one is a potential luxury gourmand. The plot thickens with an estimated 4.7 million households with a purchasing power of more than US$30,000[3] – in the Chinese context that's enough money for them to become luxury regulars. From there you move to a vast throng of would-be nibblers, a staggering 175 million who the China Association of Branding Strategy claims can afford to buy luxury brands.[4] Even if 5 percent of them actually buy a piece of luxe, you are still looking at 8.5 million shoppers, more than Hong Kong's population. And that's today.

China's real lure is the growth to come. It is only at Stage 3 of the Spread of Luxury model – *show off* – with all the serious action up ahead. With one foot pressed firmly on the accelerator, its economy is speeding at an annual GDP growth rate of 8–10 percent, while the luxury market itself is galloping at 25 percent a year. As subsequent strata of society rise and acquire the means to purchase, you can safely bet on their urge to splurge on branded luxe. The China Association of Branding Strategy expects the number who can afford luxury brands to have grown to 250 million by 2010. China's luxury market of US$2.5 billion is already significant, but it will multiply several times over in the coming decade.

Plus there's aggressive shopping abroad. We estimate the Chinese tourist is spending over US$1 billion currently, and that amount will skyrocket in tandem with the coming explosion of outbound tourism – compared to the 28 million Chinese who traveled abroad in 2004, the Economist Intelligence Unit projects a round 100 million by 2015. The Chinese, it seems, will be the growth engine of the luxury industry not only within China, but also all over the globe.

Luxury brand companies are salivating at the prospect and the general line of thinking is to get your foot in the door fast and make sure your brand name is firmly implanted on the consumers' radar screen. The takings may be modest today, but you'll be laying the foundation for a hugely profitable tomorrow and gaining valuable on-the-ground experience. The China dream beckons with such force that despite the many obstacles of doing business here, companies are making a beeline for the country, their intent reinforced by the perception that you can't afford to be left out. The prestigious Comité Colbert – the French luxury brands' association – took the unprecedented step of moving its annual general meeting to Beijing, the first time outside of Europe in its 50-year history.[5]

For brands that moved in early enough, the rewards have been well worth it. Take Zegna, which set up shop in 1991, far ahead of today's brand pack. Not only is it one of the largest menswear brands in China today, it reportedly sells more sleeve units in China than it does in Japan. Hiroshi Ogawa, who ran the Zegna business in China then and currently heads the Asia-Pacific operations of Baccarat, recalls those turbulent early days.[6] In 1989, Louis Vuitton had booked a large store in the prestigious Palace hotel, a stone's throw from Tiananmen Square, when the tanks rolled in. Vuitton decided to withdraw, and Ogawa called his boss to discuss whether Zegna should follow suit. "We are not going to deal with the Chinese government, we are going to deal with the Chinese consumer" was the boss's view. Zegna opened its first store two years later in the prime spot vacated by Vuitton, and the rest is history. Ironically, Zegna finds itself dealing with the government after all – its suits are a hot favorite with senior government officials.

Louis Vuitton, which finally opened in 1992, has done extremely well, becoming the top brand in leather goods. Serge Brunschwig, former managing director of Louis Vuitton (Worldwide), says:

One thing that has surprised us in the last ten years is the speed at which it [China's luxury market] has developed. What we are seeing today is a customer who understands a certain aspect of luxury goods and is really hungry for buying it.[7]

In this chapter we look at the unique forces spurring the growth of the Chinese luxury market: the avid consumer society that has sprung up in recent years with a great hunger for Western luxury brands; the arrival of brands to feed (and feed on) that hunger; and the fast-changing retail scene that is catapulting itself from extremely backward to cutting-edge world class in one great leap forward. China is like a fascinating social laboratory where you can observe what ordinary people do when they are suddenly let loose, allowed to get rich, permitted to choose what they do with their lives. From what we have seen so far, a trip to the luxury store is one of the first things you do, especially if that's what great-grandma did in her heyday.

BACK TO THE FUTURE, SANS STYLE

Like most things in China, the luxury brand phenomenon has "before" and "after" chapters. Centered largely in Shanghai, the before chapter goes all the way back to the heady days of the 1920s and 1930s when the Chinese version of *la dolce vita* was enacted in what was then a bustling international city with special enclaves for the British, French, and Americans. Not only was it a thriving center of commerce, it was also the Paris of the East and the Hollywood of China, with glamorous actresses like Ruan Lingyu causing as much of a stir as Greta Garbo.

We asked Lynn Pan, author of several books on the city, what life was like in those days.[8] Lynn is a picture of elegance herself, but it was her mother we were interested in, a stylish and tasteful lady tracing her lineage back to the Ming dynasty, who lived the Shanghainese high life before the family fled to Hong Kong in the 1950s. Lynn's mother wore cheongsams of silk and chiffon, lined with fine wool in winter. She owned several fur coats: lynx, otter, fox, "practically every skin known" – Lynn inherited the lynx. Her father alternated with ease between Western and Chinese clothes, his winter *changpao*[9] lined with sable from Russia. He loved horses, played polo, and raced his horses at the Turf Club. Lynn's mother rode too, tutored by a Cossack. Both loved dancing foxtrots and cha-chas at clubs like Ciro's and the Paramount Ballroom. There were parties with the men in tuxedos and the women in ankle-length cheongsams, hair up in a chignon, "very *soignée*."

Even as a refugee in Hong Kong, Lynn's mother, forced to work for the first time in her life, kept her sense of style intact. Lynn describes her mother stepping out of their run-down quarters in North Point, looking svelte in an elegant cheongsam, high-heeled shoes, handbag, not a hair out of place, rather like Maggie Cheung in the Cannes award-winning movie *In the Mood for Love*. The point is that this kind of deep-rooted fashion sensibility cannot be wiped out completely, even by a man as determined as Mao. It hibernates, like tulip bulbs under the ground in a long winter of discontent, only to re-emerge when the climate is more congenial.

While Shanghai is flowering again as a style capital, the same cannot be said about the rest of China. The love of dressing up and living it up is back, but its expression is all flash and show, strut and preen, with some awkward results. Talk to any luxury brand manager and there is a barely suppressed moan about the prevailing levels of fashion taste. Small pockets of elegance do exist – for example the scions of old wealthy families have resurfaced and they dress with confidence, Lynn being a case in point. However, the larger scene reconfirms Bourdieu's thesis that taste in cultural matters is a function of educational level and social origin,[10] exactly the two aspects Mao was intent on eradicating. He promptly "re-educated" (a euphemism for hard labor in rural communes) anyone who remotely smacked of higher social origin. The Cultural Revolution was designed to wipe out all "culture" in the traditional sense, a brutal equalization perpetrated by demolishing the élite and bringing everyone down to the same coarse level of existence, rather than raising the masses to a higher appreciation of life.

What happens when color and beauty are forbidden, when an entire nation is emptied of all traces of personal style, when a generation grows up without any visual stimulation whatsoever? What do you do when your own rich cultural heritage is erased, and a sparse and senseless monotony artificially imposed in its place? In China outside Shanghai it's like starting with a blank slate, where there are no yardsticks for beauty and elegance, no standards for what is tasteful and what is not. Developing a sense of style after living in a visual vacuum for decades is very hard indeed. Says Lynn:

It's the years of dearth, of not having anything beautiful to look at. When you are not surrounded by beautiful things, how do you learn to be discriminating? And now suddenly, there is a plethora of things, and the people go for the brightest and flashiest.

Wealth Is the New Fashion Statement

Stories of jaw-dropping excess by China's nouveau riche class are by now well known. Huang Qiaoling, who has figured on the Forbes China Rich List, built a US$10 million replica of the White House, Oval Office included; as if that wasn't enough, he threw in a scaled-down version of Mount Rushmore and the Washington Monument.[11] Appropriately enough, his staff call him President Huang, although he chooses not to work in the Oval Office, presumably in deference to the real US President. Meanwhile Li Qinfu (also on the Forbes list) thought it appropriate to respond with a facsimile of the US Capitol.[12] Notwithstanding the risk of attracting the wrath of the Chinese government and the ax of the tax authorities, usually accompanied by imprisonment and worse, conspicuous consumption *sans* taste continues for most of the new rich.

The simple reason is this: Taste is not part of the equation – conspicuous consumption is an end in itself. The more you spend and the more you flash the cash, the higher your status in society. The manifestation of wealth is more important than the degree of wealth. This sets off a beneficial upward spiral – if you are seen to be rich and successful, you attract more business deals, and you win approvals faster from officials who know you have the means to make appropriate gifts and donations. What is more, there are none of the double standards of "developed" cultures, where the tenet that wealth is ultimately power holds equally true but there are rules dictating how you display it tastefully, and the obviousness of new money is frowned on. In a land of new and newer money, there is no such baggage. The rule is loud and clear: If you have it, flaunt it.

Or as Yu Lei, managing editor of *Shanghai Tatler*, says:

If you want to be part of "high status" society, then you need something on your exterior to let others know.[13]

That China, despite its recent Communist history, is at its core a Confucian society has a further encouraging influence on luxury brand consumption. Families are important to all of us, but in the Chinese Confucian tradition they are center stage – you are part of the family and the family is part of you. It's not just for your *own* glory you're adorning yourself with visible symbols of success, it's for the greater glory of your family. With the blessings of Confucianism behind you, the question of resisting the charms of Vuitton and Versace doesn't even arise. Be good – succumb.

If the purpose of donning luxury brands is to display your successful status, then that evidence has to be clearly understood by all concerned. Easier said than done, given that most Chinese are not conversant with English – they cannot *read* the brand names, neither is "made in France" or "made in Italy" decipherable to them. (Just imagine what you would do if the tables were turned and you had to decipher dozens of words in Chinese script.) Logos and symbols, important display mechanisms all over the world, become mission-critical visual shorthand in China. Consumers often refer to brands by their initials – CD and DG are after all a lot easier to master than Christian Dior and Dolce & Gabbana.

The Chinese luxe consumer uses a variety of strategies to maximize the wealth-demonstration effect. First, and perhaps the most direct approach, is simply to leave the ticket on. In the early days especially, it was common practice to have the price tag dangling from your dark glasses, for example.

A second method is to announce proudly that you have made your purchases at home rather than abroad, meaning you have spent 15–20 percent more, as prices are higher in China by that margin.

A third fail-safe way is to choose brands that are very high priced – a bit like a novice selecting wine by pointing at the most expensive. Hermès has acquired the reputation of being the most pricey brand, prompting wealthy but relatively clueless shoppers to pick up its wares for precisely that reason. We heard an amusing tale of a customer from the Northern provinces who walked into the Hermès store at the Palace hotel in Beijing and purchased an amazing amount of china. Hermès is most sought after for its leather goods, notably the Kelly and Birkin bags, but that day just for a change the shop windows featured a display of cups, saucers, and other porcelain products. Our man from the North assumed Hermès is best known for porcelain, and promptly proceeded to buy US$75,000 worth of it. The shop was shuttered down; the sale girls emptied a shopping bag stuffed with RMB600,000 and spent the next two hours counting cash.

Even the relatively better informed big-city folk go by the popularity of a brand rather than its inherent brand image. Gu Ming, associate publisher of Hachette Filipacchi in China, best known for *Elle* magazine, comments:

Most people go with the trend rather than what suits them. It's not like "I am this sort of person so I use Prada or Vuitton." I don't think we have reached that point yet. It's more "Is this well-known?" or "Is this expensive?"[14]

With "wealth as fashion statement" the guiding force, each stratum of society from multimillionaires to middle-class salary earners is eyeing luxury goods. Even on very small salaries people make an effort to flash their status. Angelica Cheung, editor of *Vogue China*, says many young girls save up to two or three months' salary to spend on a Louis Vuitton handbag:

They may work as secretaries, but having the bag gives the impression that they come from a wealthy family or have a rich boyfriend.[15]

Hung Huang, publisher of lifestyle magazine *iLook*, claims her typical white-collar female reader, age 28, would have at least one Louis Vuitton bag, one pair of Gucci shoes, and seven lipsticks from brands like Lancôme and Estée Lauder.[16]

How do they do it on an annual salary equivalent to US$4,000? The answer lies in low living expenses and the high priority assigned to luxury goods. Young working people tend to live with parents, a bit like the Japanese parasite singles, but in China it's simply a case of staying on with mum and dad till marriage or work takes you away. As for giving a higher priority to looking good, as the saying goes: "The Shanghainese would rather spend on dressing up than filling up their stomach."

THE GREAT LEAP FORWARD

The rise of luxury brands in China is, not unexpectedly, inextricably linked to the rise of the country as an economic power. From the fateful 1978 start of Deng's "Open Policy" to becoming the world's fourth-largest economy, China's ascent has been like a rocket launched into outer space. The story of how that translated into a parallel take-off for designer brands contains some interesting twists and turns. We outline below six major drivers of luxury consumption here.

Chinese *Guanxi*, European Luxury

Half a century of purging has fortunately not dampened the spirit of private enterprise, which like a genie released from its bottle is working overtime creating magical amounts of wealth for entrepreneurs. This full-blooded capitalism is driving China's economic growth, but along with it comes a large gray zone of "gifting" necessary for building relationships, or what the Chinese call *guanxi*.[17] That's the way business works in China, all parties concerned know the rules of the game, and most talk about it as a matter of fact. It used to be hard cash in the early days, now it is increasingly being replaced by luxury brand gifts. *Guanxi*, which oils the wheels of government bureaucracy and business alike, is the single biggest factor that has spurred the growth of luxe in China.

Industry stalwarts estimate that in the early days as many as 80 percent of luxury sales were intended as "gifts" to government officials and business contacts. Since these were mostly men, China's branded market became highly male skewed – men's ready-to-wear, accessories, and watches dominate and brands like Zegna, Hugo Boss, and Dunhill are leaders. ("Own-use consumption" has risen in recent years, bringing that percentage down, but still 50 percent of luxe sales are gifted away. That doesn't mean that gifting has reduced, it just means that *other* segments of the market have grown considerably.) The result is a bureaucratic landscape peppered with luxe, or as China expert James McGregor puts it:

Everywhere one looks in China there are state-enterprise bosses and government officials sporting Armani suits, driving Mercedes or Audi luxury cars, and living in apartment buildings called Park Avenue, Palm Springs, or Beverly Hills. They golf at private clubs that charge $150 a round. Many of them earn little more than $1,000 a month, but nobody asks about their assets and nobody tells.[18]

The government's systematic crackdown on corruption is no doubt producing results – including some headline-making culprits – but there's a long way to go. (Transparency International gave China a score of 3.2 in its Corruption Perceptions Index 2005 out of a possible 10; as a reference point neighboring Hong Kong and Taiwan scored 8.3 and 5.9 respectively.[19]) The crackdown has, however, produced results on an unintended front: It has helped the case for luxury brands. People are more careful about cash gifts in the new vigilant climate, and expensive imported goods are seen as far safer.

Guanxi has always been a way of life in China – as indeed it is to varying extents the world over – but it has found new meaning thanks to the power government officials wield in allocating resources that business people need to run their enterprises, whether it's getting a loan sanctioned or obtaining land to build a factory on or having a license approved for running that factory. The law and its application in China are murky, and in this uncertain atmosphere entrepreneurs create their own certainty by establishing personal relationships with bureacrats. Gifts in cash or kind are traded for access to resources and keeping unnecessary harassment at bay.

Like plants need watering, all government departments your business deals with need regular gifting. For example, if you run a restaurant it's wise to take care of the officials who look after hygiene, fire safety, and so on, and in turn they'll look after your interests. If you need special approvals, say you are trying to get a big railroad project off the ground, the nature of gifts changes dramatically – one case we heard of involved several imported limousines. Another leading company in the technology sector chose to have its top 25 customers fitted out in made-to-measure suits, two per head. A leading European brand was commissioned, and it promptly flew down its top tailor to measure the clients in Beijing. Each suit cost between US$3,000 and US$6,000, depending on the fabric selected. The tailor came with faultless credentials, we were told, having stitched for European aristocrats and celebrities.

Imported limousines and made-to-measure suits are the exception rather than the rule, nevertheless. In most cases something small and expensive, like a diamond-studded Cartier watch, is considered ideal. For lower budgets, a wallet, a belt, a tie, a muffler, a pair of cufflinks, a briefcase, or a bag – any of these will do nicely as long as you make sure it comes from a well-known brand. Personal items like shoes and suits are gifted, but the trick here is to prearrange a process of exchange if the size isn't right. Even women's items like Chanel bags and suits are gifted, presumably to female officers or wives and daughters of government officers.

At the Palace hotel shopping arcade in Beijing, we watched with fascination as an ongoing circus of customers and purchases unfolded. Men shopping in pairs seemed to be the rule, presumably benefactor and beneficiary bonding through a bout of retail therapy. We saw one such pair, from all appearances not typical luxury goods customers, emerge from the Cartier store with four red shopping bags. They promptly dived into the Burberry outlet and had the sales girls in a tizzy pulling out several polo shirts and sweaters of the same pattern. The pair later walked out of the Chanel shop, also loaded with bags. They hailed a taxi and left – all done in less than an hour.

An interesting fallout of this kind of shopping is that most purchases are paid for in cash. It is true that China's credit card system is not well developed, but even if it were, cash payments would still prevail as nobody wants purchases traced back to them. There is plenty of unaccounted money in the system – the Political and Economic Risk Consultancy estimates that China's economy may be 15 percent larger than official figures due to the gray market[20] – and it's mostly this gray money making the rounds of luxe stores.

Every store has an amusing tale to tell of a large cash purchase, say RMB500,000 (US$60,000), where they had to close the store and count cash for several hours, and with the highest denomination of the Renminbi a mere 100, there is invariably a lot of counting to do. Even high-end cars are bought with cash payments. Customers carry their bulky wads of cash in used shopping bags, in pillowcases, or wrapped up in an old newspaper, the bundle firmly tucked under the armpit. We heard of one case where the money had an earthy smell and the sales girl suspected it had been stashed away in a hole in the ground. Sorting through a tangle of notes is time consuming, but cash is cash and a big purchase is always welcome. Cash-counting machines are becoming standard equipment at luxe stores.

Where there's a need there's a solution, and the cash-carrying need has found its solution in the Louis Vuitton "messenger" bag. This is very popular with Chinese men as its roomy interior can easily hold several thousand in currency notes. Other brands like Dior and Dunhill offer variations of this rectangular bag that sits snugly at the hip with a protective outer flap, and a wide strap securely crossing your heart.

Capitalism and Concubines

With the market opening up, foreign investment has flowed into China like a tap on full blast, and international companies from automobiles to condoms have rushed in to set up shop. Today China pulls in the largest amount of foreign investment in the world, 2002 being the landmark year when an inflow of US$52.7 billion put it ahead of the US.[21] Shanghai alone has 31,440 foreign-invested projects with a total value of US$73 billion.[22]

Along with foreign business came foreign bosses and managers, especially in the early days when China's own managerial talent was underdeveloped. A large percentage of the money as well as the manpower has come from neighboring Hong Kong (the biggest investor in China) and Taiwan, and somewhere along the line providing seed capital got mixed up with sowing wild oats. The result: a mass of mainland Chinese "second wives" (known locally as *er nais*, they are not legally married; it's an informal arrangement *à la* Hong Kong) and, more importantly, a sizeable segment of ardent female luxury purchasers. This has been the second major force responsible for the growth of luxury brands in China, providing a colorful counterweight to the male-skewed government segment.

Typically, these women are set up in a house by their Hong Kong/Taiwanese "husbands" – in cities like Shenzhen, complete "mistress villages" have sprung up – and provided with a handsome spending allowance, with the husband visiting them two or three times a month. Given the nature of their contract, these women have both the means to spend and a high need to dress beautifully, and in many cases they have a suitably besotted partner only too happy to come shopping with them. Dubbed the "morning-after syndrome," it's common to see older businessmen with sweet young things doing the rounds of expensive shopping malls, compensating for services provided the night before – typically Sunday mornings are popular for this activity, but we spotted a few on weekdays in Shanghai.

The phenomenon of the modern Chinese concubine has caught the attention of the popular press, resulting in a flurry of articles on her lifestyle, usually portrayed as lavish. Author Pamela Yatsko calls these women "the beautiful people" who "have nothing to do but go out, spend money and keep luxury stores in business."[23] In a bizarre twist, now these mistresses in turn are keeping their own men, known as "little wolf dogs,"[24] as entertainment while waiting for their partner's sporadic visits. The mistress phenomenon has also caught the eye of the Chinese government, which promptly passed a law making *er nais* illegal, but so far it seems to be legislation largely ignored in both spirit and deed.

In the meantime, the private investigator business is growing, hired by first wives wanting to get their own form of justice on their cheating husbands. Journalist Allen T Cheng recounts the case of an American wife who hired the services of a Chinese detective and used the video evidence to nail a divorce back home.[25] Appropriately enough, part of the incriminating evidence consisted of American husband and Chinese mistress walking hand in hand in a shopping mall, no doubt stocking up on some luxe essentials.

Western men used to be hot favorites – the women drawn to them by the lure of lucre, the men attracted by the mystique of Chinese beauty, and a Gucci or Chanel bag somehow finding its way into the compensation equation. In the early days Chinese women blindly equated white skin to loads of cash and perhaps a visa out of the country, but with the rapid growth of wealth in China these women have become wiser – they realize that successful Chinese businessmen are likely to be a bigger catch than most salaried Westerners, even if the latter are in senior managerial positions. "Western men are now sought not for money, but for their reputation of being sensitive lovers," one luxe store manager told us. Others think having a Western man on your arm is a status symbol, parallel to a Western luxury brand.

Wherever they come from, these men provided the necessary foreplay to jump-start the women's designer market, and, more importantly, develop the female taste buds for Western luxe.

Shop-o-tourism

Deng may not have had luxury brands on his mind when he announced his historical Open Policy in 1978, but that one act set China on a sure path to Western luxurydom. The Open Policy led to two things: It let the world into China, and it let the Chinese consumer out into the world. Both paths led the Chinese consumer to European luxury brands.

One of the results of opening the country up has been the wave of overseas returnees, Chinese men and women who have spent the better part of their lives abroad and are now coming home to take advantage of the amazing business opportunities in China. With a Western education, many are sought after by multinational companies, where their Chineseness combined with an understanding of Western corporate culture is valued. Others have set up businesses in China. Whatever they do on the professional front, these overseas returnees bring money, sophistication, and a lifestyle that rubs off on the people they interact with. Luxury brands have been a natural part of their lives, and they are now instrumental in spreading the gospel in China. Many of them still make frequent trips "back home" to the US or Europe and return with the latest editions of luxe products, which do not go unnoticed by their local colleagues and friends.

Another implication of opening up is the arrival of international companies and the resulting rise in salary levels. Initially, these companies paid mouthwatering amounts to expats – this was a hardship posting, after all – but soon the loot spread to local employees as well. The reason: China is extremely short on appropriate talent to manage its explosive growth, leading to relatively high salaries for the right local candidates. According to Jerry Chang, director of headhunting firm Barons & Company, managers in Shanghai in 1992 commanded a monthly salary of RMB$3,000–5,000 (US$375–625); a decade later it had risen to RMB$60,000 per month (US$7,500).[26] That's a lot of money anywhere in the world; in China it's a small fortune. This rapid rise in salaries has provided both the means and the desire to live the good life, and that invariably includes friends Louis Vuitton *et al*.

With easy access, the wealthy Chinese diaspora all over the world has started making more trips back home, reconnecting with family. In fact, there is a rising trend for "reunion parties" with 30–40 family members in attendance. And when they visit, they come loaded with gifts, as is the custom in much of Asia, giving face to both the giver and the receiver. You guessed it: Luxury brands make excellent gifts – conveying on the one hand the high esteem in which the receiver is held, and on the other the financial prowess of the giver in being able to afford these expensive items. Very often, relatives specify what they want, typically brands or items not available at home. Many luxury brands have started advertising in China well before their products are sold here, building awareness and desire that can only be fulfilled by buying the products abroad.

If inbound restrictions have eased so have outbound ones, allowing mainland Chinese to travel abroad, bringing them face to face with Western cultures and influences – so far they have proved to be keen learners. In the beginning, the government only allowed business travel, so it was mainly men who made the trips. They were the first to taste and try luxe products abroad, and when brands initially became available in China they were the first to buy them, contributing to a male-skewed market. During the early 1990s, it was common to see these "knowledgeable" men bringing their wives and girlfriends to designer stores and "training" them in how to wear Western products, a bizarre version of *My Fair Lady* meets *Pretty Woman* on a mass scale.

Now the government is allowing travel for tourism purposes, opening the doors for a wave of Chinese shop-o-tourism. We have already seen the vigorous impact that has had on luxury brand sales in Hong Kong – the same story is unfolding in Europe, where 27 EU countries were granted Approved Destination Status for group tours in 2004. It is their reputation as big spenders that makes Chinese tourists so attractive, and the fact that there is an endless supply of them only adds to the luster. For example, the typical Chinese tourist in Australia is said to spend an average of US$3,000 compared to the US$1,000 spent by an American or European visitor.[27] When it comes to luxury shopping, Goldman Sachs estimates that the Chinese spend twice as much when traveling abroad as they do locally,[28] tempted by the irrefutable logic of lower prices and better selection. Western countries that earlier feared Chinese as overstayers and potential illegal immigrants are taking a second look at their loaded wallets and granting visas.

While Europe gears up to meet the needs of Chinese shoppers – Mandarin language training for staff has started in earnest – Hong Kong is several steps ahead with specific marketing campaigns directed to woo them. Phone calls are routinely placed to top customers announcing new arrivals, and there's a willingness to reserve "hot items" till their next trip to Hong Kong. In the knowledge that these trips are typically short ones, often just a day, services like alterations have been speeded up – you can have trouser hems and jacket sleeves adjusted in an hour or two, and deliveries to hotels are readily arranged. Top dollar gets top service.

Mao may have said that "Power flows from the barrel of a gun," but one wishes he'd had the chance of testing the power that flows from a loaded wallet. History would have been so much sweeter for it.

The Rags to Riches Syndrome

Another factor responsible for the spread of the luxe cult in China is the "rags to riches syndrome," typified on the one hand by unbridled ambition and a great sense of possibility, and on the other by unbridled spending with no sense of proportion. This has created a "new rich" consumer society that buys luxe like chewing gum or popcorn. Admittedly their numbers are small compared to the population of China, but their financial prowess is enough to keep the luxe industry surging ahead.

To understand the mentality of these new rich, you have to understand their life experience. All of them started with next to nothing, but in their own lifetime, in fact within the space of 10–20 years, they have achieved remarkable wealth. This has taught them that a lot can happen in a decade – you can build a successful business, move into a comfortable if not palatial home, wear beautiful clothes, travel abroad on holidays, and earn the respect of family and peers. They used to ride cycles; now they have a variety of imported cars to choose from. They didn't have a fixed-line telephone in their younger days; now they change their mobile phone every three to six months just to keep up with the times. Then they look around China and see the same thing happening to the nation. The cityscapes have changed dramatically, with soaring skyscrapers and a network of state-of-the-art highways.

The natural corollary to this life experience is that a lot more can happen in the next 10 years. There is an amazing sense of possibility that drives these people's own ambitions and the goals they set for themselves. An extensive study of the new rich class done by advertising agency M&C Saatchi explored, among other aspects, their definition of personal success. The findings speak not only of glowing optimism, but also of sky-is-the-limit ambition. Maggie Sun, director of strategic planning who led the study, quotes the example of a businessman running a large construction company, whose wife shops for houses as a hobby – she has bought four so far – but who does not consider himself successful yet.[29] Hold your breath here: This Chinese businessman is benchmarking himself against Bill Gates, and only when he has a company the size of Microsoft and billions in personal wealth will he regard himself as a success. People who are older compare themselves to Li Ka Shing, the Hong Kong magnate who ranks 22nd on the Forbes Global Billionaire list.

If you think these people are nuts, think again. Hundreds of thousands of them have gone from surviving in one Mao suit, often without the means to wash it clean, to wearing only the finest Italian suits with a thread count of 120+. They are convinced that another decade or two should give them ample time and opportunity to achieve levels of success comparable to the Bill Gateses of this world. This is China's secret – a large enough class of people who are fired with intense ambition and a great belief in their ability to succeed. May the force be with them.

Another confirmation of their faith in China is this: A mere five years ago, they wanted their children to settle abroad in what they clearly imagined was a better life. Now they might send them abroad to study – "my son will go to Harvard" is the standard dream – but they are clear they want them to come back to the unbeatable land of opportunity. The vision of China as the center of the universe again is finally taking shape, affirmed by events like entry to WTO, the country's first manned space flight, and the 2008 Olympics being entrusted to Beijing. Let's face it, they're right – the Middle Kingdom is hot.

When you hold such an optimistic world view, it's hardly surprising that you're free and easy with your spending. The retail manager of a prominent luxury brand store in Shanghai, who has seen Chinese spending power in action, says:

Only 2–3 percent of the population has money, but they can really spend. Rich women will come in at the beginning of the season and spend RMB200,000 (US$25,000) in one trip.

What about the men? She gives us a knowing smile. "Chinese men can *really* spend money."

There are regional differences in spending habits. Beijing people have a reputation for spending more than the fashionable Shanghainese. One Shanghainese explained to us that Beijing being the seat of government meant that people there had greater opportunity to make bigger money by "leveraging their relationship with powerful government officials," and so could afford to spend freely. Beijing shoppers are said to be quick decision makers who spend substantial amounts in the blink of an eye. The Shanghainese, on the other hand, have a reputation for being pragmatic about money; they are likely to compare prices and eventually spend a smaller amount. Many people in the luxe industry see setting up a store in Shanghai as "more for image," whereas a store in Beijing is for "image plus business."

Capsule Cribsheets

The recent gaggle of glossies flooding the Chinese market are playing a significant role in shedding conservative attitudes and building a fashion-conscious, liberal-minded consumer. The first issues of *Elle*, which arrived in China a decade ago, ran features like "how to make a dress," complete with patterns and stitching instructions, whereas today's bunch of fashion and lifestyle magazines are more likely to run features on "how to make out with your boyfriend."

Like every other industry, China's magazine industry is booming. A veteran luxe manager says that a decade ago she looked for magazines to invite to fashion shows, but there were barely one or two. Today she can't accommodate all the magazine reporters and photographers who clamor to attend the shows – there are at least 200 women's titles, the top international titles, plus a mixed bag of domestic ones, and she can at best invite around 40 magazines.

Fashion and beauty are now simply center stage for the entire magazine industry thanks to substantial advertising support. According to media agency Zenith Optimedia, the top four product categories advertised in all magazines in China, including those for women, were skincare, boutiques and fashion, watches, and cosmetics.[30] Given that China's market is still in the early stages of development, many brands are advertising heavily to establish their image. Gu Ming of *Elle* explains:

A lot of luxury brands are investing in our magazines. They are hoping this generation will grow and when they can afford it, they will buy it.[31]

Magazines in turn run educational features like "brand stories," cribsheets that capsule the history and distinguishing features of a given brand.

Besides helping consumers change their attitude toward luxury brands, these magazines with their "demonstration effect" are changing attitudes toward life. The lifestyle advice they offer might be considered standard fare in most other countries – the usual cheeky, pushing-the-edge take on managing relationships, hooking guys, and looking sexy – but in China's highly media-controlled atmosphere it comes as a surprise. Until 2005, the country's vigilant censors seemed to be more concerned about keeping a lid on political issues and obviously didn't see a threat to the moral fabric of Chinese womanhood in consuming such flippantly forward mush packed with Western cultural propaganda. They have since woken up, and have issued a warning that that they will "safeguard state security in the cultural field" by keeping a closer eye on foreign media[32] – a case of locking the barn door after the horse has bolted. Mindsets have been changed irrevocably – for example, a survey by *Madame Figaro* magazine found that between 46 and 52 percent of university graduates in Shanghai and Beijing condoned premarital sex.[33]

The Rise of Swinging Metropolises

China is a vast country with 1.3 billion people, but the real action is in the "chosen few" cities – mostly along the eastern coastline – that have rapidly transformed into modern metropolises boasting some of the best infrastructure in the world, and rapid wealth accumulation. China's worst may well be pretty bad, but its best is truly world class. The country thinks like its Bill Gates wannabes: It doesn't bother with small steps ahead, it hurls itself headlong into cutting-edge stuff, and it benchmarks its landmarks against the best in the world, with the clear intention of outdoing them. Shanghai has the world's first maglev, a superfast train that magnetically levitates, connecting the city's airport to the new commercial development of Pudong. Or take shopping malls: China isn't just building lots of them, 600 at last count, it is emphatically after the "world's largest" titles. Beijing's Golden Resources Mall, dubbed the Great Mall of China with a 600,000 square meter floor area, is a case in point, and by 2010 the country is gunning to have seven of the world's ten largest malls.[34]

These cities' coming of age affects luxury brands in two ways: It opens up exciting retail formats of world-class standard and an atmosphere and setting conducive to the display and sale of high-end fashion labels; and it also opens up cultural hotspots – trendy restaurants, bars, nightclubs, hotels, and hangouts – where luxe consumers can display their fine acquisitions. We discuss luxury retail in greater detail in the next section.

As for the cultural scene, take Shanghai again. M on the Bund, named one of the best restaurants in the world by *Condé Nast Traveler* magazine, is a hotspot frequented by celebrities – we ran into American musician Kenny G there, his two shows in jazz-loving Shanghai sold out days in advance. Xintiandi, packed with trendy locals and tourists, is a sprawling complex of street-level restaurants, cafés, and bars. Nightclubs like Guandi and Park 97 are packed with beautiful people, the crowds throbbing to pulsating music, the bars spilling over with fashionable drinkers, everyone dressed to kill. Mao would have had a fit.

Shanghai is quite literally a nonstop party, whether it's a big bash like the MTV Awards, or the St. Regis hotel opening party that featured a Chinese water ballet as poolside entertainment, or the Chanel fashion show held at an abandoned airport. Yu Lei of *Shanghai Tatler* says he hasn't had time to make it to the dentist as there are so many events to attend. One of the most talked-about parties was the Hermès store opening, a spectacular with high-tech trapeze "elastonauts" flown in from Paris and hooked to the roof of Plaza 66's cavernous atrium – people gasped in disbelief as they "flew" through the air. Equally spectacular was the sit-down dinner for 800 guests that followed, hosted by the French consulate in the grounds of an old French colonial house. As

for the store, queues formed from 4 am the next morning and everything was sold out on opening day. Reportedly, Japanese Hermès-loving
girls flew in from Tokyo for the day.

All these parties need clothes, not to mention jewelry and accessories. Eva Yu, social editor of *Shanghai Tatler*, is of the opinion that
Chinese high society is still learning how to dress for really formal
occasions.[35] For example, men show up in a suit when a tux would be
more appropriate, and women come in short dresses instead of evening
gowns. Furthermore, she informed us, women have been spotted
repeating the same jewelry with different outfits. This is a clear indication of the immense potential for luxury brands: What's a girl to do
when there simply aren't many long dresses and cool jewels available in
the shops?

Beijing doesn't quite have the same buzz as Shanghai, but then that
would be hard with the Communist government sitting there – consumption exists in spades, but its display is not overt. There's no lack of
places and events to keep you going, though – try the trendy San Li Tun
area, home to many bars. We attended the Max Mara fashion show at
the exquisite China Club. The president of the Max Mara Group, Luigi
Maramotti, flew in from Italy, and there were a clump of VVIPs, people
from the diplomatic community, and an extensive press posse in attendance. 23 statuesque Chinese women, average height 5 feet 11 inches,
sashayed down the catwalk displaying the autumn/winter collection –
furs, long coats, suits, dresses, pants, shirts, casuals, and yes, evening
gowns. The China Club setting, reminiscent of a bygone era of high living, brought home eloquently that European fashion has entered the
very heart of the country.

Shanghai and Beijing are the top two cities, but there is enough action
in the next rung. Guangzhou and Shenzhen in the south boast very high
per capita incomes; these are boomtowns close to Hong Kong. In fact,
Shenzhen has become a party spot for Hong Kongers, who see it as great
fun at great prices. The three cities to the northeast of Beijing – Dalian,
Shenyang, and Harbin – you'd think they are remote industrial towns, but
they harbor serious wealth and prestigious retailers like Louis Vuitton and
Lane Crawford are moving in.

Other up-and-coming cities are Chengdu, which the government is
trying to transform into the Chicago of China with a heavy injection of

investment; Qingdao, a large port city with a great entrepreneurial spirit; and Tianjin, which like Beijing and Shanghai is a special municipality and has been the focus of major industrialization. It's a twenty-first-century version of the great leap forward, this time for real. Even smaller towns in the provinces are yielding good results for luxury brand retailers, who are finding that these small-town folk with few sources of entertainment are happy to come out and play at designer-label stores.

Dunhill: How it Became One of the Biggest Men's Brands in China

One of the first brands to enter China, Dunhill has had such a successful run that it now gets over a third of its global sales from Chinese consumers.[36] We spoke with Tim King, managing director, Richemont Luxury Asia-Pacific, Alfred Dunhill division, to understand how this pioneering brand became a hot favorite.[37]

It seems greatness was being thrust upon Dunhill well before it entered China. In the early 1990s, the company noticed an increasing number of mainlanders coming to its Hong Kong stores and buying several blazers and trousers in one go. One such customer even ran a parallel import shop in Beijing. The turning point came at a 10-day trade show in Guangzhou, where Dunhill products literally flew off the shelves, resulting in a stock-out on the second day. "Eyes were opened," says King, and the company started looking at China in all seriousness.

A colorful trio of entrepreneurs, including a businessman with People's Liberation Army connections, formed a company that became Dunhill's first franchisee in Beijing. Dunhill next opened in Shanghai at two department stores, Wings and Printemps. Business grew from there. In fact, it seems the Chinese couldn't get enough of Dunhill. "We were actually selling out once we had the shops established," says King.

Then came an offer to open a store in the back-of-beyond city of Harbin in China's northeast. "People said 'Why Harbin?'" recalls King. "It's cold and you need a lot of clothes, but is there any money out there?" Plenty, as Dunhill soon found out.

Dunhill's distribution strategy could well be a roadmap for other brands looking to enter China. "We began with the major cities of Beijing, Shanghai, and Guangzhou," explains King. "Then the coastal cities, then the northeast, and then we started identifying provincial cities as well." The company has built up an expansive network of over 50 points of sales in 30 cities (Figure 5.1).

Figure 5.1 Dunhill's inroads into China, number of stores by location

What was the key to Dunhill's success in China? From being an early bird, to spreading its wings far and wide, to being lucky in having a well-recognized brand name thanks to its tobacco heritage – the reasons are many, but it finally boils down to one: being the ideal men's gift in what is largely a men's gift market.

"China [its luxury market] is dominated by men who are rewarding themselves and rewarding their business contacts and friends," says King. "In our shops you will often see two guys shopping – one guy choosing products, the other will just sit and read, and then when the things are being wrapped up, he will come and pay. You bring your business contact to the shop, it's not as blatant as a red envelope with cash, but you basically say, let me buy you a jacket."

Dunhill's success lies in understanding that it is ultimately operating in the gift industry, where the value of the present should be clearly understood by the person receiving it. "It's a safe gift," says King. "It's a known brand which is worth something in terms of prestige and value. We are certainly marketing to that, to make sure people are aware of what the brand is."

THE RETAIL REVOLUTION

With Chinese cities booming, the retail scene is also growing by leaps and bounds. Most major brands already have a presence in the country, at least in the key cities. Now they are in expansion mode. They are spreading out geographically into second- and third-tier cities – for example, Louis Vuitton has extended to a dozen cities and plans to keep adding two or three stores every year. They are building bigger and fancier stores – Giorgio Armani's lovely flagship store at the historic Three on the Bund building is a case in point. They are upping the quality of their operations by closing down underperforming stores and moving to better locations that have since become available. They are increasing control over their operations by reducing the role of agents – Lanvin, for instance, parted ways with China Resources, its agent of 10 years. However, doing business in a geographic area as vast as China increases the cost and complexity of covering it effectively. This has led to a hybrid model: self-managing in key markets *and* using agents to augment distribution in other cities.

While Japan has predominantly department stores and Hong Kong has a shopping mall culture, China's retail scene is still fluid, with both department stores and shopping malls being developed. And there's a strong third category – five-star hotel shopping arcades.

The reason behind the popularity of these arcades is unique to China. Getting a retail license was difficult in the early days – you needed to tie up with a local partner, among other things – so luxury brands found it easier to use a hotel's retail license. In effect, the hotels functioned as "department stores," buying all the products and selling them on their premises.

Invariably, all Chinese cities have seen the start of luxury retail in the most prestigious hotel, whether it's the Marriott in Guangzhou, the Ritz Carlton in Shanghai, or that mother of all hotel arcades, the Palace hotel in Beijing, now rechristened the Peninsula Beijing.

When brands first entered China, the first port of call was the Palace hotel as there were few classy retail locations available. Today, the Palace has become synonymous with high-end brands. The relative ignorance of many luxury consumers has put the hotel in an enviable position. One store manager explained that even if she wanted to move to

THE CULT OF THE LUXURY BRAND

another location, the risk was just too high of losing prospective consumers, as some were barely aware of individual brand names and were relying blindly on the Palace hotel name to deliver the goods.

Realizing the goldmine it was sitting on, the Palace went about expanding its commercial space in the early 2000s. It took the unprecedented step of shifting its lobby-level restaurant to Basement 1, thus creating prime retail space in the reception area itself. This was rapidly snapped up by the likes of Piaget, Tiffany, and Cartier, which promptly expanded its existing store. Dior moved up from Basement 1 to the lobby level and sales moved up too. Prada left for a while, but was soon back. Louis Vuitton, Armani, Chanel, and Zegna stayed put at the lobby level.

The Palace hotel retail portfolio was soon shuffled like a pack of cards. The space vacated in Basement 1 was taken up by Lanvin, Dolce & Gabbana, and Ungaro, and others like Gucci, Versace, and Ferragamo expanded their operations. Burberry, Bally, Hugo Boss, and Givenchy are other notable brands at this level. Basement 2 in the meantime added Missoni and St. John stores to its already long list of existing outlets, Cerruti, Gianfranco Ferre, Gieves & Hawkes, Lagerfeld, and Longchamp among them. What started as a few stores in the early 1990s has grown into a 50-strong who's who of brands, thereby further cementing the hotel's reputation as the premier luxury destination.

If the Palace hotel is Beijing's foremost luxe location, Plaza 66 is Shanghai's answer. An ultramodern, glass-and-chrome, 50,000 square meter shopping mall on Nanjing Road, it has been purpose built for luxury retailing, and is home to the most prestigious portfolio of brands. You won't find crowds of customers here, but clearly the companies are finding business rewarding – for example, Louis Vuitton expanded its store by adding another floor. Interestingly, Hong Kong developers have spearheaded the development of China's high-end malls, giving them the same ritzy feel and world-class quality that Hong Kong's malls are known for – Plaza 66 was built by Hong Kong-based Hang Lung Group with an investment of US$500 million.

As for department stores, China has plenty of them, including the trusty old Friendship Stores that have been selling imported goods for a long time. Former President Jiang in search of the Burberry muffler went to Beijing's Scitech department store. These stores meet the needs of wealthier shoppers who don't want to be spotted, preferring to park in the basement and quietly ride the elevators up to the desired floor and then leave discreetly, often having their bags picked up separately. Department stores also play a critical role in helping luxury brands expand their distribution in the numerous smaller cities spread all over China.

ONE COUNTRY, MANY SEGMENTS

As is to be expected in a populous and self-willed country, there is a colorful cast of consumer segments, all marching to the tune of Vuitton, Cartier, Dior, and Zegna. Since it is a male-skewed market – the only country we know to be such – we look at men first and then women.

Men: The Government Leads the Way

Unlikely as it seems, leading the fashion stakes are high-ranking *government officials*, as well as those at senior positions in state-owned enterprises. Men from the ministry of foreign affairs have the reputation of being the most fashion savvy. Even the top brass of the People's Liberation Army stock up on their luxury goods rations discreetly in the private VIP rooms of luxury stores. People in this segment tread a fine line: On the one hand they willingly accept these gifts, on the other hand being seen using them has the potential to land them in trouble. The trick here is to tone down the obviousness of the brand as much as possible. As a result, French and Italian suits have become de rigueur – they have the advantage of you not being "found out" – set off with expensive watches and other accessories.

China's *business élite* comes next – entrepreneurs and businessmen, including "JV man," who until recently was that all-essential partner for foreign ventures. These are the biggest spenders, shelling out on themselves plus financing much of what is consumed by government officials. While they may aspire to be Bill Gates, they certainly don't subscribe to his laid-back dress sense. They clothe themselves in a manner worthy of their newly acquired high social status. A survey of the brands favored by China's richest men – conducted by Rupert Hoogewerf and summarized in Table 5.1 – gives a rare insight into their

Table 5.1 Preferred brands of China's richest

FASHION BRAND	JEWELRY	WATCHES
Giorgio Armani	Cartier	*Sports*
Louis Vuitton	Chanel	Rolex
Boss	Piaget	Omega
Dunhill	Tiffany	TAG Heuer
Hermès	Bulgari	Rado
Prada	Dior	
Zegna	Van Cleef & Arpels	*High Complications*
Chanel		Vacheron Constantin
	High Jewelry Watches	Patek Philippe
	Cartier	Breguet
	Piaget	IWC
	Chopard	Audemars Piguet

Source: 2006 *Best of the Best*, Hurun Report.

accepted dress code. Best fashion brands: Giorgio Armani, followed by Louis Vuitton. Best jewelry watch brand: Cartier. Best Sports Watch: Rolex. Needless to say, they set the tone for others to follow.

Most of these businessmen are nouveau riche, but there is another distinct subclass: *descendants of the erstwhile élite* who now run their own businesses. Our understanding of revolutionary history was that all the rich people either ran away from China, or if they stayed they had their wealth taken away by the Red Guards, and in fact coming from an élite background meant worse treatment and that much more re-education. However, in our recent research interviews, we were told time and again that descendants of the élite class are an important segment for luxury goods and they display confidence and good taste – that in itself sets them apart. We were told about one such customer who wore Baby Dior when she was little – presumably while the Red Guards looked the other way – and continues to be a Dior loyalist to this day. They are not in the show-off game – they are like rich people anywhere in the world, who in the natural order of things enjoy what they can afford.

Princelings, progeny of government hotshots, are in business entirely due to their ability to peddle influence and wield power. An independent analyst once recommended buying Chinese stocks with strong princeling connections, as business in the country is largely about connections.[38] While it is not known how sound this investment strategy proved, what is common knowledge is that princelings have steadily acquired a lot of wealth, and head important companies. Others are being groomed for political roles – at one Chinese People's Political Consultative Conference more than 50 deputies were from "notable families," including two children of Deng Xiaoping and four related to chairman Mao Zedong.[39]

Also known as the red aristocracy, the princelings favor the same fine suits and accessories as other Chinese businessmen, but they tend to keep a lower profile as there is considerable anger in some quarters about their blatant use of family connections.

Women: Just the Beginning

The women's market for luxury brands is finally taking off and we expect it to grow rapidly. Aside from the most developed *concubine* segment, encountered earlier in this chapter, the up-and-coming segment is *female entrepreneurs*, and China boasts a growing number of spunky women doing their bit to hold up half the business sky. Their motive for buying luxury brands is as much to gain social recognition for their financial success as to reward themselves. "I have worked so hard, I deserve the best, and the best is the most expensive" is the logic here.

We heard about one such woman – she is one of the top ten customers at a leading brand store in Beijing – who worked her way up from being a teacher earning next to nothing to making US$1.5 million a year in business. By her own admission, she spends US$250,000 on her wardrobe every year, all at the Palace hotel shopping arcade. She does have a less-than-endearing quirk, though – she loves to scream at the shop assistants. New money, at least in this case, is quite literally loud.

As elsewhere in the region, rich tai-tais – *er nais* in China – indulge in the same delightful existence of shopping and lunch. The twist in China is that they can often be wives of senior government officials, and many of them fly down to Hong Kong for their shopping sprees.

Mainland tai-tais are known to be even more extravagant than their Hong Kong counterparts. Their hobbies include shopping for houses and redecorating with a vengeance – apparently they are looking for greater meaning in their lives than the pleasurable routine of massages, beauty treatments, and socializing with the girls.

NOUVEAU RICHE TO NOUVEAU CHIC TO NOUVEAU COOL

The consumer segments we have met so far are the luxury heavy hitters, men and women who have made it rich through their entrepreneurial zeal and business acumen; along the way, the men have helped dress up government officials in luxury brands, as well as their own wives and mistresses. The common thread that runs through most of these segments is new money (barring of course the descendants of the erstwhile élite and the princelings). This *nouveau riche* class has behaved according to script: focusing on status display as much as possible, not stopping to think about style or aesthetics.

Nouveau Chic

In recent years an interesting new segment has emerged that defines itself by style – that's right, style. It's in small pockets now, but it's gathering momentum. Call it *nouveau chic*. Typically well-educated professionals or managers in senior or middle-level positions at multinational corporations who earn substantial salaries – known as "gold-collar" workers – its members hold an international mind-set thanks to workplace interactions and business trips abroad. Or they could be entrepreneurs in the more creative professions like the media, arts, music, public relations, fashion retail, and trendy restaurants and bars – services experiencing a growing demand as Chinese society evolves. More refined, more confident, more knowledgeable, members of this nouveau chic set use luxury brands to express their personal taste. One of their number is Henry Li (see sidebar overleaf).

So does status go out the window? No, this is China and overt status marking will always remain a pillar of this Confucian society. For the nouveaux chic, luxury brands are about status *and* style. As against the

Consumer Profile
Henry Li: On a One-Man Mission to Change the Way the Chinese Party

Dressed in a black leather jacket (Dolce & Gabbana) and expensive jeans (Evisu, a Japanese brand "popular even in Milan," he tells us), hair fashionably styled with blond streaks, Henry is a tall, handsome fortysomething, originally from Shanghai but now bar owner and party organizer par excellence in Beijing. His style is totally laid back, possibly a result of spending several years in Australia. He found time to talk to us before heading off for an appointment with his French hair stylist.[40]

Confident and provocative, Li clearly commands a big following – during the hour we spent at Beijing's Kerry Center coffee shop, no fewer than seven people stopped by to say hello. You instantly warm to his air of boyishness and vulnerability.

He is intent on introducing the Chinese to the "unnecessary pleasures" of life – fine wine, fine food, fine cigars, even fine conversation. To that end he has opened Club Vogue, the Public Space bar, and the Neo Lounge ("a bar is like a t-shirt, a club is like a formal full-sleeved shirt") in Beijing's San Li Tun area, popularly known as "bar street." He also runs a professional party-organizing outfit, Vogue.

On his favorite brands
"Dolce & Gabbana and Issey Miyake. I like John Galliano from Dior. I used to shop Prada and Gucci every season, but not so much now – they have stayed the same, while other brands have innovated and moved ahead. In Hong Kong, I like shopping at Joyce, they have strange things with unique taste. Roberto Cavalli is getting popular."

On his favorite shopping spots
"Milan, Paris, and Palace hotel Beijing."

On what he'd wear to a party
"Something simple but makes a statement. Say, all black outfit with a touch of red shoes."

On the Chinese sense of style
"Still not there, but getting there. They spend a lot of money, they show off, so you know this guy is rich even though the results look a bit funny. For example, a guest at last night's party wore a RMB50,000 [US$6,000] gown, kind of fifteenth-century European costume look, with a jacket on it, but she looked ridiculous."

On China's partying habits

"They throw a lot of money but they have no style. It's still old-style karaoke, very expensive whisky, hostesses, hire a room for four or five people, which costs RMB10,000 for the night. A bunch of girls sit on your lap and tell you stupid stories. What are you getting for your money? People still call you stupid.

"I want to introduce the clubbing culture in Beijing, where people can do their own thing. Look at London, New York, Tokyo, a city has to have good clubs to be a great city."

On his most memorable party

"The Lycra Fashion Awards was huge, everyone from Asia was there, 30–40 stars, Gong Li, Karen Mok. I hosted the after-hours party – I didn't let the press come in – I'm good at 'underground' parties.

"At my parties, I discourage people from talking business or exchanging business cards – if I see people doing that, I break it up with a laugh. I want people to talk about their dreams, talk about themselves. I think that's what makes my parties successful."

---

well-defined set of *ming pai* or famous brands that the nouveaux riches gravitate to, the nouveaux chic use a wider gamut of brands. They may wear a dress by a niche brand, say Marc Jacobs, and carry a distinctive Chanel bag for status-marking purposes. They give relatively subtle brands a shot – for example a Tod's leather bag, which is obvious enough but not as in your face as a Gucci logo bag. But ultimately, it's the stylish way they present themselves that sets them apart.

The nouveaux chic have effectively put Bourdieu on overdrive, soaking up a century's worth of learning in one snappy decade. It's the immersion effect, where learning is speeded up thanks to being bombarded by fashion knowledge from all sides. They read the glossies, they notice what people are wearing on the streets, they check out the local malls, they see fashion on television, they discuss it with friends and colleagues, they breathe in international styles on their travels abroad, they prowl the stores in Hong Kong and Paris absorbing the looks, and pretty soon these become their personal benchmarks.

As the ranks of the nouveaux chic grow in the coming years, it will open up exciting new opportunities for brands and shopping centers. As we saw in the case of Hong Kong, raising the style quotient further drives consumption, creating a platform for greater variety and broader use. In China's case too, the game will move from a singular focus on mainstream brands to offering a wider selection of brands. From catering to a homogeneous need for status to meeting a growing variety of tastes. From a broad retail approach to segmenting and targeting. More fun all round for consumers, shopping malls, and brands.

Nouveau Cool

While the nouveaux chic are out there in the workplace, there's another segment of luxury consumers in the making. We call this segment *nouveau cool*. Its members are China's youngsters, teens and early twenties, a generation of only children coming of age. Some are already beginning to dabble in luxury brands, but we will feel their full impact from 2010 onwards, when a sizable number have entered the workforce and acquired the means to buy luxe.

Two things define them. They are decidedly cool – they have been experimenting with teen fashion, practicing trendy looks, building up a storehouse of experience in the style department. They are also more individualistic, a "me generation" like never before – these are China's little emperors, pampered not just by their parents but by two sets of adoring grandparents.

Spoilt they might be, but make no mistake, they are extremely driven to succeed. Richard Lee, marketing head of PepsiCo China, calls them "hybrid" in that their dress sense is totally "out there" – whacky hairdos, tattoos, and multiple ear piercings, for example – but they are achievers to the core. He describes a focus group he conducted with seven teenagers – six of them planned to study abroad, thereby giving them a competitive edge over the locally educated. He says:

Two things shocked me about these teenagers. One, they had thought about it and knew what they wanted to do. Two, they were not nerds – even though they were in tattoos and earrings, they were not school dropouts, they were strivers.[41]

This is the first generation raised in a branded world, and they intrinsically understand what it's all about. The China Cool Hunt Survey conducted among Beijing and Shanghai university students found that they identify particularly well with sports and technology brands – Nike was the coolest brand, followed by Sony and Adidas – but what was surprising was the fact that BMW and Ferrari made it into the top 10, and Christian Dior almost sneaked in at No. 11.[42] Luxury is already on these young minds.

What is the implication for luxury brands? The nouveaux cool will demand an even greater variety of brands and products to help them express and differentiate themselves. They will come armed with even broader fashion knowledge and a more developed sense of style. Most significantly, luxury brands will have to learn to chime with their younger, individualistic mind-sets.

All three segments – the nouveau riche, the nouveau chic, and the nouveau cool – will coexist and grow in the future. Perhaps the greatest challenge for luxury brands will be to address their widely differing needs simultaneously.

Why Do the Chinese Love *Western* Brands?

As with most other things in China, there's a paradox to unscramble. On the one hand there's immense pride in being Chinese and jubilation that China is finally taking its rightful place at the center of the universe; on the other, there's an obvious admiration of Western objects. The market for imported luxe wouldn't be growing at this dramatic pace but for an immense hankering for Western brands. As we saw, ask the nation's richest men to name their favorite brands and you get a list of *Western* makes. Ask teenagers to name their coolest brands, and there's not a single mention of a Chinese company in the top 10. The reason? In a country where projecting status is a central theme, Western luxury brands do it best.

To an extent this is a theoretical discussion as there are hardly any local luxury brands, but even if there were, it's unlikely the Chinese consumer would go for them with the same gusto. It's the Westernness of luxury brands – and the ideals of "prestige" and "world's best" they represent – that is central to their appeal.

Perhaps the most extreme example of the lure of Westernness comes from the growing popularity of Western wedding gowns all over China.

In a delightful study of Chinese Muslim brides in Xi'an, anthropologist Maris Gillette found that these young women abandon traditional conservative rules of propriety in dress and risk angering their elders, but still they go ahead and don body-hugging, low-cut Western wedding gowns.[43] These gowns stand for "modernity, sophistication, and affluence" and allow these brides to announce to the world that's what they represent themselves. For that day at least, they're "participating in the international fashion world."

We asked Gu Ming why the Chinese edition of *Elle* consistently chooses to use Western models on its cover rather than local ones. Her view confirms what the Xi'an brides so graphically demonstrate: Western brands say "I am up to date, young, and cool" and that's what counts.

With China becoming the manufacturing base for just about everything in the world, including some Western luxury brands, pointed situations arise. Will the Chinese consumer buy Western luxe that is made in China? The answer is no, at least for now. Pierre Cardin, the master licenser and pioneer in China, made waves in the early 1980s as a luxury brand, but when people discovered he had a factory in China they said no thank you, this is for "countryside people." One brand manager explained:

The perception is how can a Chinese worker, who was a peasant yesterday, make a fine luxury product? It is not even conceivable. The French worker is better than the Chinese one in the mind of the Chinese consumer.

The classic country-of-origin effect at work. In one of the sweet ironies of life, managers of European brands in China are specifying that only product made in Italy or France be shipped to them, even if the brand also has a production facility in the Middle Kingdom.

A strange tug of war takes place in the mind of Chinese consumers. At one level there's an acknowledgment that Western is more desirable and there's a rush to adopt its culture – whether it's nightclubs blaring Western pop, or the Western styles of clothing, or the trendy cafés, bars, and restaurants that the cool crowd collects at – and it certainly helps your image to have a Caucasian boyfriend dangling on your arm while you clutch your Chanel purse. At another level, the thinking goes, "If I buy you, then I am superior." If a lovely French saleswoman plying a

French brand is showering you with sweet attention, then who's boss? In fact, one store manager we talked to brings out her beautiful female European assistant every time a male Chinese customer walks in, and apparently the ploy is extremely effective. Chinese men, it seems, are fond of more than Western brands.

WHAT IT TAKES TO WIN IN CHINA

It's easy to fall into a gold-rush mentality – but hard work, significant expenditure, and a great deal of perseverance are involved in setting up goldmines, and the question always hangs in the air as to how much gold *your* brand can mine. So what should a luxury brand do to succeed in China?

Play to the Show Off Stage

Remember China is in Stage 3, *show off*, of the Spread of Luxury model – new money looking for status markers.

So give them products and brands that raise the prestige of Chinese consumers in a *visible* way. Logo-fication is good. The Chinese have a highly developed symbol memory – thanks to a lifetime of practicing the Chinese script, which is a basically a set of symbols – so you have the opportunity to create and link other symbolic elements with your brand. That might come in handy if fatigue sets in with the primary logo.

At the top end, given their heady sense of grandeur, we believe there's a place for haute couture. China may well help revive Europe's dying haute couture industry.

Never Dilute Your International Credentials

The Chinese are after *ming pai* or famous brands – by which they mean brands that are successful on the *world* stage. International companies often make the mistake of going "local" in an attempt to meet consumer needs more closely. Be careful: The Chinese consumer is buying global success, so never reduce your international aura.

Target a Younger Consumer Profile

Wealth is in much younger hands in China than elsewhere. Take a look at the five richest men in China, three still in their 30s (Table 5.2).

Table 5.2 The richest men in China

RANK	NAME	WEALTH (US$)	AGE
1	Huang Guangyu	1.7 billion	36
2	Yan Jiehe	1.5 billion	45
3	Timothy Chen Tianqiao	1.45 billion	32
4	William Ding Lei	1.25 billion	34
5	Xu Rongmao	1.2 billion	55

Source: Hurun Report, 2005

People born before 1960 bore the brunt of the Cultural Revolution – many missed out on a decent education and are now unable to participate meaningfully in the economic boom around them. Shaped by their harsh experiences, they hang on to a conservative view of life. While there are exceptions, generally speaking these relatively older people have neither the means nor the mind-set to indulge in luxury goods.

Exactly the reverse holds true for the younger generation, for whom recent years have been a time of untold opportunity. They have money in their pockets and are extremely optimistic about the future.

So target your luxury brands at this relatively younger age group: 25–35 would be the core segment. The fact that more than half of China's population is under 35 only helps.

Go to Where the Money Is, Never Mind the Sophistication Level

The use of luxury brands is *not* linked to the sophistication level of the consumer – it answers only to the need to show wealth. Consider spreading your footprint wider than the metropolises of Shanghai, Beijing, and Guangzhou. Louis Vuitton is in more than a dozen cities and doing roaring business; Dunhill is in 30. And as China's economy grows, the money will spread to third- and fourth-tier cities, presenting further opportunities for luxury brands.

Foster the Development of Style

While the overall sophistication level is low today, it is entirely in the interest of the luxury industry to foster its development – a stylish market is in the long run a more profitable and sustainable one. Many of the lessons from Hong Kong and Taiwan apply here. Defining *what* is chic and then showing *how* to put it together, style schooling is essential in China too.

In this regard, targeting the nouveau chic segment is important. Even though their numbers are small today and they don't have the same hefty wallet power as the nouveaux riches, they will increase China's overall style quotient.

The same logic applies to the nouveau cool segment – they are natural students for style, and while their spending power is also still to come, their ability to revolutionize China's aesthetic sensibility is powerful. Promoting the development of style is going to be a win–win all round.

Beauty is the national obsession, spurring Korean women to adopt complex beauty regimens. They take their cue from movie stars like Choi Ji Woo, posing here for DiorSnow Pure skincare range.

Photo courtesy of Dior.

6

SOUTH KOREA: INDEBTED TO LUXURY

"This is just one more syndrome in Korea – like the diet syndrome, the plastic surgery syndrome, and now the luxury brand syndrome."

Hyon-Ju Cho, managing director, Starcom Korea[1]

"Ah, the luxury of it. Fashion stores line the street in Chungdam-Dong, reeking of conspicuous consumption... But on the other side of the tracks, housemaids, waitresses and restaurant dishwashers work more than 12 hours a day for 1 million won ($820) a month, the price of one handbag with an upscale logo."

News article in Korea Times[2]

You see the clash of values most starkly in South Korea. On the one hand, there is a mad rush for imported luxury brands and unrestrained consumer spending, with maxed-out credit cards pretty much the norm. On the other, there is biting public rhetoric against conspicuous consumption, the media pointing fingers at the increasing gap between the rich and the poor, and not too far from the surface simmers the notion that buying imported merchandise is "shameful." Morality and nationalism pitted against Gucci and Ferragamo.

While Japan is an unabashed consumer society and Hong Kong subscribes to the more-is-better philosophy, South Korea grapples with opposing forces. The fact that its imported luxury market has rapidly ballooned to US$3.1 billion, about the same size as Hong Kong's, is testimony enough that consumers are hungrily devouring luxe. Furthermore, an increasing number of South Koreans are shopping abroad, bringing back bags bursting with luxury purchases, so much so that the government has instituted luggage-inspection measures when they return.[3] But it seems the more impediments and luxury bashing there are, the greater the growth of luxe consumption. The social glory of a carefully displayed Hermès bag far outweighs the moral censure from society at large. If there is any residual guilt, it is safely tucked away in the suede-lined inner pockets of a Chanel bag, or stubbed out by the deft twist of a Manolo Blahnik.

This is the land where every other woman in Seoul and Pusan is said to have a Louis Vuitton piece. This is the land where Ferragamo shoes and Gucci bags are purchased on installment plans. This is the land where Burberry is so popular that "Burberry" has become the Korean word for trench coat (which incidentally leads to some provocative situations with customers walking into, say, an Armani store and asking for a Burberry). This is the land where diamond-studded Cartier watches and Hermès Kelly bags come top of the wish lists of young working women, along with BMW convertibles. This is the land where beauty is a religion in itself.

For us, one story captures the essence of South Korea's unique love affair with luxury goods. Young-Chull Kim, publisher of *Marie Claire*, *Harper's Bazaar*, and other glossies – who until recently owned Jindo Fur, one of the biggest fur retailers in South Korea – tells the tale of a working-class woman who made her money running a small eatery selling a local variety of pancakes.[4] One day Young found the woman shopping for a mink coat at his store, and he asked what she needed it for. "Because I feel cold," she said. Sure, it's upward mobility, but in South Korea that upward mobility is fur clad.

In this chapter we look at the fast-forward evolution of the Korean luxury market, the social tugs and pulls that have shaped it, the march of brands, the diverse retail scene that ranges from flea markets to a swank Rodeo Street, and the unique mind-set of the South Korean consumer who is embracing Western luxury brands with open arms, in the process turning a well-toned, Prada-clad back to the moralistic scolds.

FROM SUITCASES TO FLAGSHIPS

Nature abhors a vacuum, they say, air rushing in to equalize the imbalance. In the case of a vacuum-sealed South Korea in the 1970s with protective trade walls around it, the equalizing force was provided by "suitcase businessmen," a breed of enterprising black marketeers who sold a variety of luxury goods, quite literally from suitcases. Their source of merchandise, and perhaps even of the luggage, was said to have been equally enterprising American GIs stationed in South Korea, who smuggled in small quantities of foreign brands. A somewhat dubious start, but a start nevertheless, of what would grow a few decades later into a multibillion-dollar luxury goods market, the humble suitcase forever replaced by monumental flagship stores.

The legal luxury goods market – coming out of the suitcase, so to speak – started in 1987, when the government finally permitted the import of ready-to-wear apparel, handbags, and shoes. South Korea slowly opened up to global influences. The 1988 Seoul Olympics catapulted the country onto the world stage, and it wasn't long afterwards that the first round of luxury brand companies started coming in, Armani, Burberry, and Louis Vuitton among them.

At the same time South Koreans were allowed to travel abroad for leisure for the first time, and with increasing prosperity many took the opportunity to do so; similar to what is happening in China today. The global Pandora's box was open, and while local moralists chorused against the evils of buying imported goods, South Korean consumers started doing the rounds of shops in Paris and Milan, bringing back bags and shoes, ideas and trends. They loved wicked Western luxe and steadily transferred their affections from local brands and designers to international ones, fueling a further outcry about domestic suffering because of imported.

The growth of the market has been nothing short of explosive, propelling South Korea into Stage 4, the *fit in* phase of the Spread of Luxury model, in just a decade. Record speed, if you consider that Japan and Hong Kong took a couple of decades to cover the same ground.

What was the reason behind this supercharged growth? Korea has been a late starter – thanks to government policies – and it's largely a case of making up for lost time. The turning point was 1995, when pent-up demand met generous supply in a loud outburst of consumer spending. South Korean consumers were more than ready – per capita income, US$3,000 in the late 1980s, had tripled by the late 1990s, serious money compared to what the Chinese have today. On the other hand, luxury brands that had been testing the waters since the market opened were now set to increase the stakes. It was land-grab time in the gold rush for the South Korean market, and every brand was investing to ensure it got a chunk of the action. The strategy yielded results. LVMH Group brands grew seven or eight times in volume from the mid-1990s to the early 2000s, with Louis Vuitton occupying the familiar number one spot.[5]

The 1997 "IMF crisis" (that's how Koreans refer to that period of economic disaster, as if the International Monetary Fund caused it) did bring about an adjustment in the luxury market, with some of the smaller brands cutting investments or temporarily leaving the country, but overall luxe did not suffer much. In fact, stronger brands like Vuitton, Hermès, and Tiffany benefited by consolidating their position of strength. Strange as it may sound, many South Koreans actually grew richer during this turbulent time thanks to skyrocketing interest rates and deregulation of foreign currency[6] – anyone who had cash to spare, especially dollars, could earn mouth-watering returns on deposits. This easy money fueled the demand for luxury brands. Take Hermès. From 1997 onward it recorded annual sales growth rates of 124, 48, 60, 44, and 31 percent, multiplying its 1997 sales of 2.6 billion won tenfold to 26 billion won five years later.[7]

It was the middle class who suffered during the IMF crisis, polarizing society into richer and poorer folk with an income gap that has widened ever since. According to the Korea National Statistical Office, the top 20 percent of income earners make five times more than the lowest 20 percent, whereas in 1997 the difference was four times.[8] Ironically, this is a situation that works in favor of luxury brands.

In line with the *fit in* stage, the luxe habit is now well entrenched. According to a survey by Synovate, 12 percent of South Koreans between the ages of 15 and 64 purchased a luxury brand in the previous six months, spending on average US$600. Of these, 22 percent shopped abroad, and another 14 percent can't remember where they bought – the amnesia brought on, we suspect, by the government's strict eye on returning tourists.[9]

Some of that "shopping abroad" is happening in South Korea itself at the several duty-free shops in Seoul. The modus operandi is simple:

Before a trip abroad, you do a leisurely shop at one of the downtown duty-free outlets, collect the goods at the airport and fly abroad, and on your return you simply bring in your purchases as part of your "used" personal belongings. Which customs official can tell whether the Gucci watch on your wrist is duty paid or duty free? The number of locals shopping at duty-free outlets is on the rise, estimated to account for 30–40 percent of all duty-free sales. Recognizing this fact, the stores are targeting locals with their marketing campaigns. Arbitrage, you might call it, since the buyers are able to shave a good 15–20 percent off the duty-paid price.

Of course, the real purpose of the duty-free channel is to cater to tourists, and it has performed that role extremely well, yielding luxury brand sales of over US$1 billion. Its mainstay has been the familiar Japanese tourist – in fact, tour operators in Japan sell packaged shopping tours to South Korea. Once you have done the rounds of Seoul you realize pretty fast that whether you are Japanese or not, the major tourist attraction is shopping, and more shopping. The whole city is geared to make you purchase. Tourist maps helpfully zero in on retail districts. Hotel concierges look you straight in the face and direct you to markets selling fakes. Taxi drivers, if you find an English-speaking one, give you friendly advice about Burberry being the hot brand to buy. Many department stores, such as Lotte, have sections devoted to duty-free goods. And if you still haven't succumbed, Seoul's Incheon airport is basically a shopping mall with flight decks attached – there are fully fledged large-format stores featuring brands like Chanel, Ferragamo, Gucci, and other favorites.

SINFUL LUXURY

Taking potshots at the excesses of consumption, especially of the luxury brand kind, isn't something new or even unique to South Korea; there's plenty of it in the Western world. Undesirable, unfulfilling, unfair, manipulated, dangerous, contagious – the reasons against luxe come fast and thick, perhaps best demonstrated by the rash of books on the subject. Just look at the disapproving titles: In *An All Consuming Century*, it's about time *The Overspent American* started questioning *The*

Morality of Spending; only by *Confronting Consumption* head on and realizing that *Less Is More* can the *Luxury Fever* (which fails to satisfy anyway) be brought under control and the *Overworked American* (who is working overtime to finance his shopping binges) get some well-deserved rest.[10] That, in a nutshell, is the only way to stem the *Affluenza* epidemic.[11]

Exactly the thinking of the South Korean moralists, who keep up a melodramatic hullabaloo over the sins of luxury consumption. There are several reasons for Korea's strong anti-luxe lobby. First, while neighboring markets like Hong Kong and China don't seem to have a problem reconciling their Confucian roots with avid luxe consumption (in fact, Confucian values like the preservation of family face are significant *drivers* of wealth display in these markets), the South Korean interpretation of certain tenets is at loggerheads with luxe consumption. Frugality and moderation have assumed a larger-than-life position in the Korean form of neo-Confucian thought.

Secondly, whereas capitalism in other countries unabashedly celebrates making money at a personal level, in South Korea capitalism is dressed up and presented as something one needs to do for the national good. The logic goes like this: Because we were not economically self-sufficient we fell prey to colonial domination (the Japanese first, and then the Americans, although in the latter case the feelings are more complex), therefore to protect the nation from a similar fate we have to develop as an economic power. The country must grow prosperous through capitalist endeavor, but you as an individual must remain frugal. The Korean government took that line of thinking to its logical conclusion, promoting frugality itself as a strategy for national development, and launched a series of public austerity campaigns to that end. If you didn't blow your money on useless, not to mention morally degrading, excessive consumption, that money could be saved and invested to promote production. Get rich, act poor.

Thirdly, South Koreans tend to wear their nationalism on their sleeves (even if they are Gucci or Armani) and somewhere along the line came the notion that to be truly nationalistic they must not buy foreign goods. Just as the government was opening up the economy to international participation, it was launching a vociferous tirade against the evils of importing goods and putting in measures to curtail it. Frugality took on yet another meaning: Excessive consumption is bad, but excessive consumption of foreign goods is worse.

In the early 1990s, people who bought imported cars had their taxes scrutinized. Author Laura Nelson cites the case of a woman who purchased a used Mercedes, which she finally had to dispose of "so the Tax office would leave us alone."[12] Perhaps the most damning blow against imported luxury goods was the government's insistence that the price tag should mention the initial import price alongside the final consumer price, which was, of course, substantially higher after adding profit margins and various taxes and duties.

Such drastic measures are no longer in force, but the historical rhetoric against imported luxe continues unabated on the front pages of the daily media. The tension between the reality of growing prosperity and the prescription of frugality can never be reasonably resolved. In the meantime, Korean consumers have found their own way of dealing with the contradictory tugs and pulls: regular bouts of retail therapy.

SOUTH KOREA'S FORCES OF LUXE

Let's give the luxe-as-sin moral posturing a break, and look at the reality of life as led by millions of South Koreans as they go about spending their recently gained wealth. There are three uniquely South Korean forces that have spurred the luxury culture.

Beauty, the National Obsession

Whether it is landing a good match in marriage (often egged on by an ambitious mother), or hanging on to a husband (notorious for their late-night drinking and womanizing), or getting a good job (appearance is an important criterion for hiring women) – without beauty your chances are considerably reduced. In the new Korea beauty is quite literally power, and women do what they can to get ahead, giving rise to a nation of budding Cleopatras.

While milk baths may have been the height of pampering for the Egyptian queen, a range of establishments have sprung up to cater to our perfection-fixated South Korean belle – cosmetic surgeries, dermatology clinics, beauty parlors, hair salons, fitness centers, spas – making South Korea a very attractive market for beauty products and services.

For the Korean woman the most important aspect is a flawless complexion, and she is willing to go to extreme lengths to achieve it – even a pimple or a small blemish is enough to give her sleepless nights. She gets professional help on a regular basis, and this can vary from facials at the beauty parlor to weekly consultations with a qualified dermatologist. As a result, the most sought-after professional course at university is dermatology, and it is next to impossible to get a place on it. Little wonder, then, that skincare sales account for two-thirds of the South Korean cosmetics market.

As in the rest of Asia fair skin is coveted, and skin-whitening products account for a third of the market. The fixation in the Korean context is linked to a desire to project high social status – in Korea's version of the caste system, those engaged in manual labor were considered low class, and were typically marked by their darker skin, a result of working in the hot sun. Fair skin, on the other hand, cued upper class.

But beauty in Korea isn't merely skin deep. Women go under the surgeon's knife to create *ul-jjang* or "best face," today's buzzword. The plastic surgery trend has become so endemic that 50 percent of women in their 20s are estimated to have undergone some surgical upgrade.[13] This is a country that thinks like Michael Jackson – Seoul boasts a street with 400 clinics, nicknamed "Plastic Surgery Street." Even schoolchildren are going for surgery, and "eye jobs" have become routine high-school graduation gifts from proud parents. Actors and popstars get complete makeovers – 90 percent of female talent is estimated to have had some plastic surgery.[14] The standing joke is that when a young female actor comes on the scene she has her own distinct features, but give her a few years and she starts resembling the others.

The potency of the call for self-beautification is illustrated by the story of top South Korean fencer Nam Hyun-hee, who was booted off the Olympic team for two years because she underwent plastic surgery. She had treatment to fix an eye problem that was impeding her vision, but while in hospital she decided to get some plastic surgery done to enhance her cheeks. Her swollen face meant several additional days of missed training, leading to her suspension.[15]

In one of our group discussions with women professionals, each of them strikingly lovely, we asked why there was a need to alter such naturally beautiful faces. They giggled and teased: "How do you know we haven't had something done?" The high cheekbones, sculpted faces with slanting eyes that we admired so much, were seen as "bland" by the women themselves, necessitating a nose job to lengthen the nose, "slimming" the face by shaving the cheekbones, and creating a fold on the eyelids "to add interest to the face." (Breast enlargements are also on the rise, but not spoken about as freely as facial alterations.) As they say, beauty lies in the eye of the beholder, and South Korean women are an exacting lot.

Whatever their secrets might be, we have to say that we met some of the most attractive women we've ever seen in Seoul – utterly feminine, petite, and delicate, with radiant complexions and warm hearts. Their dress sense is characterized by simplicity and elegance, most women preferring classic skirt suits, quite like the Japanese. Of late the suit trend is softening – if it was Armani suits earlier, it's knitted twinsets now, with the rich favoring cashmere knits from Hermès and Loro Piana at US$2,000 or more a set. Sarah Kim, retail manager of Fendi, comments:

Until the late 1990s, it was hard to do business without a good range of suits. But now women are looking beyond suits.[16]

With the spotlight squarely on beauty, there is a parallel surge in luxury brand products – natural accessories to producing *ul-jjang*, after all.

Consumer Profile
Lee Hyuen-Suk and Kim Mi-Jung*: From Fakes to the Real Thing

A palpable bond of friendship binds this delightful duo. Both women are in their early 40s, they hold senior managerial positions, and they have been colleagues for over a decade. They laugh easily, girlish pride in their voices as they describe their recent shopping escapades. Hyuen-Suk, the "older and wiser" one, wears a Gucci watch and a silver Tiffany necklace and ring, while Mi-Jung looks radiant in a soft brown wool Max Mara coat and Missoni muffler. We meet over dinner, not easy as they are both on a diet, but there's plenty of food for thought.

*Names changed.

On the transition from fakes

Hyuen-Suk: "We used to buy a lot of fakes, you know from Dongdaemun – Louis
   Vuitton and Gucci bags – I didn't think anyone could tell the difference. Younger colleagues would urge me to try the real thing. I finally gave in, but I am the last in the
   office to start buying luxury brands."

Mi-Jung: "My colleagues kept asking me, 'Why do you buy fakes at your status?' It's
   funny, now that I'm buying originals, I have to declare to everyone, 'Hey, this is
   real!'"

On why they buy luxury brands

Mi-Jung: "Earlier I thought luxury brands were a waste of money, but now I feel 'I
   deserve it,' I have worked so hard for 20 years, after all."

Hyuen-Suk: "We still buy t-shirts and things from Dongdaemun – like I might get a
   black high-neck top from Dongdaemun and wear it with my Armani jacket."

On their favorite brands

Hyuen-Suk [without hesitation]: "Mont Blanc – I first bought the fountain pen. I just
   loved the design. Then I bought the ball pen and pencil too, and it all fits into this
   neat black leather case. [She shows us the case] I like taking it out at client meetings [laughs] – it's a symbol of my status."

Mi-Jung: "Cartier – I was going to buy a Cartier watch at the duty-free shop, but Hyuen-
   Suk said wait a little bit more."

Hyuen-Suk [nods]: "It's very expensive, better to think for a few days if you really want
   it."

On what brands their colleagues favor

Men will wear Armani suits and Cartier watches. Women will go for Ferragamo shoes,
Louis Vuitton/Prada bags, Gucci/Cartier watches, Hermès scarves.

On the popularity of luxury brands

Hyuen-Suk: "Koreans have an abnormal love for luxury brands, every woman has to
   have them. They want to show they belong to a higher class."

Mi-Jung: "In Korea we have a saying: 'You eat poor, but you have to wear well.' Other
   people may not bother about their appearance, but for Koreans looking good is very
   important."

On the South Korean standard of beauty

Hyuen-Suk: "Very slim, beautiful skin, we like the facial features to be of a certain kind
– so everyone is doing plastic surgery of eyes and nose, even schoolgirls. Even Mi-
Jung is thinking of getting her eyes done."

Mi-Jung [who, in our opinion, has the most beautiful almond-shaped, upward-tilted
eyes]: "Yeah, just to get a fold on the eyelid, it'll look much nicer, won't it?"

Quick on the Draw with the Card

From Confucian frugality with a stress on savings, South Koreans have
swung to the other extreme, spending way beyond their means thanks
to the easy-credit culture that has taken root.

If South Korea's 1997 crisis was brought on by indiscriminate corporate debt, in the early 2000s it was followed by indiscriminate consumer
debt. South Korea's economic recovery after the IMF crisis was fueled by
encouraging consumers to spend, with the government lowering interest
rates to make it easier to borrow money. South Koreans didn't think twice
before doing the "patriotic" thing – they borrowed heaps and spent heaps
too. They bought houses. They bought cars. They also bought little Fendi
purses on credit-card downpayments with 12 easy installments. As we saw
earlier, this was the period of explosive growth for the luxury industry.

The speed at which South Koreans took to credit is mind-boggling.
Five years after 1997, the country's household debt had doubled,
amounting to 73 percent of its gross domestic product, not far from the
79 percent level seen in the credit-saturated US.[17] More worryingly, an
estimated 2.5 million South Koreans were behind on their credit-card
payments. A series of "credit-card suicides" came to light, mostly young
people in their 20s and 30s. Some 24,500 people killed themselves in
2001 and 2002, often over an accumulation of bad debts.[18]

How could an intrinsically frugal people collectively lose their financial balance almost overnight? While an over-aggressive credit-card
industry certainly takes part of the blame, that doesn't detract from the
fact that South Koreans *chose* to spend. With the economy escaping
from the jaws of death, the nation's mood was optimistic. Many people
made money on property and stocks; others cashed in on the internet
boom. And while some had real wealth to splash, others joined the

spending bandwagon with borrowed funds. South Koreans don't like to be left behind.

Outdoing the Kims and Lees

Unlike Japan where the overpowering need is to conform, where "nails that stick out are hammered in," South Korea is a highly competitive society that takes keeping up with the Joneses to the next level: outdoing the Kims and Lees. This is characterized by constant comparisons with friends and neighbors – your house, your possessions, your accomplishments, your children's accomplishments, your husband's job, everything is compared. There is immense pressure to measure up otherwise there is loss of face, which is painful and unacceptable, leading people to spend way beyond their means. One woman told us her sister-in-law, who had been raised in the US, found the competitive talk of friendly fellow moms so stressful – apparently little Johnny never quite met Korean standards – that she packed her bags and left, little Johnny and husband in tow.

The compare-and-compete culture of Korean housewives is a central theme for prominent novelist Pak Wan-so. The following passage from her story "The Identical Rooms" illustrates this tendency strongly in a middle-class context:

I tried so hard to make my room fancier than hers but ended up with nothing so special. The color of the curtain and the placement of the furniture all turned out to be just the same... Just as my apartment resembled Cholhee's, all the other apartments in our neighborhood, on the left and the right and up and down were alike.... I was sick and tired of this sameness, but I saved money to buy the washing machine which Cholhee's mother had.[19]

This is peer pressure taken to pressure-cooker levels, and the tale of the identical rooms repeats itself in luxe consumption. The result is that when a luxury brand trend catches on it spreads furiously, and then pretty soon the stakes get raised, with the élite set wanting out and moving on to something that puts them ahead of the mass market. (This is a modern-day Korean version of Georg Simmel's classic trickle-down theory of fashion, but more on that in Chapter 9.)

Take the national obsession, Ferragamo shoes. Until recently the élite were happy to flaunt them, but now they see office ladies and university students doing the same. Looking to put some distance between themselves and the *hoi polloi*, they are moving up the ladder to more expensive brands like Hermès. Or even within "mass luxury" brands such as Gucci, the élite are selecting higher-priced items like clothing. Other distance-increasing devices include jewel-encrusted Cartier watches, or a high-carat diamond from Tiffany.

As a sign of the times, we heard how a Louis Vuitton salesgirl who used to "sniff out the spending power" of customers by noting the brand of shoe and bag they were carrying has now had to change tack. "Everyone has a branded bag or shoe nowadays," she says. So now she has taken to checking out their watches and jewelry.

Luxury brands have become everyday necessities in South Korea. You wear them every time you step out, whether you are going to the supermarket, the beauty parlor, to work, or to school. In this close-knit claustrophobic milieu, you can't afford to let your guard down. Friends and neighbors are watching.

FLAGSHIPS TO FAKES

Shopping is the soul of Seoul, with every conceivable mode of luxe retailing deployed here, including a few that headquarters in Paris and Milan wouldn't have conceived of. You go from exclusive flagship stores, absolute temples of sophistication, to the hustle-bustle of local markets like Dongdaemun, where dozens of Ferragamo shoes and Burberry bags are displayed on open stalls like so many potatoes and carrots in a vegetable market. There are mammoth upscale department stores with an array of luxe brands, each with its own prestigious enclave and white-gloved service; then you walk into a family-run multibrand store round the corner, Dior bags happily mixed with Gucci and Louis Vuitton, and the distinct smell of a meal being prepared in the background. Luxury is truly accessible to all.

Similar to Japan, department stores are the mainstay of luxe retailing – in fact, Japanese department stores came to South Korea in the early 1930s during the Japanese occupation.[20] Today all the major department store chains – Shinsegae, Lotte, Hyundai, Galleria, LG, Samsung – are South Korean, but they are modeled closely on the Japanese ones.

The imposing twin-structure Galleria in the trendy Chungdam-Dong area is undoubtedly the plushest of them all, with a separate building devoted to imported brands. This is luxury at its most concentrated, Armani to Zegna with over 100 brands in between, covering ready-to-wear, leather goods, watches, jewelry, accessories, cosmetics, and homeware. The place has a rarefied air, with an Alice in Wonderland, surreal quality to it, where time slows down and customers decked out in long fur coats, prominent designer bag at hand, move leisurely from store to store, or sip lemon tea with other fur-clad women in the stylish café upstairs.

In sharp contrast, the Shinsegae department store, next to the Marriott hotel, has a more active demeanor, crowds streaming in and out, luxury shoppers drawn from a broader cross-section of society. It's a 10-story behemoth, and with Christmas round the corner when we visited, there were high-wire mechanical Santas doing tricks in mid-air in the gigantic atrium. The power names, known locally as *myongpum* brands – Louis Vuitton, Gucci, Ferragamo, *et al.* – are at street level and other brands are stacked up on succeeding floors.

While department stores are where most of the luxe sales are made, it is the flagship store phenomenon that has elevated Seoul to the fore-front of fashion retailing. The trend started in the booming mid-1990s, and soon Seoul had its very own Rodeo Street with a line-up of major brands. Admittedly these are not built on the same scale as the flagships in Japan, but they are large, free-standing stores all the same, typically two- or three-story vertical blocks with massive glass frontages. What we found puzzling was the lack of customers. Even a power brand like Louis Vuitton, with a beautifully rendered store, did not have a single customer during the hour we spent in the shop – a totally different position from the Louis Vuitton flagships in Tokyo, which are under siege by customers willing to wait their turn. What could be the reason? The answer lies in the breathtaking speed with which the luxe culture has spread in South Korea. While legions of consumers are buying luxury brands, they don't necessarily feel comfortable in the awe-inspiring atmosphere of the flagship stores. They flock instead to the department stores and night markets.

No description of Seoul's retail scene would be complete without a visit to the famous local markets – Dongdaemun, Namdaemun, and several others like them. Throbbing with life late into the night, these markets are stuffed to the seams with trendy fashion goods, moderately priced, of reasonable quality.

Take Doosan Tower, one of several market buildings in Dongdaemun. It can best be described as a vertical flea market with row upon row of small 8 foot by 10 foot stalls, each piled high with merchandise, displayed vigorously on every square inch of available space, and a couple of enterprising salesgirls in attendance. It has a carnival atmosphere, Western pop music blaring from the loud-speakers, lots of young people milling around, crowded escalators snaking up and down. You enter a sea of denim jeans, every kind you can dream of – faded, patched, torn, embroidered, appliquéd, all in a variety of colors. You are handed a big skirt that functions like a waist-down "changing room," and you try the jeans on right there on the spot.

For luxury brands you head down to Basement 2, and again you're swimming in stalls selling imported goods – Ferragamo shoes, Louis Vuitton wallets, Burberry bags, Armani leather jackets, DKNY jeans. Mind you, this is all supposedly genuine stuff, parallel imports, brought in by individual travelers. Your mind reels, first to see brands in such abundance and variety, and then by a 20–30 percent discount on regular prices. These objects of desire look almost homely shorn of their customary refined surroundings – in a flagship store you might have one bag displayed in splendid isolation, here hundreds are stacked in the same space. But while the flagship stores are quiet, here you find a crowd of willing shoppers.

Head up to the fourth floor, and now you are swallowed by a tide of fake LV bags, and to a lesser extent Gucci, Prada, and several other brands. Stall upon stall is chockablock with fakes of every quality, openly displayed. The minute you show interest in one of the items, the shopkeeper wrinkles his nose and says, "Oh, that's C-grade" – then he pulls you inside the tiny stall and produces the A-grade imitation. They don't come cheap – an A-grade fake LV bag starts at US$125, but with haggling can be yours for US$100. And if you don't like what's on display, there are fat Japanese catalogs picturing every brand and every style of product, complete with model number and specifications. Just point to the one you like and, as if by magic, it emerges from somewhere within the belly of that tiny stall.

Extremely Discreet to Highly Conspicuous

In line with the *fit in* stage of the market, South Korea's luxury consumers come from a wide cross-section of society. The twist here is that the luxury gourmands have gone underground, making a fine art of *inconspicuous* consumption, while the rest of society openly parades designer brands. Let's understand how that came to be, and the role luxury brands play in the lives of different segments.

Inconspicuous Gourmands

While the daily diatribe against conspicuous consumption is a factor, the real reason the super-élite make themselves "invisible" is the anger and frustration that people harbor against them, believing they have gotten rich by a combination of favoritism and corruption. Many of them belong to powerful industrial families, part of Korea's famed *chaebol*, who grew into gigantic corporations with multiple businesses due to the close connections they enjoyed with the state. Just how heavy these fat cats became is best demonstrated by this statistic: In 1974, the aggregate net sales of the top ten *chaebol* equaled 15 percent of South Korea's GNP; by 1985, it had swollen to 80 percent of GNP,[21] leading to super-concentration of wealth in the hands of a small segment. *Chaebol* were favored with easy access to low-interest loans – opportunists to the core, they apparently played the illegal curb market for unlisted stocks with these borrowed funds (which were earmarked for export-oriented production and hence carried low interest rates) and raked in huge profits.[22] Avoiding taxes, circumventing laws for personal gain, using insider knowledge to advantage – the extent of corruption in élite circles is hard to gauge, but the general *perception* that the moneyed are corrupt has stuck.

As a result, a whole world of extraordinary wealth and social influence exists solely behind closed doors. These super-gourmands' expenditure on luxury brands is phenomenal – a divorced tai-tai told us she enjoyed a "bottomless account" during her marriage – but the consumption has to remain invisible. Even charity balls, the ultimate photo opportunity, are held away from the prying eyes of the media. The same applies to luxury brand parties – if your brand caters to the tip of society, then party by all means, but keep it suitably toned down. For example, Giorgio Armani's South Korean flagship launch party was a relatively discreet affair.

These customers demand the utmost privacy when shopping. "The rich are targets of criticism, not enjoying respect from other people, so affluent people want to be discreet," says HS Jun, managing director of Hermès,[23] pointing out the case of the company's store at the upscale Shilla hotel, which has some 40 loyal customers, absolute *crème de la crème*. "They don't want to shop if any other customer is in the store."

From *Yoksim*-Charged Housewives to the Missy Generation

The underlying theme in South Korea is good old upward social mobility practiced vigorously and visibly. Women in particular play an aggressive role. They have discovered that generations of Confucian pigeonholing into lower social strata can be done away with by making money and displaying it smartly. Grandma may have worked the rice fields in some remote village, but chances are mother has raised her family in the comfortable setting of urban middle/upper-middle-class Seoul, while daughter trawls the malls dressed in this season's Gucci bests that look swell on her silicon-enhanced bust, liposuctioned derrière, and surgically elongated legs. Luxury brands are the handy palette with which this broad new class paints its fresh identity.

What stands out is astonishing ambition matched by amazing entrepreneurial zeal, best exemplified by the older generation of housewives, now in their 50s or later. Whereas in most other Asian societies there is a division of labor – men make money, women spend it – in South Korea this older generation of housewives played a large hand in enhancing the family fortunes through shrewd investments. Most of these women led a strange, female-only existence, while their husbands engaged in "higher-order," nation-building activities in the corporate

The Ferragamo Fetish

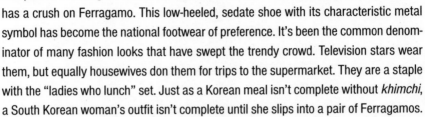

If Japan has a thing for Louis Vuitton, South Korea has a crush on Ferragamo. This low-heeled, sedate shoe with its characteristic metal symbol has become the national footwear of preference. It's been the common denominator of many fashion looks that have swept the trendy crowd. Television stars wear them, but equally housewives don them for trips to the supermarket. They are a staple with the "ladies who lunch" set. Just as a Korean meal isn't complete without *khimchi*, a South Korean woman's outfit isn't complete until she slips into a pair of Ferragamos.

Over time, the Ferragamo shoe has acquired a life of its own – it has gone from an object of desire to a social necessity. Park Mee Jung of *Elle* puts it simply: "Everyone owns Ferragamo, so you have to have them too." What has made this rather simple, comfortable court the national obsession?

Conservative Korean taste
The shoe's classic elegance has struck a chord with South Koreans. Broadly speaking, simplicity is the height of fashion here. The well-groomed "good girl" look is in.

Status marker par excellence
Ferragamo has invested heavily in building its prestigious image in South Korea and has become the most recognizable symbol of owning a luxury brand. For starters, its prominent metallic emblem and ladylike bows let everyone know in a jiffy that you're in Ferragamos. The company advertises heavily, taking prominent inside and back covers of fashion glossies, its ads often placed next to brands like Hermès, Chanel, and Cartier. It has a chic flagship store on Rodeo Street. It has snared prime locations in department stores. In a nutshell, it has done its marketing extremely well.

Value for money
Ferragamo has consistently positioned itself as high-end luxury, which indeed it is if you're buying a sweater or jacket where prices start at US$1,000. But when it comes to its shoes the price point is relatively low, starting at US$300. It's this "high image, affordable price" equation that makes it such good value for money.

Salvatore Ferragamo, a Florentine shoemaker who made his name in the 1930s, would never have dreamed that an entire nation would one day march ahead in his shoes.

Photo courtesy of Ferragamo.

world, working late in the office before they went "missing in action"; that is, bonding with male colleagues over drinks and more. As many as 20 percent of South Korean men aged 20–64 buy sex once a week, resulting in a sex industry that accounts for 4 percent of GDP, according to the Korean Institute of Criminology.[24]

While the men were occupied, gainfully or otherwise, their wives acted as "fund managers" for the family, taking their husband's income and investing it with finesse in the multitude of opportunities offered by Korea's booming economy. A series of sobriquets emerged to describe these financially savvy wives: Mrs. Realtor, who bought and sold land and houses for speculation; Big Hand, who lent large sums in the unofficial money market; Swish of Skirts, who used informal networks to influence people in public positions; Madame Procuress, who made large sums of money by arranging marriages.[25]

You can taste the sting in those nicknames, and indeed the moralists had a field day deriding the women's naked ambition and vulgar display, but when all's said and done these housewives collectively changed the fortunes and lifestyles of Korea's middle/upper-middle class. The key to understanding this generation of older women lies in their humble backgrounds, their childhoods spent in abject poverty, their families displaced by the Korean War, firing them with an immense hunger to improve their lot – a particularly potent *subjugation* phase, Stage 1 of the Spread of Luxury model. The Koreans term this hunger *yoksim*, variously meaning greed, fierce ambition, a relentless craving for wealth and social recognition. Like an army of Scarlett O'Haras these *yoksim*-charged women rebuilt their lives – with little help from their absent husbands – moving into larger, well-appointed homes, putting their kids through good schools, wangling successful marriages for their sons and daughters, and accumulating social assets with the same savvy as they did their financial ones. Superwomen, no less.

Imported luxury brands are an important part of their lives today, but they tend to purchase the bags, shoes, fur coats, watches, jewelry, and other accessories. When it comes to clothes, the slim-fit styling of imported brands is a problem as these women tend to have rather matronly figures, leaving them no choice but to turn to local designers. A fashion magazine stylist explained:

First wives favor Korean designers, and often have their outfits tailored at absurd prices. Second wives head into Fendi or Gucci for the latest international trends – they have the figure to carry it off.

The younger generation of housewives is a different story altogether. They may be married, but they dress like a much younger college student, taking pains to present a trendy, girlish image. There's even a term for this chic wife – "missy," because they look like young misses.[26] Keeping a hold on their husbands is of course an important motivation, especially when the streets of Seoul are inundated with strikingly beautiful females, but there's also plenty of peer pressure from other women. Missydom lies not only in what you stand for – a young, sexy, and seemingly single girl – but what you don't stand for – an unsophisticated housewife of modest means. A dream situation for the luxury brand industry, with hordes stalking department stores, purchasing all the essential doodads to put together the sizzling missy look.

The final irony comes from the bar hostess segment. While missy housewives are adding oomph to their everyday look, some "room salon" hostesses are going the other way. Room salons are a common fixture of Korean night life, bars offering private rooms where pretty hostesses serve drinks and light conversation to male clients, extremely expensive setups frequented by managing directors and company presidents. The hostesses have the reputation of being exquisitely beautiful – "better than popstars and entertainers even," we were told. They don't dress cheaply and flashily; they endeavor to project an intellectual image in line with the stature of their high-ranking clients. They often dress in suits, Chanel being a favorite. They also love Cartier watches and the omnipresent Ferragamo shoes.

Sacrificing Nibblers

In a replay of what's happening in the rest of Asia – and if anything, the luxe urge is amplified in South Korea due to the overemphasis on beauty – office ladies and university students are buying small amounts of luxury brands. Young-Chull Kim of *Marie Claire* comments:

Young people will eat cheap instant noodle soup. But they'll buy Cartier and Louis Vuitton.

Students take part-time jobs to finance their luxury needs. Office ladies put aside money every month for a luxe bag. Like in Japan, there is a growing trend for "freelance" sex[27] to finance brand purchases. When all else fails, they "charge it" to a handy credit card, which they stretch and stretch, often, as we have seen, with disastrous results.

Why don't they buy the abundantly available fake products rather than go through all this financial pain? The answer is that many are ardent buyers of counterfeit goods, but for others fakes don't cut it, especially as there's the risk they might be ridiculed by brand-savvy fellow students if they're discovered. Also, while Louis Vuitton and Gucci bags are easily available as high-quality fakes, that's not the case with the highly sought-after Ferragamo shoes, necessitating the purchase of an original pair.

BUSINESS LESSONS FROM SOUTH KOREA

South Korea is a case study of how swiftly the cult of the luxury brand can establish itself in an emerging Asian country. There are important business lessons here that can be applied to other markets, especially China and India.

Pump Up the Beauty Industry

South Korea demonstrates most graphically the link between beauty and luxe – promoting one leads to a natural growth in the other.

Cosmetics and skincare products are an easier sell in an emerging market to begin with as price points are significantly lower, making it easier to launch a beauty culture. That awakens the desire to look good on other fronts, a natural upping of personal standards of grooming and presentation, and a desire to be in fashion – steps that lead to branded bags, accessories, and clothes in due course. India is a good example of a luxury market at the initial stages. Promoting its incipient beauty market would help the case for brands here, and indeed some companies have begun to do so – for example, MAC has teamed up with *Verve* magazine to hold make-up workshops. China has covered significant ground – an estimated 20 percent of professional women between 20 and 50 use beauty services[28] – but given its sheer size, there's still a long way to go.

The fact that most luxury brands have beauty products as part of their range – or the parent group has beauty brands in its portfolio – gives them the levers to influence the development of the beauty culture.

Power Through the Obstacles

Nearly every weapon that can stop the development of a Western luxury culture has been deployed vigorously, yet South Korean consumers have gone ahead and embraced luxe. As we have seen, the government and the media have tried the whole arsenal, from moralizing against conspicuous consumption to playing up patriotism in the fight against foreign goods, but to no avail. The government even took specific measures at various times to control the luxury goods phenomenon – for example stringent checks of incoming luggage, harassing conspicuous users with income-tax reviews, and insisting luxury brands confess their initial import price on the retail price tag. But none of these obstacles dampened the growth of the luxury culture.

In emerging markets like India a similar gamut of obstacles is likely to play out – the signs are already appearing. Should luxury brands be discouraged? South Korea's experience points to an emphatic no. You can't stop human nature: New money will always triumphantly display its wealth.

Western Brands Hold the Trump Card

South Korea puts to rest the debate about whether Asians intrinsically prefer Western brands or are choosing them only because there are no local ones of stature. Thanks to the government keeping the economy tightly closed till the early 1990s, a significant domestic design scene flourished in the country. But the minute Western luxury brands entered, consumers promptly abandoned local in favor of Western.

Admittedly a few designers like Jee Chun Hee and Lee Kwang Hee still enjoy an exclusive clientele, but for the most part local talent has taken a knocking. The craze that is sweeping South Korea is emphatically that of *Western* luxury brands – that's what consumers consider aspirational, cool, and status enhancing.

Many Korean fashion brands – Time, Giovanna Botticelli, Banilla B, ninesix ny – carefully present themselves as Western, using Western names and Caucasian models in their advertisements. Local editions of fashion magazines almost always use Caucasian faces on the cover – both Dong Min Park, editorial managing director of Hachette Nextmedia, which publishes *Elle*, and Young-Chull Kim, who brings out *Marie Claire*, *Harper's Bazaar*, and *Esquire*, have tried putting Korean models on the cover, only to see sales of that issue dip by half. Even the frantic plastic surgery movement is ultimately aimed at looking more Western.

Young offers an interesting insight:

In the Korean language, we don't have the word "fashion." Imported goods are regarded as fashionable, and the word "imported goods" has come to represent "fashion."

Being fashionable, it seems, means being Western.

Shop-o-tourism is a theme that runs through Southeast Asian countries. This publicity still pitches Singapore as a luxury shopper's Mecca.

Photo courtesy of Singapore Tourism Board.

7

SINGLE-SEASON SISTERS: SINGAPORE, MALAYSIA, THAILAND, INDONESIA, & THE PHILIPPINES

S outheast Asia is collectively a presence that cannot be ignored in the global strategies of luxury brands. It can be likened to a charm bracelet: Each individual charm is a well-crafted entity in its own right. String them all together and they become an irresistible ensemble. In the same way, Thailand, Malaysia, Indonesia, and the Philippines are niche markets with the promise of further expansion as standards of living continue to rise, and Singapore is undoubtedly the jewel in the regional crown, thanks to a high per capita income that puts it in the developed-nation league.

In just a decade, much of Southeast Asia has transformed itself from a house of cards in the 1997 crisis to a firm emerging market of over 400 million people, with a rapidly growing middle class and style-hungry consumers, who are spending in increasing numbers on fashion wear, accessories, and high-end cosmetics. The luxury brand market in the region is already worth US$1.5 billion and with the return of economic confidence – GDP growth rates have averaged 4–5 percent for these countries in recent years – it is set to grow. Designer malls springing up across the region are a reflection of this bouyancy, all dedicated to the present and future of luxury retail.

The markets themselves are at very different stages of luxe evolution, a fairly straightforward reflection of their level of affluence (Figure 7.1). They range from Singapore, where luxury is a *way of life*, to Indonesia and the Philippines, which are at the *start of money* stage.

Luxury brands battle an unexpected rival here: perennial summer. With the equator cutting through its belly, and most of the region falling 15 degrees north or south of it, you get the same warm, humid weather

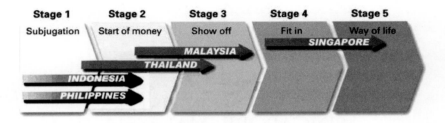

Figure 7.1 Southeast Asia: Stages of luxe evolution

all year round. In a business that revolves around spring/summer collections followed by fall/winter lines, you have the ultimate anomaly: the "single-season sisters." This puts a cap on what even the most determined fashionista can do in terms of designer wear – fur-trimmed boots and sable stoles are obviously ruled out, as are a whole host of more practical fall/winter items.

What's more, all-year hot weather makes for a more casual dress code – people don't "dress up" in Singapore and Kuala Lumpur the way they do in Hong Kong or Seoul on an everyday basis. This shapes luxury brand consumption in interesting ways. There is a greater emphasis on accessories like expensive watches and designer bags. The more casual bridge lines like Armani Exchange and Polo Ralph Lauren do well. Local designers have a higher than usual sway – their clothes incorporate European fashion elements in fabrics and sizes suited to the weather and the physique of the local consumer.

Southeast Asia provides a fascinating testing ground for the influence of religion, if any, on luxury brand consumption, representing as it does every major religion from the predominantly Muslim Indonesia and Malaysia, to Buddhist Thailand, to the Catholic Philippines (Table 7.1). The business-savvy and extremely wealthy Chinese diaspora that has an overarching presence across the region – a three-quarters majority in Singapore, between 2 and 24 percent in other countries – practices a mix of Taoism and Buddhism. We examine specific consumer behavior in the country sections that follow, but the top line is this: When money comes, luxury brands follow, irrespective of religious background. The strong need for marking status as well as the very human desire for beauty and self-enhancement finds expression even in the face of the strict dictates of Islam. Interestingly, Arab tourists from the far more conservative Middle East societies are a growing force in Malaysia, their

Table 7.1 Southeast Asia's main countries: Key facts[1]

COUNTRY	POPULATION (MILLION)	MAJORITY RELIGION	GDP PER CAPITA (US$)	CHINESE DIASPORA (% OF POPULATION)	LUXURY BRAND MARKET (US$ MN)
Singapore	4	Buddhism	24,621	77%	750
Malaysia	24	Islam	5,003	24%	300
Thailand	65	Buddhism	2,845	14%	300
Indonesia	245	Islam	1,100	3%	100
Philippines	89	Catholicism	1,021	2%	50
TOTAL	427				1,500

petrodollars gushing like oil from a newfound well at Kuala Lumpur's trendy stores.

THE UNIQUELY SINGAPOREAN MIND-SET

In Singaporean English, the expression "one kind" refers to a person with unique, probably quirky characteristics. It can be a term of admiration, mystification, or even contempt, depending on the context. Singaporeans are themselves "one kind." Their defining feature is the pursuit of success. This translates into a dogged quest for excellence in education and the accumulation of wealth. Combine Chinese cultural values with the immigrant's determination to succeed and you have an affluent consumer who demands value for money.

Singaporeans are often seen as docile and compliant, allowing a benign dictatorship to rule the island-state. The truth is that they don't care, as long as the economy functions and society is free of crime. They speak freely and frequently about the government (often in the back of taxis). Again in local-speak, "Singapore people are famous for complaining," but they know they're getting value for their money from their government.

After all, it's all worked out exactly as promised. Today GDP per capita is over US$25,000, comparable to the UK, Germany, Canada, or France.

Since the 1970s there has been no underclass of low-paid Singaporean workers, as the island steadily moved away from manufacturing into service and knowledge industries. Above all, thanks to government schemes, Singaporeans do not carry a mortgage burden and are comparatively lightly taxed, with a top rate of 20 percent. Result: A nanny state where the cosseted citizenry has a lot of pocket money left over to spend.

But a well-endowed purse and free-spending ways are two different matters. Singaporeans are obsessed with the price of everything. They are entirely free of the Western reticence to discuss income and expenditure. It's routine in conversation for a Singaporean to ask: "What is your salary? How much is your rent? What did you pay for those sunglasses?" Whatever you did pay, a Singaporean can tell you where you could have got them cheaper. In local parlance this is *kiasu*, fear of losing out. There is no dichotomy, for a Singaporean, in loving a bargain and flaunting wealth, both at once. For example, a street hawker described a Rolex-wearing customer who jumped out of his Mercedes, opened a wallet thick with notes, and then argued for a considerable time about the number of oysters he should have in his Sing$2 (US$1.25) omelette.

Rolex provides more insight. This Swiss marque was the pioneer in stand-alone luxury retail. Singaporeans have a desire for the watch that verges on obsession. Reasons are manifold: The design is easily recognizable, prestige is high as every aspiring owner knows the price, and it fetches a good resale value. Characteristically, a Singaporean will buy a plain Rolex but upgrade it by adding a diamond bezel bought from the local jeweler. Status is achieved without unnecessary expense.

The theme of "visible status at a reasonable price plus resale value" is carried through at every level of the luxury market. Thus a Gucci bag, a Mont Blanc pen, a Tag Heuer watch are all coveted by the status-conscious Singaporean. Unless jewelry is recognizable as Tiffany, Cartier, or more recently Chanel, pragmatic Singaporeans will stick with their 18K or 22K gold from local jewelers. Reproductions are tolerated, but have to be as good as real – for example an excellent Cartier replica (real gold, top-class workmanship) bought on holiday in Hong Kong.

FROM QUAINT TO WORLD-CLASS RETAIL

Retail in Singapore used to be very different in the 1970s. There was a little street called High Street. It boasted a department store, Metro, a popular dress shop, Hilda's, and a variety of Indian silk stores selling fabrics, electrical goods, semiprecious jewelry and some branded goods, mainly pens and lighters from Cartier, Dunhill, and Dupont for tourists. Not too far away, in Raffles Place, was the epitome of the British department store, Robinsons.

High Street's challenger was People's Park in Chinatown, especially for dress fabrics. (Interestingly, Singapore's old money still maintains the tailor-made dress tradition.) The fabled shopping mile of Orchard Road was just a collection of low-rise buildings, including the Chinese-style wooden building of CK Tang department store and Antoinette's, the only boutique in town that sold hats, nobody knew to whom.

There was an enclave of designer elegance in boutiques such as the now-defunct Glamourette, unglamorously located behind Fitzpatrick's supermarket, and Singora, in the Hilton hotel. But overall, shopping in Singapore in 1970 was quaint.

Then everything changed. The economy boomed. Tourist arrivals soared. Property values in the land-scarce country began a steep upward climb, which was checked only by the 1997 crisis. Everybody had money. Everybody had leisure time – and Singapore's retail rapidly traded up.

Orchard Road came into its own. Shophouses were replaced by shopping centers. Five-star hotels shot up. A world-class precinct emerged over 12 city blocks, which today offers something like six million square feet of retail space. In the 1990s, many Orchard Road complexes were retrofitted and revamped, born again as temples of high fashion and home to the big brands.

Competition reared its high-rise head in the form of Raffles City, a hotel–retail complex on Beach Road. A short walk away, a *Blade Runner-*like warren of malls opened, linked by underground walkways: Marina Square, then Suntec City and Millennium Walk, forming a rival to Orchard Road. Other attractions in the vicinity such as the landmark Raffles hotel shopping arcade and Bugis Junction bolstered the appeal.

Has the onslaught of new pretenders pushed Orchard Road off the shopping map? Far from it. Families flocked to the Marina with enthusiasm, but Orchard Road took on greater luster as the precinct of choice for luxury goods retailers. It has a mystique, like Ginza, which keeps it at the high end of the market. It is a wide street, tree lined, with generous tiled footpaths. Its profile is not high rise, so there's no suggestion of a concrete canyon here.

The buildings are sophisticated in architecture and facilities, such as the giant Ngee Ann City, home of Takashimaya, the largest store in Southeast Asia. They are glamorous, such as Paragon, which houses several luxury brands, and Palais Renaissance, which specializes in beauty and fashion. Forum The Shopping Mall, Wisma Atria, Shaw Centre, and Pacific Place are just a few of the Orchard Road complexes with luxe representation. The area's heart is the junction with Scotts Road, which is the address for the stylish Scotts hotel.

Five-star hotel galleries – hosting international luxury brands – augment the shopping complexes. Fashion powerhouse Club 21 has several brands in the Hilton arcade and Four Seasons.

Just like the city itself, its retail has come a long way – it's now modern, plentiful, attractively laid out, and extremely well run.

FREE-PORT FASHION

Like Hong Kong, Singapore relies on a two-pronged strategy – a hearty tourist trade plus significant local demand.

Right from its founding in 1965, the island republic capitalized on a key asset: its free-port status. At a time when neighboring countries slapped punitive duties on everything from cameras to fashion goods, Singapore became a shopping Mecca, whether it was the trusty Japanese tourist stocking up at lower-than-Tokyo prices or regional labelistas looking to replenish their wardrobes with the latest European attire and accessories. Free-spending Indonesians, in particular, have been a welcome fixture. Even the spendthrift prince of neighboring Brunei did some of his famous bingeing here.

Soon the luxury bug spread to the general public. It was a gentle progression, starting with cosmetics, perfumes, and accessories before moving on to diffusion lines, then the hardcore designer clothing lines.

The 1980s saw the rise and rise of luxury brands. Gucci was an early entrant with a big investment in Orchard Road through its distributor FJ Benjamin. Armani made an impressive debut in 1988: Christina Ong, owner of Club 21 brands, launched the designer with his Emporio diffusion line since the market was relatively unsophisticated. Income and taste levels have evolved to accommodate big names the length of Orchard Road, such as Louis Vuitton, Gucci, Prada, Burberry, Versace, Ferragamo, Paul Smith, Yohji Yamamoto, Calvin Klein, and Dolce & Gabbana. Singapore also has a high number of diffusion line outlets – such as D&G, Versace's Versus, Gaultier Jeans, and Armani Exchange – which are estimated to account for as much as 50 percent of the turnover of brands, a comment on the warm weather-led casual lifestyle.

The 1997 financial crisis was a blow. Tourism dipped. A number of designer outlets closed, including Gigli, Ungaro, Sonia Rykiel, and Valentino. Although Singapore tourism bounced back with a vengeance, the experience underscored for luxury retailers this sector's dependence on the tourist dollar, a point reiterated by the SARS crisis in 2003.

In the meantime the local market has shaped up nicely enough, although per capita luxury spending is never going to be quite as gung-ho as Hong Kong's due to the value-for-money mind-set on the one hand and the perpetual hot-and-humid weather on the other. Just how much that can hurt luxury sales is evident from these research findings from Synovate[2]: While per capita incomes are comparable, the average Hong Kong luxury consumer spends *twice* as much as his or her Singapore counterpart (i.e., US$1,300 compared to US$600 in six months). While 22–24 percent of Hong Kong luxe shoppers plump for expensive brands like Gucci and Louis Vuitton, the comparable number for Singapore is 13–14 percent. At the same time, while only 6 percent of Hong Kong luxe shoppers bother with mid-priced diffusion brands like Polo Ralph Lauren, twice as many Singaporeans go for them.

The warm temperature, and the resulting relaxed dress code, has produced an unexpected winner: local designers. With a deeper understanding of local consumers, homegrown designers are producing a wide variety of alternatives more suited to the climate, their tastes, and, yes, their pockets. The fact that Singaporean names are beginning to pack a punch on the international scene – Jonathan Seow of Woods & Woods is showing in Paris and exporting to Europe; Jo Soh of Hansel sells well in the US and Australia; All Dressed Up by Tina Tan, owner of Link Boutique, is another brand with a big future on international racks – is in turn winning over the domestic consumer.

Another exciting spin-off of the warm weather is the Californian look, which is hot among the young crowd. "The tanned skin, sun-streaked hair, and gold hoop earrings – they love that here," says Kenneth Go, fashion director of *Harper's Bazaar*. The favored uniform among pretty young things is a skimpy top – a tube, camisole, or tank – with a short skirt. The willingness to show skin is unusual in the Asian context, and is certainly not the case in nearby Malaysia or Indonesia, where women sweat it out in modest headscarves. To a large extent, the answer lies in the role models that Singapore's young women look up to as fashion icons: Mischa Barton in *The OC*, Sarah Jessica Parker in *Sex and the City*. There's even an emerging beach cult – typified by Ibiza-style bar KM8 on Sentosa island – which is creating a fetish for jewelry and branded watches to accessorize swimwear. This obsession with the body beautiful has opened up a market for luxury branded swimwear and resort wear.

"It" Bags and Pink Dollars

Singapore has its old money, from rubber, shipping, and trading houses; it has its slightly newer money, from manufacturing, oil trading, banking, and property development; and it has its very new money, fortunes made in property speculation and the expansion of retailing. It is this *new money* that underpins the designer boutiques and supports the upper stratum of local designers.

Then there is the *expatriate community*. This used to be a major force in high-end retailing, but its importance has dwindled as many corporations are appointing local senior staff, and the numbers of expatriate wives with too much time and too much money are reducing.

Young Singaporeans form the next segment. Formidably well educated – many in Commonwealth Anglo countries or the US – and back home in professional jobs earning high salaries, they spend a considerable amount on luxury brands, but here's the thing: They home in on the trimmings, such as handbags, wallets, and belts, but give luxury brand apparel a miss. "They accessorize clothes from BCBG, Mango, or

Zara [relatively inexpensive brands] with a good bag, good shoes," says Kenneth Go. Douglas Benjamin, president of distributor and retailer FJ Benjamin, concurs: "The Singaporean luxe shopper is younger but very savvy – they understand quality which is why they look for things such as leather goods which last."

That they are savvy shoppers plugged into the latest fashion trends is best illustrated by the "it" bag phenomenon. Singaporeans know the Chloé Paddington, Balenciaga Lariat, Mulberry Roxanne – whatever is the reigning "it" bag – and they want it. But a lot of women stop there. Go says: "They just get the bag and nothing else. That's their investment for the season and it says, 'I have achieved, I have arrived, see, this is my bag.'"

The power of the "pink dollar" is also not to be underestimated. The gay population in Singapore is very visible but is more likely to spend on a gym membership and boutique-style holidays. Gay men do invest in good designer bags and shoes – Diesel, Armani Exchange, and DKNY are favorites – but they're more into active wear. Designer suits are down the totem pole, since the weather does not demand formal dressing.

The larger male market is not so developed. The average man – in line with the uniquely Singaporean DNA – prefers to put his money into watches, cars, and property.

MALAYSIA: MONEYED AND DOWN TO EARTH

Kuala Lumpur usually fails to register a blip on the radar of fashion's highfliers. But any outsider who has spent even a short time in the Klang Valley – as the Malaysian capital's conurbation is called – learns there is more to it than meets the eye.

You need to know where to look for the money. The wealthy élite, long the mainstay of luxury brands, are not usually inclined to put their assets on parade – at least not to casual observers. One *mak datin*, the Malaysian version of the tai-tai set, sighed during the 1997 crisis: "Instead of buying five Dior bags at a time, now I have to buy one." But her indiscretion is the exception, seldom the rule.

The restraint has to do with a mix of Islamic modesty and a lingering sense of immigrant frugality among the Chinese and Indians, with an overarching British reticence from colonial days. But money sweeps through the upscale malls and trendy theme restaurants as quietly and swiftly as a stealth bomber.

Brands are lining up to tap the ultra-high-end dollar. Asprey has opened its flagship Asian store, spread over an expansive 4,000 square feet, in the Starhill Gallery, the David Rockwell-designed mall that rivals Hong Kong's Landmark, along Bukit Bintang in the city's so-called Golden Triangle of shopping and entertainment. Audemars Piguet has opened its only global flagship store at the mall, as has Jaeger-LeCoultre. When Mercedes-Benz produced a limited series of ten sedans, five were reportedly sold to Malaysia, for MR3 million (US$800,000) each.

Shopping in this wealthy set is underpinned by a value quaintly called *kam cheng*, a Hokkien term that translates roughly as closeness or kinship. B B Ong, founder of upscale shoe boutique Shuz, which introduced brands like Manolo Blahnik, Guiseppe Zanotti, and Christian Laboutin to Kuala Lumpur, says:

Regular customers tend to put their trust and judgment in familiar sales staff. A sort of understanding and loyalty develops. Sometimes, when a good salesperson goes, clients will follow.

The brand manager of a coveted label says whenever her sales target falls short for a month, she only has to call up a big-spending loyal customer. "She will just ask me, 'How much do you need to make this month?' and spend the difference."

THE MIDDLE CLASS: LOOKING FOR A RETURN ON INVESTMENT

While the upper crust has always shopped for luxury brands, often on trips abroad, with Malaysia's economic ascent – per capita GDP is US$5,000, the highest in the region after Singapore – the luxury passion is fast percolating down to the middle class. The mind-set in this group is similar to that in neighboring Singapore. Alistair Tan, lifestyle editor of *The Star* newspaper, comments:

Malaysians like to get a return on investment. An outfit can be recognized after two outings, but a watch or bag has a long use-by date. Usually, a middle-class customer will save and buy a watch or bag that has durable style.

As a result the accessories market is buoyant – bags, shoes, and especially watches, which deliver both as a social investment and as a financial one – but high-end fashionwear remains a relatively thin wedge of the luxury pie. Factor in the hot weather and Islamic reserve – Singapore's Californian rendition of sun, skin, and skimpy clothes wouldn't fly here – and the case for pricey designer wear remains somewhat limited. Bridge brands do fare well, however – more affordable, more in tune with the casual dress mode – just as they do in Singapore.

Bagging the Tourist Dollar

Malaysia has been extremely successful in growing tourism – the average annual growth rate of tourist arrivals from 1998 to 2004 was a whopping 18.9 percent,[3] the highest by far in the region. But tourist spending on *shopping* hasn't been quite as high as Malaysia would like – the average tourist spends 22 percent of their budget on shopping here, whereas tourists to Singapore or Hong Kong spend 50 percent.[4] So Malaysia is vigorously repositioning itself as a retail paradise, prominently featuring luxury brands as bait in its advertising campaigns. Suria KLCC – the mall at the base of the world's tallest twin towers – Starhill, Avenue K, and the Pavilion (open in 2007) form the platform of Kuala Lumpur's ambitions as a world-class luxe-shopping destination.

Of the 15 million tourists that visit Malaysia annually,[5] the two most promising segments for luxury brands are the Arabs and the Chinese. Post the 9/11 terrorist attack on the World Trade Center in New York, Malaysia has seen a sharp rise in Middle East tourists. Their spending prowess is in a different league: MR6,000 (US$1,500) per head, more than triple the average tourist spending of MR1,800.[6] These high rollers travel with family, and that might include more than one wife, so there's plenty of shopping on the cards. A Starhill boutique owner comments:

Some Arab women shop for the thrill. They don't wear the clothes, but MR4,000 is a steal for them. They give the stuff away.

Malaysia is pulling out all the stops to cater to this loaded segment. Bukit Bintang, Kuala Lumpur's main shopping district, now operates late into the night to suit Middle Eastern habits. Dozens of Arab restaurants have sprung up. The tourism board has even developed "Arab Square," a park with an Arab teapot-like fountain as its main feature.

The new-rich Chinese are a different kettle of fish with their unique scrimp-and-splurge strategy. In Hong Kong, for instance, they spend only 10 percent of their budget on accommodation, but a wholesome 69 percent on shopping.[7] The comparative figures for an American tourist are 45 percent on accommodation and 25 percent on shopping. Malaysia is vigorously promoting itself to the Chinese with package holidays and shopping vouchers.

Watch out Singapore: If things go to plan, the Chinese bonanza could move to Malaysian stores.

THAILAND: A STYLE CAPITAL IN THE MAKING?

Thais are no strangers to luxury. It is second nature to people who revere the royal family, whose patronage of Thai arts and crafts symbolizes their cultural heritage. Appreciation for fine things has matured over generations. A gentle grace is deeply ingrained. With Western engagement that began in the nineteenth century – the country was never colonized – it is no surprise that luxury purveyors have had an élite following in Thailand for generations, including successive queens.

But the ambitions of the style merchants have broadened. Since the Land of Smiles emerged as an economic tiger in the late 1980s, a growing base of new-rich businesspeople and middle-class professionals has enlarged the consumption rate for the likes of Hermès, Louis Vuitton, Prada, and other high-end labels. These new consumers of luxury are admittedly a sharp contrast to Thailand's old money – as against quiet good taste, you get a hearty display of newfound status, not unlike China's. Couple that with an estimated 12 million visitors[8] – tourism is the country's top dollar earner – and the luxury sector has growth potential far beyond its current comfortable niche.

The teeming metropolis of Bangkok has become a Southeast Asian address where every serious luxury brand must have a flagship store.

The world's most prestigious brands have all opened for business at the swank new Siam Paragon, the biggest mall in the region. Dubbed the Pride of Bangkok, the massive 500,000 square meter mall, located in the heart of the city, has sparked a race to upgrade and expand among its posh rivals. The Emporium, for instance, which houses several luxury brands, went for a 500 million baht (US$13 million) makeover, to create a Paris-like ambience. The company behind Gaysorn Plaza – a swish, luxe-studded mall – is contemplating building one more shopping center at the Ratchaprasong intersection, one of Bangkok's prominent shopping districts. This busy area already has the Central department store and Erawan Bangkok retailing luxury brands.

Ironically, it was Thailand's 1997 financial melt-down that led to a strengthening of the luxury brand scene. Before the bubble, most brands were franchised to local operators. The regional crisis hurt them badly – many went under – bringing principal companies in to salvage the prestige and sales of their products. Unlike franchisees, the owners are in the market not for immediate profits but as long-term investors. The big guns committed sizable budgets to push their designer logos. They put up lavish boutiques in prestige malls, with the intention of not just generating sales but also communicating the power and creativity of their brands. They roped in celebrities to promote their products. The fashion glossies, heavily dependent on advertising support, enthusiastically pitched in with editorial coverage. The result: The luxury brand culture spread beyond the "hi-so" – as the high-society crowd is locally referred to – spilling over into the lives of Mr./Ms. Average and even the occasional lo-so.

In the meantime, Thailand has emerged as a major tourist destination and colorful shopping Mecca. For tourist-shoppers Thailand does seem to have it all – they can buy Patpong fakes (for fun), Thai designer attire (affordable and outstanding back home), and luxury branded goods. Brand flagships such as Gucci and Prada are practically tourist destinations themselves. A retail insider estimates that tourists, many of them Japanese, account for 70 percent of business at Louis Vuitton, and about 60 percent at Hermès. "They go to see the Buddha, then they come here," says a sales associate at Gucci in Gaysorn Plaza. Shopping for visitors is sweetened with a 7 percent VAT refund.

The trendy bar and restaurant circuit – nothing whatsoever to do with the seedy nightclub stereotype – has added an element of chic and creativity to the nightlife. The restaurant and nightclub Bed, for example, is a never-ending expanse of mattresses and pillows, everything in crisp white linen, where you lie down and enjoy a top-class meal with friends. The Met Bar, Sirocco, Eat Me, and Koi are all buzzing, drawing weekenders from as far as Kuala Lumpur, Singapore, and Hong Kong, weary of their own jaded scene. Typically, these stylish eateries are the brainchild of hi-so youngsters, mostly foreign educated, bringing home a Western design aesthetic and marrying it – quite successfully we might add – to the local one. No doubt, Bangkok's vibrant gay scene has helped this high-end design revolution.

If this city of 7 million people is not hip central for the region yet, it's not for lack of effort on the part of the Thai government. It is pumping at least US$40 million into the Bangkok Fashion City project to outgun Singapore and Sydney as the fashion capital of Australasia. The project has involved a series of fashion shows in Bangkok promoting a promising crop of local designers, and a road show taking Thai garments and jewelry around Asian and European capitals before winding up in the US. With so many factors working for it, it is only a matter of time before Bangkok matures into a style capital for the region.

INDONESIA: BLING-BLING OPULENCE

Indonesia is a mass of contradictions. A country of 3,000 islands, it swings between extremes as far flung as its archipelago. The faithful crowd into mosques for Friday prayers, but the men's clubs are busy every night. Religious campaigners lobby for Islamic law, yet alcohol is there for the asking. The malls feature the latest fashions for Muslims – colorful headscarves and designer tunics – but also blare out Christmas tunes to the masses nonstop throughout December. Many in the world's fourth-largest nation (population 245 million, mainly Muslim) are still mired in poverty – per capita income US$1,000 – yet its wealthy élite boasts homes the size of boutique hotels that host fleets of cars. The visitor leaves with an unanswered question: Are there really two Indonesias?

The luxury market targets the 1 percent of the population known locally as *orang kaya baru* (OKB), literally "new rich people." The equivalents of Japan's office ladies and the middle classes of Seoul and Taipei, who help to drive luxury consumption, are unknown here.

OKB are concentrated mainly in the capital Jakarta – with subcenters in upcoming Surabaya and Bandung – and are a motley mix of industry executives, top military brass, young entrepreneurs, entertainment stars, small-time politicians who've suddenly made it big, and children of the old rich who've found new and interesting things to do with Daddy's money. They are a clearly defined species in designer clothes as they cruise effortlessly through Jakarta in steel-and-chrome chariots: Maseratis, Ferraris, and Mercedes, which are often created exclusively for this demanding market. They hold executive memberships at prestigious clubs and live in mansions that come from the pages of glossy magazines.

Privileged or poor, one unique Indonesian practice is a great social leveler: *arisan*, a custom in which money pooled monthly by a group of friends can be won in a lottery. More importantly, it's about networking. A 23-year-old socialite, recently returned from abroad, comments:

I think that's how the ladies stay in touch. Somebody shows off what she has bought, talks about where to buy it, the latest discounts, and so on. It's pretty harmless.

Some luxe goods distributors even use the system to promote their brands. A fashion retailer explains:

We bring our products to the arisan, *and educate them about the brand. It's a subtle and effective way of marketing.*

Top-end consumers are split into the *ibu-ibu* – the Indonesian version of the Hong Kong tai-tais – and the affluent young things home from an expensive education in the US, the UK, or Australia, who lead a lifestyle empowered by near-bottomless lucre from their parents. There are three must-haves for every young debutante, according to one beautiful actress:

She must have diamond stud earrings no less than one carat of the highest clarity, Gucci or Louis Vuitton logo bag, and a Rolex watch. We know our stuff, and must be first to have something. It's like a race!

Their mothers, the *ibu-ibu* set, are wives of mega-rich businessmen or top government officials, who faithfully stick to the ladies-who-lunch routine. They are seen at their best at all times. Chauffeured from one place to the next, they never *walk* unless it's inside upscale malls such as Plaza Indonesia or Plaza Senayan, housing designer-brand boutiques. They spare no expense on the upkeep of their looks, but every high-maintenance *ibu-ibu* looks as though she comes from the same designer cookie cutter: same hairdo, same makeup, and same dress code. A designer bag, usually Louis Vuitton, is obligatory.

Indonesian men haven't evolved into fashion-conscious metro-sexuals yet and prefer to spend their money on boys' toys – but what toys! High-end mobile phones, costing upward of US$700, are familiar favorites, and some models are created specially for this discerning market. Luxury car sellers have a similar happy tale to tell. Handmade imported shoes and limited-edition watches are garden-variety embell-ishments for the seriously rich.

The downside of all this zest for life is a total lack of any trendsetting spirit or originality. It's a bland sameness that shouts even from the bill-boards and television commercials that feature models from an assem-bly line of the same hair, makeup, and pose. The girl who sells Lux soap looks like the girl flogging Pond's cleanser and like the girl hyping Nokia phones. "It's a look Indonesians like, and it sells," notes a talent agency operator.

They may not be on fashion's constantly moving edge, but that does not hold back the Indonesian passion for overseas shopping. Singapore is a casual fling and Hong Kong is a familiar stomping ground, but a serious binge entails a business-class swoop on New York, London, or Paris for the world-class jet-setter. As a result, Singapore is the bench-mark that the luxury retailers in Jakarta hold themselves against. Kiki Moran, vice-president of leading fashion brand distributor PT Mahagaya Menara, explains:

Prices are controlled not more than 10 percent higher than Singapore. We also have to watch out for "sale" periods in Singapore. All brands have to be up to date, to compete with overseas markets. Customers can walk in with maga-zine pages asking for the product, and if we don't have it, they go elsewhere.

With all the frantic spending, there must be reasons for dressing up. Besides travel – boutiques thoughtfully stock the winter collections for these world travelers – fashionistas can count on a busy social calendar that regularly requires diamonds and gowns. There are also plenty of new bars, restaurants, boutiques, and galleries – like in Thailand, these are operated by young moneyed entrepreneurs who prefer the glamorous hospitality business to the boring family firm – offering welcome venues to put their latest luxe acquisitions in full sight of their peers.

PHILIPPINES: MALLING CULTURE

The Philippines can rightly claim to be the Asian country with the most Westernized taste, after nearly 500 years of colonial rule under the Spanish and the Americans. The upper class of *mestizos*, Spanish and native Filipinos who consider themselves Western, and the expanding middle class were just as comfortable with the milieu of European luxury. Decades of erratic governance, however – not to mention political turmoil and endemic corruption – have contributed to a huge wealth gap, not unlike Indonesia's. The per capita GDP of this predominantly Catholic nation of 89 million people is US$1,000.

But setbacks have not dampened the Filipino appetite for life. Shopping – or "malling" as it is known here – is the national sport. "Rich or poor, the people in Manila like to shop," says Allan Chan, creative partner of Salabianca, a Malaysian-based fashion chain with Filipino outlets. It's a social activity that calls for dressing up among people imbued with European manners.

Nevertheless, luxury brand shopping is a relatively exclusive sport, with the Greenbelt, Ayala Center's ritzy mall, serving as the city's luxe nerve center. It's supported by two levels of consumers: the rich rich (old and new) who, with their European pretensions, would never be caught dead without logos, and a broader group of more modest means and formative tastes who keep the cash registers going at luxury accessory stores such as Tod's and Kate Spade in Manila.

The couture crowd demands exclusivity for the bucks they pay, since no high-born Filipina wants to be seen on the busy social circuit as a body double for another party diva. That's one reason Filipino designers, who can produce limited editions and one-offs, continue to thrive. Wealthy sophisticates create their own exclusivity – they jet off to nearby Singapore, Hong Kong, or even New York to renew their wardrobes with pieces not available in Manila stores.

With their love for malling, fondness for dressing up, and high degree of Westernization, Filipinos are natural consumers for designer brands. Yet the luxury market remains a niche phenomenon – "people power" may have arrived a couple of decades ago, but economic power for the mass of the population is still to come. In the meantime, luxury shopping remains largely in the hands of the Imeldas.

LESSONS FROM THE SINGLE-SEASON SISTERS

A mixed bunch they may be, but there are important lessons from these warm-weather markets, especially applicable to India where half the country (including key cities like Mumbai, Bangalore, and Chennai) lives in perpetual summer.

Create Special Lines for Warm-Weather Countries

So far all the developed markets – Europe, the US, Japan, Hong Kong – have fallen neatly into the four-season mold. Ditto for the emerging "big prizes" of China and South Korea. Singapore is an affluent city, but its tiny population isn't enough to prod luxury brands into major reengineering. Result: Luxury brands have not figured how to cater to, and fully exploit, the opportunity that single-season markets present.

With the economic emergence of Southeast Asia, the impending rise of the other big prize, India, and indeed the growing clout of the Middle East shopper, building significant single-season expertise is going to be increasingly profitable. Specially designed collections that provide a full-blooded warm-weather fall/winter collection are a necessary first step, as is addressing the climate-dictated casual dress code. Fabrics that can tackle heat and humidity, clothes that can be washed thoroughly (dry cleaning doesn't do justice to sweat-drenched armpits), staying cool while modestly dressed (Hermès *hijabs*, anyone?) – these are all areas deserving greater attention.

The roaring success of Dubai as a luxury-shopping destination is a handy lesson in how Islamic restraint and unabashed enthusiasm for luxe can happily coexist in a custom-designed *abaya*, hot weather notwithstanding. Dubai is putting up massive malls at a breakneck pace – the region already has 4.65 million square meters of retail space and another 2.5 million are under construction[9] – and every luxury brand of stature is here. Upscale retailers like Saks Fifth Avenue and Harvey Nichols have dropped anchor early in the game, and Dubai has given rise to local luxury retailers like Villa Moda, who are now expanding into other countries. The local consumer is lapping it up, demonstrating that it is entirely possible to sizzle with the latest fashion under wraps, to be revealed in women-only settings – designer jeans and figure-hugging tops are everyday wear, while special occasions like wedding parties call for designer gowns. The veil is no threat, just another accessory in the hands of a determined fashionista. Accessories take on a heightened role, having to do all the talking in public places. Designer handbags are a must-have and women go out of their way to adorn their hands with high-end jewelry from the likes of Cartier and Chopard.

Add Hospitality to Your Service Mix

Along with warm weather, it seems, comes warm hospitality. While excellent service in the luxury business is a given, Southeast Asian cultures bring home the importance of an added dimension: hospitality in service. In Singapore, for example, everyone knows everyone – six degrees of separation are far too many – and fashionable women are personal friends with boutique owners and distributors of fashion lines. In Jakarta, as also in Kuala Lumpur, social gatherings are a popular way to shop because customers enjoy the camaraderie and assurance of buying among friends. As luxury brands grow and stores multiply, channeling this warmth and hospitality into formal staff training is essential.

Besides being a growing opportunity in themselves, the single-season sisters are an excellent practice ground for a vast emerging market, India.

Bollywood top star and former Miss World, Aishwarya Rai served on the Cannes Film Festival jury. Chopard took the opportunity to promote the brand to Indians by decking out Ms. Rai in its jewelry.

Photo courtesy of Chopard.

8

INDIA:
THE NEXT CHINA?

"The potential is massive in India... we will develop a new generation of customers in India, people who are very aware of what's happening in the rest of the world."

Yves Carcelle, Chairman LVMH[1]

In his Paris office, Carcelle keeps a photo of Shanghai's Nanjing Road, chockablock with bicycles in 1992 when Louis Vuitton opened its first store there.[2] Today, the street is packed with international cars and world-class buildings have sprung up on either side, including the posh Plaza 66 that houses Vuitton's expansive global store.

The heightened interest in India today is because of the unprecedented success of luxury brands in China. A decade ago China hardly looked like the place for brands – today the Chinese consumer is the darling of the luxe world, and the companies that have prospered most are the ones that braved it in early, like Vuitton. The magic more than 8 percent economic growth rate and the emergence of a moneyed class did the trick. Now India's economy is tearing ahead, posting similar growth rates, and a new splurging class is making its presence felt, snapping up cars, mobile phones, and home appliances. India looks a lot like China did a decade ago, and no luxury brand wants to miss the chance of getting in on the ground floor. Xavier Bertrand, head of Chanel in India, says:

We were successful in China in a short time. India is also an emerging market and we wanted to be among the first to start here.[3]

While India's luxury market is still small, an estimated US$100 million at best, this India-is-the-next-China logic has been driving a steady pilgrimage of industry top brass, who come as much to pay their respects and make a media splash as to size up the market and firm up business plans:

* Carcelle was one of the first to send in a team in 1999, linking up with Tikka Shatrujit Singh, great grandson of the Maharaja of Kapurthala, who helped smooth the way for Vuitton's first store in New Delhi's tony Oberoi hotel in 2003. (The Maharaja incidentally was a prized personal customer of *Louis Vuitton* himself, who made 50 trunks for him in the 1890s.)
* Chanel's chief, Françoise Montenay, visited several times to understand the "unique social and cultural aspects" of India, before finally dropping anchor in 2005 with an ultra-chic full-range store in New Delhi's exquisite Imperial hotel.
* Valentino dazzled Mumbai's high society with a fashion show staged on the steps of the historic Asiatic Society building.
* Donatella Versace went a step further – she played judge on a television fashion reality show, taking the winner back to Italy to do an internship with her. In the process, her blonde mane was plastered all over the media, and she was fêted enthusiastically by India's upper crust.
* Giorgio Armani dressed up Bollywood diva Aishwarya Rai for the London premiere of *Bride and Prejudice*, generating reams of press back home in India.

In a near-virgin market, the rewards are almost instant – research conducted by the Federation of Indian Chambers of Commerce and Industry found that Louis Vuitton was the most prestigious accessory brand, while Armani topped the charts in the apparel category, followed by Versace and Valentino.[4] After all, you can't admire brands you don't know about.

Vijay Murjani, the man partnering Gucci and Jimmy Choo in India, comments:

Interest in India is just amazing. Every single week I have people here from abroad, from some of the biggest brands, just trying to get a handle on this market.[5]

As a sign of the times, the World Luxury Council has opened an Indian operation. Devyani Raman, the woman who spearheaded its launch, says that India is the most desirable market for international luxury brands today. She should know – she has gone on to launch Leading Brands of the World, a company that aims to help luxury brands make a soft landing in India.

In terms of our Spread of Luxury model, India is squarely at the *start of money* stage – the emerging middle class is upping its quality of life, making its first foray into washing machines and air-conditioners, while a small élite segment indulges in luxury brands. The twist in India is that they have been shopping abroad for decades. This brand-savvy élite are no doubt the first customers of luxury brands in India, but eventually they will be a sideshow compared to the extravaganza India's feisty economic growth is producing. A second movement of luxury, the kind that we saw in Japan, China, and South Korea, is taking shape in parallel, a movement based on the hearty creation of new money and the inevitable democratization of luxury, which is putting designer handbags and Rolex watches into the grasp of a wider band of consumers. If the old money élite was a gently gurgling, remote mountain stream, what is emerging is an imminent tidal wave.

While India may be the next China in terms of eventual market size, the forces shaping its development are quite different. If China's starting point was a slate wiped clean by Mao, India's is a chalkboard covered with myriad traditions, religious beliefs, colorful festivals, a there-but-not-there caste system – all sewn together into a vocal democracy.

* Everyone was uniformly poor in China; in India a feudal aristocracy has always coexisted alongside extreme poverty.
* Private enterprise was snuffed out in China; India's socialist route allowed industrialist families to flourish alongside state-owned enterprises, creating a sizable vault of old money with suitably refined tastes.
* Education was almost eradicated for a generation or two in China; Indians have always placed the highest value on education, putting scholars at the top of the caste system. Even today, India's economic resurgence is linked to knowledge-based industries, creating a segment of "educated new money" that behaves differently from China's garment-and-toy-manufacturing new money.

✳ Religion was blanked out in China; spirituality remains the core of India. Hinduism, Islam, Christianity, and a multitude of other religions have a following here, leading to a potpourri of festivals, customs, and dress.

If the task in China was to fill a near vacuum, in India luxury brands have to find a way to blend in with the milieu of local traditions. China abandoned the Mao suit in a hurry, switching hook, line, and sinker to a Western dress code, making the country a natural fit for Western luxury brands. While Indians too are moving toward Western clothing, they continue to wear ethnic outfits proudly. Celebratory occasions, in particular, have an Indian dress code. A Chinese bride dreams of a Vera Wang gown and Cartier jewelry; an Indian bride does not dream of parting with her traditional finery – although she happily packs her trousseau in Louis Vuitton trunks, custom built if Daddy is loaded.

To this complex scenario add a Noah's ark full of biosocial diversity. Think of it as an *n*-dimensional matrix defined by a range of not only religions and castes, but also regions, languages, skin tones, physical builds, and, most importantly, value systems. For example, the Louis Vuitton store in Delhi has been successful from day one, even building up three-month-long waiting lists for hot items, whereas the business in its Mumbai store has been much slower. Shobha De, celebrity author and piquant society observer, attributes it to Delhi's "cash combined with flash" mentality:

There's a basic identity crisis there – you have to prove you have money to be someone. In Mumbai you have to prove talent, brains, something other than money. You'll never find a Ratan Tata or a Shapoorji Pallonji, or even an Anil Ambani or Kumaramangalam Birla going to LV and shopping there.[6] *[All captains of industry and, except Tata, Forbes billionaires.]*

As for the stunningly beautiful Ms. De, which brands does she use? Eyes sparkling, she shoots back:

I would never let a brand define who I am. I will define who I am. I consciously avoid brands, and always have. I don't wear Indian designers for that matter. I am snobbish in the other way – I would never be caught dead with a brand.

We said a quick prayer for Messrs Vuitton *et al*.

From reverse snobbery to cash and flash, from Bollywood glamour to a gung-ho middle class, in this chapter we dissect the many contradictory faces of India and what it will take for luxury brands to succeed here. India is in the midst of a social revolution, a massive silent earthquake that is altering the lay of the land, putting money in new hands, changing once-rigid social structures, rewriting old value systems. The ideal setting for luxury brands to enter and do what they do best – help redefine identities.

INDIA SHINING

"India Shining" sums up the dichotomy of India. It was the campaign slogan of the ruling Bharatiya Janata Party in the 2004 election, a confident report card of the nation's proud economic strides under its stewardship. A booming economy, a stock market on the up and up, an IT sector that was making waves abroad, a burgeoning middle class, rising living standards – instead of the usual litany of broken promises, this government had solid achievements to talk about. And yet it lost the election with a resounding thump. It didn't do its math right. India shone brightly enough for the top quarter of the population, but the masses of the poor remained just as miserable as before, and they voted with their feet.

There's no denying that India is predominantly a poor country – its per capita GDP is around US$700 – but more of its people are making more money than ever before. In 1995, at the beginning of liberalization, 4.5 million households were classified as middle class, falling within the broad income band of Rs.200,000 to Rs.1 million (US$4,700 to US$23,300), according to SK Dwivedi of the National Council of Applied Economic Research.[7] A decade later that number had almost quadrupled to 17.3 million households, which translates into 90 million individuals, dubbed the "great Indian middle class." In that same decade, the number of upper-income households (annual income over Rs.1 million) grew sixfold to 1.7 million.[8]

At the top end, the number of high net worth individuals with over US$1 million in financial assets went from 50,000 in 2002 to 83,000 in

2004.[9] And there was some serious money added in the billionaires club – in 2004, India had nine billionaires on the Forbes List, collectively worth US$31.9 billion; by 2006, there were 23 billionaires with a combined booty of US$98.8 billion.[10]

As is to be expected, this economic upsurge has transformed the social landscape, creating distinct consumer segments with widely differing mind-sets. We take a closer look at four key groups that luxury brands could target: India's old-money industrial dynasties for whom luxury is a way of life anyway; the new-money entrepreneurs who are raring to show it off; the gold collars of the corporate world, who earn substantial salaries but show shades of the frugal Gandhian mind-set; and the BPO generation, young and fresh, for whom making money and spending it is the new religion.

Old Money: Industrial Dynasties

This segment was always there – industrial families of long standing, some tracing their business roots to pre-independence days, passing the mantle from one generation to another. What changed in the post-liberalization era is that the contorted caste-combined-with-socialism logic of "making money is bad" evaporated. These families got the respect they deserved, or as Gurcharan Das puts it, "they finally became old money."[11]

Tata, Birla, Godrej, Bajaj, Thapar, Mahindra – these are some of the prominent dynasties. Their businesses span every major industry from steel to automobiles, telecommunications to consumer products. Many are widely diversified conglomerates, with different members of a joint family heading parts of the business. Despite the squabbling siblings that make the headlines, ties among business families are still strong, the glue provided by a respected head, who deals with a very even hand. Quaintly enough, the fairness extends to luxury brand purchases. We heard of instances where the matriarch orders five identical pieces of the season's latest handbag: two for her daughters-in-law, two for her daughters, and one for herself.

The current generation of old money are a sophisticated lot. They've been schooled at Harvard and Wharton, Cambridge and London Business School. Their business interests take them all over the world.

They speak faultless English; they are equally fluent in Hindi and their native tongues. They do wine and cheese; they do samosas and *chai*. They wear Zegna suits and John Lobb shoes; they also wear *kurta* pajamas and *kolhapuris*. They are as much citizens of the world as they are Indian. Naturally, they're brand savvy; they have been shopping in London and New York for years.

Take Anuradha Mahindra – wife of Anand Mahindra, head of automobile company Mahindra & Mahindra – who runs fashion and lifestyle magazine *Verve*.[12] She's a beautiful woman, with twinkling eyes and a warm smile, the picture of elegance. What brands does she like? She wears Ralph Lauren and Donna Karan for "everyday kind of thing." She's fond of Chanel, Vuitton, Prada. For leather goods, she's partial to the Italians – Bottega Veneta seems to be a weakness. She favors classic brands – "I'm more a classic person." She admits "going in for the odd trendy accessory," and points ruefully at the Balenciaga "it" bag that her daughter made her buy – "I'll pass it on to her next month." She's planning an accessories museum at the Verve office, to feature items from her personal collection. "My husband says what are you going to do with all this – I have stuff which is 25 years old, almost like vintage."

In terms of a sophistication index, Anuradha is several notches higher than most other luxe consumers we interviewed across Asia – and we don't mean her choice of brands, but the way she carries herself. That's what adds to the challenge of luxury brands entering India.

India may be an emerging market, but the existing luxe consumer base is among the most knowledgeable in the world. Prasanna Bhaskar, former retail manager of Louis Vuitton in India, says that certain customers are so well versed in the latest happenings in the fashion world that they will reserve a product two or three months *before* it comes out.[13]

While this segment will form the backbone of the market in the initial years, their numbers are not enough to support ongoing growth. Luxury brands need to spread their net far wider for that.

New Money: Many Faces of Entrepreneurship

With liberalization and the gradual dismantling of the license raj – the need to get government licenses or approvals for business projects – India's entrepreneurial spirit has got a second lease of life, producing an eclectic bunch of new businesses and an equally eclectic bunch of the newly prosperous. They are prime targets for luxury brands, but unlike the industrial dynasties, this segment is new to luxe.

The first Forbes India's 40 Richest list confirms that new money is the order of the day – 19 people on the list are self-made.[14] Technology and pharmaceuticals, relatively new industries, have been money spinners – 11 people made their fortune in technology, 9 owe it to pharmaceuticals. Many are highly educated entrepreneur-professionals, and while their money may be new, it doesn't necessarily strut and preen. In fact, several tech entrepreneurs are based in South India, a region known for its "simple living, high thinking" philosophy. Infosys's legendary NR Narayana Murthy is a tech billionaire, but insists on traveling economy class.

Switch tracks to the newly rich farmers from the north, from Punjab and Haryana, and you have a case of "high living, limited thinking" at work. No surprise, then, that the highest number of luxury cars is not in Mumbai or Delhi, but in the Punjab town of Ludhiana. Reminiscent of those businessmen from China's industrial northeast, these farmers are trooping into Delhi, cash in hand, in a hurry to splash it.

Rural India is turning out some unlikely luxury takers. Ashish Chordia – who runs the uber-cool multibrand store Thanks in Mumbai, featuring brands such as Fendi, Dolce & Gabbana, Stella McCartney, and Paper Denim & Cloth – is surprised by the flow of small-town buyers. One of his early customers was a 60-year-old man who had driven all the way to Mumbai on the strength of a newspaper article about the store's opening. He had never heard of any of the brands, but was thrilled to try these new wonders. "He shopped a brand like Dolce & Gabbana," says Ashish with surprise. Another pair of men walked in asking what was the most special thing in the store, and left with two Fendi spy bags, each costing US$4,000. Ashish comments:

When you see them you won't believe that they'll buy the spy bag because they are not dressed according to that. They didn't know what a spy bag was.[15]

Whether in small towns or big towns, the fact that new money is not necessarily sophisticated looking is reiterated by Kamal Bharucha, who runs the Mont Blanc store at the Taj in Mumbai:

The kind who buy don't look like they can afford it. They're not Page 3 peo-ple. They are not the society sorts. Many of them don't speak English.[16]

Mont Blanc has made an effort to make the store environment approachable – for example, the sales staff are purposely not in suits that might intimidate this "very local consumer." Clearly the strategy is working – the store is abuzz with customers.

In Delhi society showing off has always been the rule, and now with entrepreneurial zeal at full throttle the showing off has taken a turn for the luxe. Ruchika Mehta, who edits lifestyle supplement *Rouge* for the *Times of India*, says if you walk into a high-end party, "there is so much display of designer wear that it is dazzling." You see Louis Vuitton bags and shoes, D&G jeans, Versace jeans, Chanel tops, and Prada, which is "a big favorite with all the women here."[17]

Zainab Nedou, formerly with the World Luxury Council, concurs – in Delhi, it's the "bling factor" that counts. "Louis Vuitton has become like Surf [a common brand of detergent in India]; everyone has it," she says, referring to the top band of society.[18]

From down-to-earth Punjabi farmers to Bangalore's high-tech entre-preneurs, from Maharashtra's rural businessmen to the razzle-dazzle of Delhi society – luxury brands will have to tune in to the many nuances of India's new money to be able to dance to it successfully.

Gold Collars: Trapped in Between

Their fathers worked at government jobs, on relatively low salaries, leading frugal lives, glorifying Gandhian simplicity. They had the best Indian education at the IITs and IIMs (India's famed institutes of tech-nology and management) – you'd be surprised how little a world-class education costs in India. They joined the corporate world, rising up the ranks, occupying senior to middle management positions. Like every-thing else, salaries have multiplied in the last decade, and they take home a sizable income plus plenty of perks – top jobs pay over US$1 million. These are India's "gold-collar" workers.

Drawn from the 35–55 age group, this is a paradoxical group that has the money but not the mind-set to spend on luxury brands. They live in upscale, company-provided homes with the best addresses in town. They are chauffeured around in top-end, company-provided cars. They travel abroad on business, often flying first class. They live the luxury lifestyle, with one important difference: They are loath to spend money on "indulgences," suddenly hit with the previous generation's Gandhian qualms. They send their children to prestigious local schools, and when the time comes they will enter US/UK colleges – *that's* money well invested – but they won't buy a US$1,000 suit. They take their families on vacation abroad – *that's* OK, that's for the family – but their wives won't buy a Louis Vuitton bag. They speculate on the stock market, they invest in the rising property market – *that's* smart, making money grow – but they tut-tut at the thought of spending US$400 on a pair of Prada shoes. People earning a fraction of what they do in Hong Kong or Shanghai would have a wardrobe chock-full of luxury brands.

So how does luxe unlock this segment? At two levels. First, it's about *creating* the cult of the luxury brand in a way that touches their lives. As things stand they don't need luxe to define who they are – where they work, where they live, where their kids study, and where they holiday are already doing an excellent job of marking status. Luxury brands are so new in India, there hasn't yet been the necessary time and the critical mass of users for them to become the norm, so smart marketing is key. Secondly, it's about playing to their mind-set. They may not buy a US$1,000 suit but they can be persuaded to buy a US$10,000 watch. They may not buy a Louis Vuitton executive bag for personal use, but they could be persuaded to buy a classic LV bag as an anniversary gift for their wives. As long as it can be classified as an investment – whether financial, emotional, or social – not an expense, you pull them in. And once they start down the luxury brand path, there's no turning back.

BPO Generation: Spending Mind-Set, Growing Affluence

Call them liberalization's children. Bereft of all the accumulated money-related baggage of earlier generations, for India's youth *money* is the new religion. These 19–29 year olds form the core of employees in India's burgeoning business process outsourcing industry. The lowest-level jobs are in call centers – all they require is a reasonable command of English (which comes easily enough after 12 years of schooling in that language) and a willingness to work at odd hours fielding calls from the US or Europe. These are footloose youngsters, ensconced comfortably in their parents' home, ferried back and forth from the call centers, even fed dinner there. With no living or working expenses, they spend their entire salary – typically US$4,000 a year – on themselves. Snazzy mobile phones, trendy clothes, sports shoes, iPods, movies, cafés, discos, pubs – they live it up, incessant nibblers.

Go up the ladder to jobs needing higher qualifications, paying higher salaries – programmers, software engineers, accountants, lawyers, doctors. The demand is so high that even fresh graduates are being hired off campus with salary offers of Rs.3.5–7 lakhs (US$8,000–16,000).[19] Salaries for MBAs have skyrocketed, with the cream of the crop being offered salaries in the US$75,000 range by Indian companies, while those hired by multinationals get twice that.[20] (Top salaries for MBA campus placements cross US$200,000.) That's several times more than what their fathers earn. It's making cash registers ring in cities across India, and it's not just mobile phones and other cool doodads, it's also 42-inch flat-screen televisions, cars, and apartments, helped along with handy credit-financing schemes.

Big money within arm's length is firing the dreams of a whole generation of youngsters. Fed on a staple diet of Bollywood movies and television shows, they have vicariously acquired a global mind-set, a desire to be just as hip and trendy as their Western counterparts, a desperate urgency to catch up. They're hungry for the same good life, the latest gizmos, and fashionable clothes, and they're very willing to slog their butts off to get it.

Alex Kuruvilla, former head of MTV India and now leading Condé Nast's entry to the country, gives the example of two college girls he met in a small town in the state of Kerala. Their single-minded ambition is to get to Bangalore and land a job in Infosys or Wipro, and to that end they are both learning programming. (Infosys has become the techie's Mecca – it gets 1.4 million applications annually; fewer than 2 percent of those applying are offered a job.) Forget marriage, forget making a home, forget starting a family – the traditional dream of Indian girls; instead there's a feverish desire to break free from the shackles of frugal living. "These two would be the poster girls of the BPO generation," says Kuruvilla.[21]

With the economy booming on several fronts, avenues for young people to make money have multiplied. Malls are springing up all over the country. New hotels are being added. New airlines have started up and existing ones have expanded. The telecommunications industry is on fire. Media is exploding. The consumer banking sector is expanding, and relatively untapped areas such as credit cards, housing loans, auto finance, mutual funds, and investments are being marketed with a vengeance. Lifestyle-related industries are taking off – yoga, fitness, beauty, grooming, fashion, clubbing, interior design, even wedding stylists are suddenly in demand. Everywhere the theme is modernity and greater professionalism. This surge in a broad swathe of service industries is creating a requirement for fresh blood and bright minds. The natural corollary is new money in young hands.

Can the luxury industry seriously target this young segment – brands on the arms of babes? The closest parallel is the parasite singles phenomenon in Japan, but the opportunity in India is potentially bigger. There are some 200 million Indians in the 20–30 age group today, and with a heavy-bottomed population pyramid there's an ever-increasing supply of people crossing into their 20s. (For example, the 15–19 segment is 110 million strong.) These young professionals' aggressive "study hard, work hard" mind-set will take them places. Even the call-center youngsters see the job as a stepping-stone, a short money-making binge; most return to college for higher education and progress into higher-paying jobs.

This generation is already showing a propensity to spend on premium goods, at least what's available locally. Murjani, whose Tommy Hilfiger brand has done extremely well in India, comments:

These kids are going out and buying the Rs.5,000 Nike shoes and designer watches. Salaries are going up in a dramatic way and that's where the consumer is coming from. Will they want luxury? Absolutely, like everywhere else in the world, they are going to want these brands. It's a matter of trading up and how quickly they trade up… going from a local brand to a brand like Tommy, to Calvin Klein, to Coach, to Gucci.

That luxury brands can tap into this broad segment is proved by the success of De Beers. India is traditionally a bastion of gold, the biggest market in the world. De Beers' marketing campaign aimed squarely at the young, making diamonds what young people gift. The results have been remarkable: Not only has gold been repositioned as old hat for "auntyjis and mummyjis," but De Beers' Indian brand Nakshatra grew to a Rs.100 crore (US$23 million) business within five years of launch.[22]

Kamal of Mont Blanc finds her base of customers is getting younger. She tells the story of a young salesgirl in the Taj hotel cake shop – down the row from the Mont Blanc store – who had her heart set on a pen as a gift for her boyfriend. She saved for a few months and walked off triumphantly with her trophy. "She didn't ask for a discount," recalls Kamal. Mahindra of *Verve* confirms there are lots of "young aspiring people":

Even a 25-year-old graduate might save up and if there's a spring/summer bag in a particular shade that's in she'll get that, and then she may not buy anything for six months.

Zainab says young working women will eat "*dal chawal* [a basic meal of rice and lentils] for three days" after a luxury purchase. These statements echo the luxury nibbler mindset found elsewhere in Asia.

The BPO generation has the spending mind-set and will grow into gold collars in a decade or so – luxury brands would be wise to start engaging them from the start and groom them into full-fledged luxe users over time.

RETAIL SPACE: SCARCITY AMONG PLENTY

Ask anyone in the luxury industry what the number one problem is, and they tell you with feeling: the lack of retail space. Ironically, it's a case of "water, water, everywhere, but not a drop to drink." India is in the midst of full-blown mall mania – 96 new malls have already sprung up, and by 2007 there will be 358 malls with 87.8 million square feet of retail space[23] – but none of the malls so far has the necessary class and quality for luxe retailing. India's traditional shopping districts don't offer much hope either, defined as they are by utter chaos and appalling hygiene.

The answer for the moment is the tried-and-tested five-star hotel – the Taj, the Oberoi, the Imperial, the Sheraton – borrowing their prestige, catering to their well-established and well-heeled client base. But unlike China's Palace, Hong Kong's Peninsula, or even Taipei's Regent, few Indian five-star hotels have a large enough tranche of retail space to house 15–20 luxury brands in comfort. (An opportunity waiting to be tapped!) The result is extreme fragmentation – in New Delhi, for instance, Louis Vuitton, Hugo Boss, and Bulgari are at the Oberoi hotel; Chanel sits in solitary splendor at the Imperial; Aigner, Mont Blanc, and the multibrand watch store Regent are at the Maurya Sheraton.

Mumbai fares somewhat better thanks to the Taj Mahal hotel's ingenious efforts to create luxury retail space. A beautiful colonial heritage building, the Taj shuffled around its cake shop and beauty salon to make room for a stunning street-side, sea-facing Louis Vuitton store in 2004. Alongside are Mont Blanc, Canali, Gerard Perregaux, and an assortment of prestigious Indian retailers who have been there for decades. The Taj then converted ground-floor senior executive offices – some occupied by the likes of the legendary JRD Tata himself – thereby accommodating Burberry, Fendi, and Moschino, but many more brands are knocking on the door. "There's more demand than we have space," says Shirin Batliwala, the woman managing Taj's retail portfolio. Big brands are asking for lobby presence, wanting to take up the bell desk, the reception counters, even suggesting the hotel closes down some of its popular restaurants. Shirin gives a weak laugh: "We *are* in the hotel business!"[24]

The Grand Hyatt, which opened in 2004 in North Mumbai – a 90-minute drive from the Taj – built a substantial luxe shopping arcade as an integral part of the hotel. But repeated delays and changes in its retail space allocation – for example, its anchor department store Vama cut its presence from two floors to one – has translated into a slow start and a tenant mix that doesn't quite come together. It lacks top-tier brands so far, but houses the likes of Aigner, Hugo Boss, Bally (which counts Bollywood megastar Amitabh Bachchan as one of its clients), Charriol, Lalique, and a multibrand watch store, alongside a smattering of Indian retailers.

Other brands are dotted in lonely dribs and drabs all over Mumbai. Tiffany, Chopard, and Hugo Boss are at the Oberoi hotel and Zegna is at Crossroads, a distinctly middle-class mall that is damaging the company's stature. When we visited the small store, tucked away in a rabbit warren of random retail outlets, it was having a sale, giving a 30 percent discount on last season's merchandise, but what was shocking was its sloppy get-up – for example, shirts in plastic bags were strewn on the floor, being unpacked for display. Omega and Swarovski have street-facing stores at CR2, a mall with a haphazard mix of premium brands. Daks sits at the other end of town in InOrbit Mall, rated as India's best mall. The Courtyard is quaint and classy with two rows of Indian designer stores, but not a single customer in sight when we visited. Phoenix High Street features Indian designer Ritu Kumar – a lovely store spread over three floors, with superb service and doing brisk business – but the rest of the mall is pegged below luxury level.

One of the hotly debated questions in India is whether five-star hotels are suitable for luxury brand retailing. Those in favor argue that this "self-selects" the élite crowd, effectively keeping at bay the great unwashed (who presumably would be all over the place in a mall); those against say that the intimidating atmosphere is screening out potential customers, especially the new-money lot who feel out of place in plush five-star surroundings.

Is India's new money with all its rough edges intimidated by sophisticated environments? We didn't see much evidence to suggest that. In New Delhi's Imperial hotel, elegantly restored to its Raj glory, we saw shoppers at the Chanel store who seemed to have come straight from Ludhiana (known as the Manchester of India). A girl in her early 20s wore a *salwar kameez* with Nike sneakers, her friend was dressed in an awkward skirt-and-cardigan ensemble and gold-colored sports shoes – both brandished Louis Vuitton monogram bags, holding them smack up front on their folded arms. They stood coolly checking out Chanel's latest offering of handbags. Nearby at the cosmetics counter, a mother-and-daughter pair in shiny *salwar kameezes* sniffed perfumes and tried on lipsticks. A couple of salesgirls hovered around.

Martine Beaumout, the store manager, kept a watchful eye – she's a remarkable woman who combines French chic with warm, welcoming eyes and a nonjudgmental attitude. So what does she think of Indian shoppers? She does an elegant side step: "They are curious about Chanel."[25]

Chanel, for its part, has brought its full range of products to India, allowing it to address a wide range of shoppers – the mother-and-daughter pair could walk out with a Rs.1,250 (US$25) lipstick, the Vuitton-brandishing ladies could splurge Rs.75,000 (US$1,500) on a bag, and women from Ruchika's party crowd could happily fork out Rs.100,000 (US$2,000) or more on clothes. And all three would be at ease in the classy Chanel store. With money comes confidence.

At the heart of the debate about five-star hotel outlets are differing assumptions as to who the luxury consumer is. If you believe luxury is for the élite, then you build fortresses that regulate entry. If you believe luxury is for a broad-based clientele, you build accessible shopping centers. In our view it's not one or the other, but both. By all means cater to the Indian old-money élite, but do also allow for the inevitable democratization of luxury and provide access for other segments.

What's the best way to reach customers? There's a range of options. The equivalent of Beijing's Palace hotel with its 50-strong contingent of luxury brands would do just fine with the élite, whether new money or old, as well as the gold collars. Ditto for a parallel to Shanghai's Plaza 66, which delivers the same mix in a classy mall milieu. Something like Hong Kong's Pacific Place would please all four segments, its trendy, accessible ambience appealing to the BPO generation, whereas the rarefied upper floors cater to the élite.

India's retail scene is looking brighter, with a few new developments reaching completion. Delhi property developer DLF is opening Emporio, a 300,000 square foot luxury mall in Vasant Kunj, anchored by Saks Fifth Avenue and housing top brands such as Gucci, Cartier, Burberry, and Fendi. Citywalk Dome, another development in Delhi, aims to top a premium-end mall quite literally with a dome housing luxury brands – it has signed up Ferragamo, Aigner, and Ferretti. Crescent at the Qutab, designed by architect Mario Bellini, should considerably lift prevailing design standards – at 40,000 square feet, it will be a small luxury precinct, accommodating Western brands on the ground floor and Indian designers on the first floor. In Mumbai, plans are afoot to restore a heritage building on Ballard Pier. Vinita Saxena of Jones Lang LaSalle, who is steering the idea, gave us a tour of this grand old colonial building overlooking the Arabian sea, which could make a lovely luxury destination à la Three on the Bund in Shanghai.[26] In addition, DLF plans to build another luxury mall in Mumbai.

In the meantime, the Indian government has allowed foreign investment in real estate, and this should bring in international developers and international standards, much as has happened in China. On the retail front too, the government has allowed foreign companies to own a controlling interest of 51 percent in joint ventures operating single-brand stores, a move that will increase the involvement of parent brands and therefore standards.

While the luxury brands are wringing their hands at the appalling lack of luxury space, the cheap and cheerful malls are playing an important role: They're giving Indians a taste of how much fun shopping can be. Away from the heat and dust of standard shopping districts – not to mention potholes and parking nightmares – these malls are full-fledged entertainment destinations, a place to eat, see a movie, let the kids play, hang out with friends, and yes, shop too. Importantly, they are exposing Indians to branded retailing, and getting them used to paying higher prices.

ACCELERATORS

While economic growth and increased spending power will be the prime drivers, there are other inherently Indian cultural and social factors that will speed up the development of the cult of the luxury brand.

Indian Weddings, *Izzat*, and Hinduism

The great Indian wedding is the best example of how Indians are culturally programmed for conspicuous consumption. Elaborate four-to-five-day affairs, weddings involve a succession of extravagant parties in lavish settings, each themed around a ritual – the *mehndi* lunch when women have their hands painted with henna, the ladies' *sangeet* when the groom's family and friends gather for a night of singing and dancing, the *shagun*, an exchange of gifts… right up to the Hindu wedding ceremony and reception. From the invitation card to the ornate sets constructed for each event, from the selection of delectable cuisine to the live entertainment – each step is an opportunity to dazzle.

The bride's trousseau consists of many sets of exquisitely embroidered outfits – what Hollywood stars wear on Oscar night pales in comparison – and several sets of fine jewelry. Wealthier families commission Indian designers to do couture outfits for every family member. On top of this is the dowry – not allowed by law but practiced often, bridegrooms demand and receive a substantial dowry from prospective in-laws: hard cash, gold, cars, white goods, all the latest status symbols.

With the economic boom, the trend toward opulence is increasing by the day, setting India's US$30 billion wedding industry rocketing upward. Even people on modest incomes save up for a lifetime for an all-out splurge on their beloved daughter's wedding. At the top end palaces are hired and Bollywood stars flown in to provide glamour and entertainment.

Indian steel billionaire Lakshmi Mittal takes the cake for opulence – he spent US$60 million on his daughter's wedding, hosting 1,500 guests over six days of festivities, hiring some of the most spectacular locales in France, including the Palace of Versailles (for the engagement) and the Tuileries Garden in Paris (for the *sangeet*), and in the process outspending Spain's Crown Prince Felipe, whose marriage, held around the same time, cost a mere US$35 million.[27] While Mittal was cash and flash on overdrive, the wedding of hotelier-socialite Vikram Chatwal and model Priya Sachdev brought a touch of cool to unabashed bling. Chatwal flew in planeloads of international jet-setters and celebrities – Bill Clinton showed up to make a toast – and hosted parties, including a masked ball, in Udaipur, Mumbai, and Delhi, spread over the obligatory seven days. Impressed guest Fern Mallis, producer of New York Fashion Week, counts it among "the best international parties I've heard of."[28]

A ton of shopping is involved when an Indian couple tie the knot, and luxury brands have already entered the marriage scene. Before the 2005 wedding season, Louis Vuitton stores ran a prominent display of trunks decked out in gold ribbons, positioning them as ideal for trousseau storage. Mont Blanc pens are finding their way into the elaborate exchange of gifts. Whereas earlier the groom might have worn a custom-made Raymonds suit (a leading Indian brand that has consistently linked itself to the wedding market), now he is looking at Canali or Zegna. Mittal's son-in-law sported a multicolored Moschino jacket for one of his events.

While the degree of ostentation varies depending on family status and whether the wedding is held in the cash-and-flash north or the relatively sober south, the point is there's no such thing as a simple Indian wedding. It's the Chinese concept of "face" at work, what the Indians call *izzat*, whereby to maintain social standing you put up a grand show. If personal finances are not enough, why then, simply borrow. Stories of brides' families ruined by the expenses abound – a fate more acceptable than losing face.

In a sense, India's majority religion Hinduism plays a corroborating role in the love for riches and their display. Temple deities are richly clad, draped in fine silks, smothered in gold and precious jewels. Hindu gods were mostly wealthy kings – a contrast to other major religions where central figures come from humble roots. The key Hindu festival of Diwali has the nation praying to the goddess of wealth, Lakshmi, lighting up the house and surroundings so she can find her way in easily.

Vishal Chawla of Indian luxury brand Ravissant – who also represents several international ones such as Cartier, Wedgwood, and Rosenthal – sums up the connection between Hinduism and the Indian love of opulence:

My god is not Mahatma Gandhi with a dhoti and danda. My god is Rama, who was a king of this part of the world. Indians all over the country, north to south, have this affection, this magnetism towards richness. We are all aspiring to a luxurious lifestyle. I pray to a god who is wearing gold… I also want to wear gold.[29]

Luxury, the path to god. A godsend for the luxury industry.

The "Cash" Economy

When Indians talk of a "cash transaction," or say that Delhi has more of a "cash culture," or that the going rate for an apartment is "60 percent cash," they're talking about a special kind of money. Variously known as black money, number two money, undeclared money, and monkey money – call it what you will, it is basically tax-dodged money, kept in currency notes, hence known simply as "cash." Like China, India has a substantial parallel economy, and the same extensive "gifting" culture among politicians and government officials, which has now spread to other walks of life. Ironically, as we saw in China, gray money is the perfect amniotic fluid for luxury brands to develop in.

The cash economy has its roots as much in human nature as in India's post-independence socialist route, which made it extremely difficult to do business honestly and hang on to the money you made. The license raj came to symbolize the political and bureaucratic attitude of "I'll keep you hanging unless you pay me." Income tax rates were so high in the past – going up to as much as 97.5 percent for higher income brackets in 1975[30] – that they literally drove people to evade tax altogether. While the salaried classes were taxed at source, giving them little leeway, entrepreneurs and businesspeople perfected tax evasion into an art form, giving rise to a well-oiled parallel economy, which by some estimates could amount to 50 percent of reported GDP.[31] From there it became part of the system. For example, try buying real estate without black money and your choices are extremely limited – almost all residential, commercial, or retail property on the secondary market has an official price to be paid by check, plus a cash price to be paid in currency notes. As NR Narayana Murthy, chairman of Infosys, put it:

It is very clear that corruption is now an accepted phenomenon in the psyche of Indians from all walks of life.[32]

While India's liberalization process has made significant progress in dismantling controls and lowering taxes, cash and corruption have become so inherent in the culture that they are going to be difficult to dislodge. Luxury brands are already part of the picture. One businessman told us that when Mont Blanc first entered the country, suddenly "every government guy wanted one." The new refrain was: *"Aapki file move karni hai to* (if you want your file moved), I will need a Mont Blanc." Now with the advent of advertising, "governmental awareness" is increasing, the same businessman laments, which translates into specific demands for higher-end Mont Blanc models. Apparently this has spawned a neat business in recycling luxury pens – specialized dealers take back pens gifted to government officials and pay cash.

Even lower-level public servants are raising their demands. A restaurateur told us the policeman on his beat is now asking for two bottles of Black Label whisky. "He's the sort it was okay to give Rs.500 earlier," he says. China, *déjà vu.*

The Indian government is trying to regulate the use of cash in shopping with a rule that cash purchases of over Rs.20,000 (approximately US$500) must be accompanied by the buyer's income tax identification number. We found little evidence of the effectiveness of this measure. At Delhi's Maurya Sheraton hotel we watched the cash-rich generation clanking money within everyone's earshot. The setting: the glitzy multibrand store Regent, stocking a wide range of expensive watches and pens – Cartier, Corum, Audemars Piguet, Dior, and several others. Loud bargaining seemed to be the norm. One customer haggled heartily with the salesgirl over the price of a Corum watch (stated price Rs.10 lakhs; US$20,000), and then announced loudly, "I'll have the cash sent tomorrow." Another father-and-son pair complained about the price of a pen that had caught their fancy, setting the stage for another round of noisy negotiations. Yet another couple wanted to know why they can't have "yesterday's price" – presumably lower – for a Cartier watch. And so it went.

We asked a watch store manager in Mumbai whether the new income tax rule was affecting his business. He seemed surprised at the question; clearly it wasn't. "We take down whatever PAN number the customer gives – we don't go out of our way to check if it is correct."

The Power of Bollywood

Celebrity endorsement is big anywhere in the world. In India, thanks to a manic obsession with Bollywood, it takes on magical proportions. Producing over 1,000 movies a year, the Indian film industry is the largest in the world. Every day an estimated 14 million Indians go to cinema halls[33] – that's over 5 billion hits annually. Now there's a spurt in the construction of multiplexes – thanks to the boom in shopping malls where they're located – which is tapping into a more sophisticated audience. On top of that there's television, which not only airs movies but also has substantial film-based programming. Popular music is largely film based. There are "filmi" magazines dishing out a constant stream of star gossip. Mammoth film posters dot Indian cities, with larger-than-life images of matinée idols staring down at you. Bollywood *is* larger than life: Its overpowering presence permeates the daily life of India and shapes the collective psyche. Rich or poor, no one is immune.

The very existence of such unbridled star power can make a qualitative difference to luxury brands. Think of what the Oscar red carpet parade does for luxury brands. Think of what *Sex and the City* did for Manolo Blahnik and umpteen other brands. Now multiply that many times over – that's the power of Bollywood waiting to be tapped.

Mahindra of *Verve* sees this as India's unique advantage. Referring to China's film industry, which is a drop in the ocean compared to Bollywood, she points out:

China is a faceless market. India will get the numbers that they [luxury brands] are looking for, but they will also get celebrity endorsement. Other places don't have the same celebrity power.

She gives the example of a feature her magazine ran for Louis Vuitton's 150th anniversary – eight Bollywood divas were photographed with their favorite Vuitton bags. This is the equivalent of Angelina Jolie, Julia Roberts, Nicole Kidman, and more – unbeatable endorsement indeed.

Bollywood's ability to be a stylesetter is beyond question. For instance, the spectacular success of *Bunty aur Babli* brought about a trend for colorful kitsch – the film's clothes, designed by Aki Narula for popular actress Rani Mukerji, became the defining style for the season. Even in the most traditional area of weddings, Bollywood's influence is palpable – the corset with a long skirt the same Rani Mukerji wore in a *mehndi* sequence in *Hum Tum* has been mirrored in the bridalwear market.[34] And men's fashion is just as susceptible to Bollywood influence. Here's an excerpt from a review of fashion trends in leading newspaper *The Hindu*:

Pink made a definitive entry in the Indian male's wardrobe courtesy Saif Ali Khan in Salaam Namaste. *In fact, if there was any lasting trend this year it was the Indian male's increasing propensity to dress anti-style. If Abhishek, whose box office success helped the trend gain currency, dared to sport a collared shirt with* sherwani *(again by Aki Narula) in* Bluffmaster, *Farhan Akhtar appeared in* Nach Baliye *in a round-neck* kurta *with a conventional blazer.*[35]

Bollywood films have an equal ability to affect brands. For example, the film *Kuch Kuch Hota Hai*, which struck a chord with teens, helped create awareness for brands such as Tommy Hilfiger, Adidas, and Reebok.[36]

Luxury watches have already started deploying Bollywood and seen results. Thanks to star backing, brands like Tag Heuer and Omega, once totally out of reach, are now spoken of as casual friends, and figured among "most prominent" in the watch category in the FICCI survey.[37] In the meantime, Aishwarya Rai has worked her magic for Nakshatra, De Beers' diamond brand in India. Again, De Beers ranks as one of the top five favored jewelry companies.

STEPPING-STONES TO SUCCESS

Despite the hype and hope that surround it, the reality is that India's luxury market is just at Stage 2 of the Spread of Luxury model. Near-virgin terrain, it will have to be developed from the ground up on *every* front, just as China was. This was hard work in China, and it's going to be no cakewalk in India.

For early movers, the prize is the same: domination of potentially the second-largest market after China. The consumer's mind is still wide open and there's a rare opportunity for a brand to own that space. As Thanks's Ashish puts it: "The market is like a sponge right now, they will learn anything, absorb anything." He should know – he is successfully hawking avant-garde brands like Paper Denim & Cloth and Dolce & Gabbana to the totally uninitiated.

What will it take to win in the Indian market? We look at the road ahead and lay out four key stepping-stones to success.

Look Beyond the Old-Money Élite

The fact that India actually has an old-money élite is proving to be a red herring. A significant chunk of people we spoke with in the industry hold the view that luxury in India will be an élitist phenomenon, a view that is coloring their thinking and action plans. For example, they are extending the behavior and needs of this extremely brand-savvy élite to be representative of the Indian consumer in general.

Nothing could be further from reality – the old-money élite has nothing in common with the rest of the country. Think of India as one huge China – of a decade ago, that is – topped with a tiny sliver of America's high society. So while a few Rothschilds and Kennedys carry on with the privileged lives they are used to, the rest of the Wangs and Zhous are busy acquiring new money and finding ways to display it. Service the Indian Rothschilds well – they will always be a visible segment of high spenders – but remember the real prize lies in developing the Indian Wang-and-Zhou market.

Democratization of luxury is inevitable as India moves into Stage 3 of the Spread of Luxury model, *show off*. Think of the needs of the new-money entrepreneurs, who will be prime customers during this phase. And as the country progresses into Stage 4, *fit in*, increasingly bring the gold collars and the BPO generation into the fold. A decade from now, if the luxury industry has done its job well, the old-money élite will form less than 5 percent of the market.

Meaning Manufacture

When you look at the Wang-and-Zhou market, luxury brand knowledge ranges from clutching at stray bits of information to not having a clue. Ask the somewhat better informed among this segment to name a few luxury brands and they confidently rattle off Louis Vuitton, Mango, Hugo Boss, and Tommy Hilfiger. Don't even try suggesting Mango and Tommy might not be in the luxury category – these are early days and consumers are simply feeding back the few random brands they have heard of.

The whole "meaning-manufacturing" process has to begin in earnest. From straightforward awareness to building a nuanced understanding of a brand, a lot of marketing ground needs to be covered. Chanel's Xavier says that the maharajas may have been conversant with luxury, but it will take time to build understanding among the vast majority of Indians, all newcomers: "Chanel is taking a long-term view. We are here to introduce what the house is all about – Madame Chanel and the story behind it."

Unlike China, India's glossy magazine market is still in its infancy with barely a handful of titles, and even the likes of *Elle* have until recently focused on Indian brands and designers because that's what was locally available. Both quantitatively and qualitatively the glossies' game will have to be significantly raised. The impending entry of Condé

Nast in 2007 will be a shot in the arm – it plans to bring in fashion bible *Vogue* and subsequently other titles like *Glamour, GQ,* and *Vanity Fair*.[38]

It's only when luxury brands get established as reliable status markers, their sign language understood by a sufficiently large group of people, that Indians will see value in paying Rs.40,000 (US$850) for a monogrammed canvas bag.

Provide Rungs on the Ladder

In India today, there are the super-luxury brands like Chanel and Louis Vuitton and then there's a steep drop to a premium brand like Tommy Hilfiger. All the traditional bridge brands are still entering India, leading to a temporary price chasm that is far too wide for most Indians to jump across. As a result, the usual process of graduating from a relatively inexpensive brand to a more expensive one, to an even more expensive one, until you finally plunge into the luxury category, is simply not there. It's like a jungle with a lion, a tiger, and a few rabbits – the whole ecosystem has to be developed. Of course, it's only a matter of time before this anomaly is corrected. Brands like Mango, Zara, Esprit, Morgan, and Guess are building their presence, becoming the necessary stepping-stones to eventual luxury consumption.

In the meantime, luxe brands can help provide rungs in the ladder in two ways. They can pull in consumers to their lower-price-point items, the perfumes and lipsticks, the wallets and name-card holders, bringing them into the brand's embrace and then graduating them to more expensive items. Secondly, the opportunity for diffusion lines is significant, giving consumers the chance to work their way up from Armani Exchange to Emporio Armani to Giorgio Armani.

Invest in Understanding the Local Mind-Set

Indians wear bright colors; Mumbai has one season; the wedding market is huge; Diwali is a time for new clothes and gifts; 60 percent of watch sales happen during the festive months of October to January; and so the list goes on. India has its own peculiarities, and luxury brands have to invest time and money in understanding Indian consumers, their different segments and regional differences. "Respect the consumer in bold letters," is Murjani's advice.

For starters, India may be a luxury hinterland, but try selling last season's goods here and you won't find takers. Thanks to the presence of a well-traveled élite, luxury brands have been forced to bring in the latest range. The same goes for pricing: You have to be sensitive to the fact that Indians compare prices with London and Dubai, pet shopping destinations, and won't pay much of a premium. It's not the money, although that counts too, it's the mind-set of seeking maximum value. Given India's high tax and duty structure, many brands are absorbing some of the hit in an attempt to keep prices parallel to other markets. As India continues to liberalize, this should become easier.

The value mind-set extends to an investment mentality, therefore promoting products like watches that play to this is a good initial strategy. Jewelry, on the other hand, is a tradition-bound area. "What is the weight?" "Is it 22 carat gold?" These are ingrained first questions and paying umpteen times the value for a Cartier bracelet or a Tiffany necklace – 18 carat at that – is going to be a hard sell for some time to come. The Chopard store manager told us people come in and enquire about the weight of a gold necklace – he struggles to explain that the value lies in its superior design and craftsmanship, as well as the brand name.

Even the super-rich are not immune from this value mind-set. As Shobha De explains, "not even a Tina Ambani would buy branded jewelry" although she would buy a "watch for Rs.5 crores [US$1 million]" (her husband, Anil Ambani, weighs in at US$5.5 billion on the Forbes India's 40 Richest List[39]). "Which she does possess," De adds. "I think it is a custom-made Chopard."

On the clothes front, thanks to the country's rich and varied crafts tradition, the Indian woman is used to intricate embroidery and embellishment, vibrant colors, and rich fabrics, whereas Western prêt-à-porter ranges are simpler, emphasizing silhouette, cut, and styling. Will Indians be willing to pay US$500 for a plain white cotton shirt from Prada, elegantly cut, this season, when for the same money they could get a locally made outfit in silk with embroidery, perhaps more to their taste? Imported brands will have to make adjustments to cater to their tastes and values.

India may be the next China, but ultimately luxury brand marketers will have to think Indian to win India.

PART THREE

BEHIND THE
CULT

It might look like a roomful of clothes, shoes, and bags, but the "press collection" is a powerful cult-building tool. When deployed on hot Hong Kong actress Cecilia Cheung, seen here in a Fendi evening gown at the Hong Kong Film Awards night, it generated reams of press coverage.

Photos courtesy of Fendi Asia Pacific.

9

HOW THE CULT
IS CREATED

"Louis Vuitton is the godhead of the nation's real state religion: the worship of brands."

Time *magazine article commenting on Japan's love for luxury brands*[1]

I t's time now to cut through the haze of glitz and glamour and look at exactly how the luxury industry has gone about building not only Japan's "real state religion" but also a powerful and unstoppable cult across the rest of Asia. Stepping away from relying solely on traditional marketing, the luxury industry has instead developed a highly successful alternative method – something that should be of interest to any brand looking at forming a mass following in Asia.

As we saw earlier in the book, the gospel itself is created at global headquarters in Paris and Milan – it is sacred, centralized, controlled, every nuance just so. Fall/winter, spring/summer, the collections are all designed here at the hands of chief creative officers, the originators of the cult. Every aspect that goes into building the experience is determined at headquarters – defining the brand concept, creating the advertising campaigns, setting the guidelines for store designs, product displays, merchandising – so that wherever in the world today's globe-trotting consumers encounter the brand, they experience the same universal truth. "Brands impose a lot of rules," says Yolanda Choy, former marketing and communications director of Fendi in Asia. "We can only do so much outside head office, we reinforce the brand's [pre-defined] image locally."

It is in the *spreading* of the gospel that *local* marketing teams of luxe companies come into their own. In this chapter we step behind the scenes to unearth the cult-creating formula, examining the principles behind it, its key components, and how it is practiced.

The Exclusive–Inclusive Paradox

At the heart of this new kind of marketing is the constant attempt to resolve two opposing forces. After all, the very phrase "luxury brand cult creation" has a delightful in-built contradition – luxury is by definition exclusive; a cult by definition has a large following. How do you balance these opposing forces?

Let's look at Louis Vuitton again, which excels at doing just that: being the ultimate symbol of luxury for millions of Asians. Vuitton's genius lies in realizing that in today's world "scarcity is not part of the definition," as former managing director Serge Brunschwig puts it,[2] and defining luxury instead in terms of high quality, a century and half of French heritage, a fine design tradition that still bubbles with creativity.

Vuitton's key principle is this: Pump up the status, pump out to the mass market, both done *simultaneously*. It takes its product range up into the realms of utmost prestige by offering made-to-order products to VIP customers – as it did to the maharajas of yore – while simultaneously extending its range down to entry-level products like the canvas monogram bag that legions of Japanese office ladies carry. Its pricing ranges from the stratospheric to the relatively within reach – for example, a men's astrakhan long coat would set you back US$20,000 while you could buy a key chain for less than US$100. LV has exclusive programs for VIP customers that it will never talk about publicly, while simultaneously bombarding mass media through high-decibel advertising and PR campaigns. It has VIP rooms that are out of bounds to the common public, yet it extends its distribution network far and wide, making its products readily available. With magnificent flagships, it ensures that the store experience is larger than life. It hosts parties that are nothing short of spectacular, inviting a city's who's who. Vuitton knows how to create exclusivity at the top, while simultaneously delivering luxury to the population at large. Pamper the élite, delight the office lady – élitism and democracy in the same breath, managed harmoniously.

While Vuitton is a master in a league of its own, other brands use the same basic principle to create their own cult.

TRICKLE DOWN OR TIPPING POINT?

How do large numbers of people – who don't even know each other – collectively decide to throw their weight behind a particular style of bag? Or a certain brand? Or a set of brands and styles? Or the broader category of Western luxury brands, as is the case in Asia today? There are many theories explaining the spread of fashion and how social epidemics are created. We look at three key ones here as stepping-stones to creating a model that explains the Asian luxe cult.

The "trickle-down" theory of fashion was proposed by Georg Simmel in 1904. In his view, styles and status symbols emerged from the upper classes and then trickled down to the masses, who imitated them in an attempt to climb up the social ladder.[3] In the meantime the élite kept a close eye on the classes below, and promptly moved on to newer styles once the earlier ones became too common. Over the last century, the theory itself has been contested, revised, and updated several times over – fashion doesn't necessarily trickle down, for example, it also slides sideways from group to group, and can even bubble up from street culture – but still the core of the trickle-down theory remains relevant to Asian society today. In certain markets, it works as is. As we have seen, members of the Korean élite are shedding their favorite Ferragamo shoes as they find secretaries and university students sporting them; they are moving up to Hermès, which thanks to its sky-high price range stays firmly out of the reach of most people.

Having said that, we must add our own Asian modifications to the age-old trickle-down theory. Certainly, it is no longer a *natural* sociological process – it is carefully *engineered* by luxe companies. And while those in the social élite still play the critical role of fashion leaders, luxe companies are influencing *multiple sources*, such as local journalists and editors, or indeed an entire market – the Japanese, for instance, who serve as style leaders for the rest of Asia. Today it's a *superaccelerated* version of trickle down, more of a gush down really. The speed with which the whole process is managed means that the élite and the rest are often picking up the latest status symbols within days of each other.

While Simmel's theory has class differentiation as its motivating force, Herbert Blumer makes the case for "collective selection" guided by what he calls the "direction of modernity."[4] He looks at the fashion process in the modern world – from designers at fashion houses to buyers from retail establishments – and argues that they all converge on the same set of styles every season because they are all anticipating the "proximate future" as interpreted by their understanding of broader trends in the world of art, culture, fashion, and consumer tastes. Feeding as they do from the same well of inspiration, these highly secretive designers from competing fashion houses, and equally secretive buyers from competing retail chains, all end up "collectively selecting" a small set of styles. And that becomes the fashion of the season.

In contrast, Malcolm Gladwell's "tipping point" model draws on the principles of disease epidemics to explain social epidemics.[5] At its core is the idea that there is one dramatic moment when a small increase in the number of people infected with a contagious virus causes the situation to tip over into an epidemic. You can manipulate the tipping point by fiddling with one of three factors: the infectious virus itself, the people who transmit the virus, or the environment in which the virus is operating. In effect, play god and create your own epidemic – exactly what every luxury brand is doing in Asia.

The epidemic, of course, is magnified and multiplied many times over because it's not just Louis Vuitton or Gucci, it's dozens and dozens of brands at work, each deploying an array of cult-creating tools to reach the tipping point and trigger its own infection. And once the job is done for the fall/winter collection, the brands get busy developing the next round of epidemics for the spring/summer collection. In Japan, in Hong Kong, in South Korea, in one Asian country after another, it's relentless. It's like hundreds of influenza viruses let loose – multiple brands, multiple locations, multiple seasons. Forget epidemic, we're talking about a full-scale *luxeplosion*.

THE LUXEPLOSION MODEL

Here's the formula, tried and tested, that luxury brands use to create the cult in Asia. We call it the Luxeplosion model (Figure 9.1).

The starting point is a good set of **cult tools**. Not surprisingly, the first tool is human – *social networkers*. Hire high-profile individuals with links to the city's A list, and put them to work on the brand's behalf. The second tool is the *press collection*, one set of the season's range of bags, shoes, ready-to-wear, and accessories, which will be used to generate press coverage. The third tool is *the spin*, a nice sticky story fed to the press.

The next step is to apply these tools on **cult catalysts**, select groups of influential people, who if seen endorsing the brand, whether directly or indirectly, will generate a buzz around town. Think of them as super-infectors, few in number but powerful in their contagion-spreading influence. *Celebrity parties*, *fashion/social editors*, and *VIP customers* are three of the best catalysts. Host a few parties with a heavyweight guest list, and the media will swarm all over them. Get your brand's crystal-studded evening gown worn by the hottest star in town, and it will be splashed all over the press. Win the affection of fashion editors and positive editorial coverage is likely to follow. Ditto for the society page editors. Pamper your VIP customers, different from celebrities in that many of them maintain a low media profile, but they're extremely influential in the social circles that spend big money. Prime the catalysts, impregnate the queen bees, put the yeast in the dough and wait for it to rise.

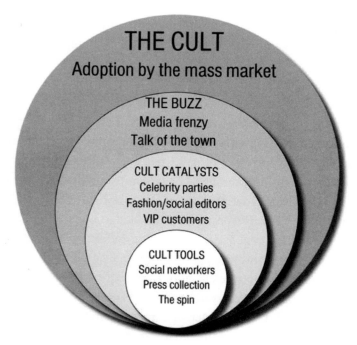

Figure 9.1 The Luxeplosion model

If you have done it well, with a light and winning touch, there will be a nice **buzz** around town. Two things will happen – fingers crossed, of course – there will be a full-scale *media frenzy* surrounding your brand, and it will become the *talk of the town*. Your brand will be covered extensively in the local press, recommended by fashion editors, endorsed by celebrities. It will generate a lot of talk: Hey, have you seen that cool TechnoMarine watch, or the new Dior bag that celebrity X is carrying? The season's hot looks are locally defined. The endorsement of celebrities sets an aspirational example. The nexus with high society pumps up the brand's status. The lavish parties that serve as backgrounds for promoting the brand further enhance the high status of the brand. "Pump up the status" is in full action.

This buzz is consumed by a wider cross-section of society: They absorb the hot looks of the season, they seek out what the celebrities are wearing, they buy the brands that are in, they discuss them with friends and colleagues. The demand spreads furiously now, or as Gladwell would say, it tips. It spills from the domain of celebrities and socialites to the mass market. The **cult** is created. For this season. For this brand. For this country. And at varying levels and for differing consumer profiles, the pattern repeats itself for several other brands. For Louis Vuitton, for Ferragamo, for Hermès, for Gucci. All adding up to a larger social epidemic – a luxeplosion.

Aren't we missing out on advertising in all of this, you might ask? Advertising plays an important role, of course: It provides the background music to the buzz-creating activity. Luxury brands spend an awful lot on advertising – the LVMH group lays out 11 percent of sales, the Gucci group a corresponding 12 percent.[6] It builds greater awareness, a larger-than-life presence, a glamorous predefined image. But finally it is the "buzz" that consumers trust more and act on. The luxury brand category works on insider knowledge, the pride of knowing what's in. The more expensive a piece, the more you rely on word of mouth, or word of print, to form opinions and purchase decisions. For example, in the last two weeks I have been told by three separate individuals about the outsized watches from Panerai – one of them is a watch connoisseur, proud owner of a rare Panerai piece "only 40mm wide." I'd be blind not to realize that Panerai is hot, but I don't recall seeing an advert for its watches.

Let's take a closer look at the individual elements: the cult tools, the cult catalysts, the buzz, and how the cult-building art is practiced in Asia's luxury industry.

CULT TOOLS

Simple things, but make or break when it comes to cult building. We look at three of the most critical tools here: social networkers, the press collection, and the spin.

Social Networkers

Since the cult-building process hinges on spreading the bug *first* to the upper echelons of society, it is essential to have individuals on the brand's payroll who are able to connect with the élite on a one-on-one basis, and fill up a room with A-list guests for events. The upper crust prefers dealing with its own kind.

In the old days of the agent-franchisee, he or she *was* the social networker, well placed enough in society to be on backslapping terms with the élite. For example, many of the agents in Hong Kong in the 1980s were wealthy tai-tais for whom luxe retailing was as much a business as a social activity, and they were extremely successful *because* of their social skills. "The way it used to be was the rich guys ran the business anyway so it was all part of the social scene, sort of like a club," says Ian Hawksworth, executive director of Hongkong Land. But with the buying back of licenses and professional managers in place, those close social links have snapped. Says Hawksworth:

Probably the focus of the European managers who run these brands is to actually get out and know these customers. But it's fairly difficult as they are never going to be in that social set.[7]

The answer is to hire someone who *is* in that social set. Many brands have a policy, unstated as it may be, to have socially prominent women, and indeed sometimes men, as marketing managers, PR managers, image directors, and so on. The key qualification on their résumé is the extent of their social network, and the key skill their ability to move in the same circles as the city's élite. We met quite a few of these socially gifted PR/marketing women – whatever the brand, whatever the country, their profile is very similar. They are a distinct tribe. Beautiful women in their own right, with a striking sense of style, dressed in the brand's clothes, sporting the latest bag – you immediately know this is no ordinary PR manager you are talking to. Their offices may be relatively modest, but their persona instantly conveys class. For example, Bonnie Gokson, stunningly beautiful and impeccably groomed, was image director of Chanel – she is also a prominent figure on Hong Kong's social scene and sister of Joyce Ma, the pioneer of luxury retailing in Hong Kong.

In addition, luxury brands hire local celebrities as brand ambassadors. Well-known actors, pop stars, models, beauty queens, and the like are signed on for the sole purpose of wearing the brand and making appearances at parties and other events the brand hosts. The extent of their commitment varies depending on the deal struck. It may be an exclusive contract, which means the celebs wear that particular brand's watch or bag every time they step out in public. Or it may be limited to a designated number of events, say three or four a season, where they are expected to appear draped in the brand's finery.

"A lot of brands hire super-idols to be their 'image boy' or 'image girl,'" says Wendy So, editor-in-chief of fashion and lifestyle magazine *Zip*.[8] Their job is to be photographed wearing the brand – a female actor might wear a Gucci dress to a film premiere, a male singer might dress in Dior for one of his concerts – so it makes "the brand appear among the public." Often they get a "shopping budget" to pick up what they like from the brand's store.

Siri Udomritthiruj, former editor of *Elle* Thailand, has had a ringside view of how trends build up in Asia:

The trend usually starts with a celebrity. You have a celebrity walking around, wearing it all the time, so it gets publicity, so it's up to the PR person to get the right celebrity wearing it.

Press Collection

Work backwards. There's a stack of local newspapers with extensive coverage of the Hong Kong Film Awards night, the local Oscars so to speak. Four of Hong Kong's hottest actors/pop singers, the equivalent of Julia Roberts, Nicole Kidman, Jennifer Lopez, and Britney Spears, hog the limelight. There's picture after stunning picture: arriving for the evening, walking up to present an award, mingling with other famous faces – it's as if the media can't get enough of them. Guess what each of these four leading ladies is wearing? Fendi evening gowns. It's a piece of brilliant product placement on Fendi's behalf, a coup that generates an avalanche of media coverage of the highest quality possible.

The evening gowns that Cecilia Cheung, Karen Mok, Kelly Chan, and Chu Yan wore for the awards night were "loaned" to them from Fendi's press collection. It sounds basic – after all, you can't get press coverage without product – but a decade ago the concept of a press collection was alien in Asia. European head offices didn't see the point of it. Local agents didn't see the point either, as it meant investing money. But with professional management taking over luxury brand companies, the press collection has become an essential marketing tool. The path breaker was Dior, under the tutelage of Yolanda Choy, a champion of the concept. "Dior was the first brand to have a press collection in 1996," she says. "It was number one in editorial coverage that year." Simple cause and effect.

The Spin

In an industry where fashions change every season and brand fortunes rise and fall, what is the key to remaining successful in the long run? The Japan head of a leading luxury brand says it is about creating the "excitement story" and presenting it to the market. Do that well and you are halfway home to building your cult. The spin is over and above advertising – it is what you say to the press and how you say it. Whether you send out a simple press release or arrange an interview with Giorgio Armani, you are providing essential media content.

There are two kinds of stories through which spin is created: the "excitement story," designed to provide a thrill a minute to keep a short attention-span audience wide-eyed and hooked; and the "educational story," aimed at enhancing consumers' knowledge of the brand's history and craftsmanship.

A large part of the excitement story is created in Europe, starting with the season's catwalk shows in Paris and Milan, which are closely analyzed in the Asian press. The next level of spin is locally manufactured. These are stories about new stores, new products, fashion shows, dazzling parties with local heartthrobs – the usual suspects are pulled out of the armory, creatively packaged, and trotted out in a series of press releases, interviews, photo shoots, and event coverage. The stickier the stories, the greater the excitement – if you can pull fashionable artist Takashi Murakami out of the bag, pair him with designer Marc Jacobs, and feed their creation to the Japanese consumer, then forget excitement, you are well into the realms of frenzy.

The educational story serves a different purpose. Barring the Japanese, who probably know more about European brands' history than the Europeans themselves, knowledge in the rest of Asia is sketchy to nonexistent. It's a cart-before-the-horse world here – consumers have rushed into luxury brands for their status-enhancing capacity, but they don't know much about the credentials of the brands themselves. However, as tastes mature, Asian consumers are going to need more justification for paying astronomically high prices. If it takes nine years of training before an apprentice is ready to handcraft an Hermès bag, then of course, it's worth paying thousands of dollars for.

It is this sort of solid luxury credentials that the educational story aims to build, employing a variety of methods to so. History lessons prove extremely effective. Cartier has paraded the famed five-layered Patiala necklace, one of the most expensive pieces of jewelry ever made, through various exhibitions.[9] LV regularly spotlights antique pieces from the Louis Vuitton Museum in its stores in Asia. Fashion glossies from Japan to China have a history column as staple fare. Gu Ming, associate publisher of *Elle* China, was pleasantly surprised by the enthusiastic response the magazine's brand history column, "icon," got from readers:

Chinese readers are really interested in the history of brands. They want to know what's behind the brand.[10]

Educating journalists is an important intermediate step, so they're equipped with the facts and processes that go into the creation of these high-value items. Where does the best fur come from? What is the difference between Siberian fur and Fendi fur? What are recent innovations in treating fur? How is lightweight fur made? Is it comfortable to wear in relatively moderate temperatures? Educate the journalists and they educate consumers through their writings.

It's all part of the spin: The more consumers appreciate the brand's traditions, the complexity and skill involved in making them, the higher their perceptions of the value and quality of the products. Here's what Hong Kong businessman and watch connoisseur Conrad Ng has to say:

My knowledge about watches is almost all from magazines. It's not as if I bought specialist books on the subject. You'll be amazed by the effect print titles have on brainwashing people.[11]

He should know, he's been collecting luxury watches for the last 18 years and has invested a sizable fortune in them, relying on the spin created by diligent PR managers.

CULT CATALYSTS

Celebrity parties, magazine editors, and VIP customers – get these three potent catalysts to endorse your brand and they ignite a chain reaction.

Celebrity Parties

Flick through a magazine or newspaper in Hong Kong and you will conclude that this city does little else but party. Not any old party, but extravagant, celebrity-studded affairs with the inevitable luxury brand connection. Ian Hawksworth comments:

I don't remember going to any innovative parties in the early 1990s. Now everybody is trying to outdo each other with what's the coolest way of doing it.[12]

Dior: The Anatomy of a Party

Dior launched its biggest flagship store in Asia Pacific with twin parties that rocked Hong Kong, generated reams of press coverage, and became the buzz of the town. Not the easiest thing to do, considering it had a surprise guest, the SARS virus, to contend with. We sat down with Peter Cheung, Dior's debonair regional marketing director, Asia Pacific, to talk about what goes into the making of a great event.

On the planning for the party

"We were facing a dilemma at that time... we have Asia Pacific region's largest boutique opening, and you have an unforeseen viral epidemic outbreak... what are we going to do?" Worried if the city was ready to come out and party, Dior held a small test event where the response was overwhelming. Fingers crossed, it planned for the big day.

On what makes a great party

"Originality, creativity, and a very fresh kind of mix of the *right* people. We had business élite, we had society élite, we also had local celebrity élite – which I must say rarely comes together under one roof – it gave the evening a really interesting *energy*."

On adding glamour

"We rolled out the red carpet in the neighborhood. We had the police, the paparazzi was out there, the onlookers. It was really Oscar like."

The high-powered guest list included (from left to right) Anita Mui, Pansy Ho, Nicholas Tse, and Janet Ma.

On finding an original venue

Having an original venue is half the battle won. "A new venue is so hard to come by in Hong Kong... We had the penthouse of One Peking Road [same as the store], 360° sea views and skyline views of Hong Kong. It was a raw space... never been used before."

On the program

❖ Cocktails in the boutique.
❖ Move to penthouse venue, via red carpet.
❖ Four-course dinner catered by Grand Hyatt.
❖ Fashion show of fall/winter collection.
❖ Surprise act by Canto-pop singer William So.
❖ Auction of Dior jewelry and handbags for SARS-affected children's charity Blossom, conducted by Sotheby's managing director.

On the results

❖ Huge editorial coverage – "the press were so supportive."
❖ Although meant to be just cocktails at the store, interest was so strong it turned into a "shopping frenzy."
❖ 100-strong queue outside the store the next morning despite rain – "we actually opened the store a few minutes early to let people in."
❖ First-day sales were equivalent to two weeks' sales in any other store.
❖ HK$0.5 million raised for charity.

But Cheung had a much more ambitious objective: to revise Hong Kong's flagging SARS-afflicted spirit, "by bringing back a feeling of glamour, of luxury, of fashion," which are Dior's core values. So apt for a city that has luxe coursing through its veins.

Photos courtesy of Dior.

Celebrity parties are extremely effective buzz generators, and what holds true for Hong Kong applies in varying degrees to every Asian metropolis. The local press is all over these affairs and photographers come armed with their own ladders to gain a vantage point. In Tokyo, they're called the party paparazzi.

The distinguishing characteristic of these parties is that they're professionally managed experiences – think of them as interactive performances with lavish sets and a cast of celebrities to be snapped by the cameras. Take Louis Vuitton's legendary store-opening parties, each one masterfully orchestrated to the smallest detail. The invitation is an inscribed bracelet, a collector's item in itself. The guest list comprises the city's who's who plus regional celebrities, to ensure press coverage in other cities. The party starts with the store opening, Veuve Clicquot flows, and then there is a spectacular transfer to the real party venue, where an extravaganza unfolds. The Omotesando party had Vuitton take over Tokyo's national museum, converting the grounds behind into five tents, each offering a taste of a country's cuisine, ambience, and entertainment – for example a full desert scene was recreated in the Turkish tent, complete with a camel in attendance. The New Delhi launch party was held at a plush farmhouse on the outskirts of the city, a breathtaking setting with an artificial lake lit up from below and LV symbols high in the sky like guiding stars. Food, wine, entertainment – everything is top notch. Result: The parties invariably go on till dawn, they are extensively covered in the media, and they become the talk of the town. Their impact is so high that guests remember them nostalgically even years later.

With dozens of events taking place every week, the party scene itself has become overcrowded. A typical socialite might have a dozen luxe events to attend in a month, not counting the other social meetings that crowd her calendar. People from the media have an even more jam-packed diary. "I could go every day of the week to some event or the other," says Udomritthiruj. When we met Eva Yu, society editor of the *Shanghai Tatler*, she was contemplating how to be at two parties at the same time that night. In the meantime, she had done the only sensible thing a girl can do in such a situation – shop for something nice to wear.

How do you distinguish your event, how do you ensure the celebrities turn up, more importantly how do you ensure the press is present in full force? The answer is a hot party organizer, someone with the clout to pull in the big names and the imagination to create a memorable evening. For example, G-Spot Productions in Hong Kong, run by party boy and local celebrity Gilbert Yeung, has acquired a surefire anything-it-does-is-red-hot reputation. Henri Li is fashionable in Beijing, priding himself on intimate underground parties.

Fashion Editors/Social Editors

Fashion editors are powerful anywhere in the world, but they hold even greater sway in Asia due to the lack of fashion confidence among new-money consumers. Even extremely wealthy people seek reassurance. Bonnie Gokson, former image director of Chanel, explains: "A lot of Asian women want to see a total look – how it goes out in the show, or how the shop matched it."[13] Some customers, especially wealthy ones from mainland China, buy entire sets – a handbag for one outfit with matching shoes and accessories – and since their wardrobes are so extensive they label the sets together lest they forget which bag goes with which dress.

There's a symbiotic threesome with the interests of luxury brands, editors, and consumers converging neatly – brands want to sell products, editors want to sell magazines, and consumers want to devour information about fashion and brands. Companies try to align themselves with the magazines' editorial needs, providing up-to-the-minute information, products for photo shoots, ideas for articles, doing whatever it takes to remain top of mind among fashion journalists, increasing their chances of getting written about.

With luxury brands going mainstream, it's not just fashion glossies that are writing about them, but also newspapers and general-interest magazines. An article on gift recommendations for Father's Day would include luxe, for example. Extremely specialized magazines have also sprung up – Japan has a lineup of fashions-for-your-dog magazines, or those that cover just shoes. In this scenario, luxury brands have to mold the perceptions of fashion journalists from a wide cross-section of publications. The catalysts themselves are growing in number.

As an example of how the nexus works in the Asian context, take a "Dress like Beckham" feature in Hong Kong's Chinese-language *Ming*

Pao Weekly.[14] David Beckham has a huge fan following in Asia and an analysis of his unusual dress sense – whether he is in "CASUAL CHIC" OR "SMART LUXARY" (sic) – is guaranteed to be closely studied, including the lineup of zany hairstyles. What makes the cash registers ring are the brands recommended to create the Beckham look, among them Gucci, Dolce & Gabbana, DKNY, and Diesel – the implicit statement being wear these brands and you'll be a step closer to your super-idol. The brands couldn't have asked for a stronger sales pitch.

Social editors are another make-or-break category of catalysts to be treated with kid gloves. All those brand parties would remain a closely guarded secret if it were not for the tribe of social editors who give them full-blooded coverage on the society pages of newspapers and magazines, splashing photos of celebrities with logos figuring prominently. Favorable writeups are not guaranteed – brands first have to ensure that this set of journalists is favorably disposed to them.

VIP Consumers

The third set of catalysts consists of the VIPs, ultra-high-spending consumers – the top ten customers might spend in the region of US$250,000 a season with their favorite brand. With that kind of spending power under their belt, this group is exceptionally influential. Admittedly there is some overlap between celebrities and VIPs, but contrary to expectations, for the most part the heavy-spending consumers are not well-known celebrities. Gokson says:

The real spenders, you would not know them. They are a very tiny percent of working women... and tai-tais, pretty bored, of course.[15]

Away from the media glare, VIP consumers work as catalysts through personal and social influence. Take the tai-tais – the central themes in their lives are shopping and lunching with girlfriends, where the day's shopping expeditions figure prominently as part of the discussions. One Hong Kong tai-tai, new to the wealthy set, told us she had accomplished the switch to luxury brand usage because her friends kept egging her on – she has evolved into a high-spending VIP consumer in the space of two years.

Little wonder, then, that luxury brands roll out the red carpet for this all-important group, shaping their opinions quite literally on a one-on-one basis. There are private viewings of the season's latest collection of clothes and accessories, and yes, these can be arranged at home. Some stores have their own VIP rooms, and with the growing trend toward outsized flagship stores, an entire floor can be devoted to servicing VIP customers. Upscale shopping malls like the Landmark in Hong Kong offer a salon that luxury brands can hire by the day for VIPs, where a couple of models will do a private show.

Luxury brands go all out to nurture close relationships. They bring out the social networkers on their payroll to socialize with the VIPs. The store managers and sales staff get attuned to VIPs' special needs, understanding their likes and dislikes, assessing what pieces from the current collection would suit them best, often doing the pre-selecting on their behalf. They call up to announce new arrivals, give them first rights on hot items, and provide flexible shopping hours and a whole host of privileges to pamper them. They shape these women's perceptions, and in turn what the VIPs wear and say shapes the perceptions of their wealthy friends and acquaintances.

THE BUZZ

Buzz: Think of it as the collective consciousness of a city and its people. Suddenly, as if by magic, they all have the same thought on their minds. If David Beckham is coming to town for a football match, expect nationwide frenzy – men, women, young, old, everyone's heart is abuzz, thousands queuing up for tickets, fans snapping up Beckham merchandise, youngsters dressing like him. If it's the launch of Ferrari's latest Enzo, the men are agog, it dominates their conversation. In car-crazy Hong Kong, the *South China Morning Post* deemed fit to give the new model front-page coverage in its City section and devoted an editorial to it. Here's the twist: Eight cars were snapped up on day one, but being left-hand drives they *cannot* be driven on Hong Kong's roads.[16] A status marker that will adorn the driveway, presumably.

If a hot television star sports a new look, suddenly all the women are abuzz, promptly adopting her style tips. The whole *ganguro* girl craze in Japan, where legions of teenagers darkened their faces and went about in whacky and wonderful outfits, tripping along on impossibly high platform shoes, was started by a hot porn star who "dressed" like that.[17] The *pinjok* look that swept South Korea was the complete antithesis – here faces were made up pale and the dress was a demure skirt suit with low-heeled Ferragamo shoes – but it began the same way, when two South Korean female actors portrayed the look on a television show, their hair pinned up with a diamond-studded hairpin (the *pinjok*), and suddenly that was the buzz around town.[18]

In our Luxeplosion model, buzz is the direct output of the actions of the cult catalysts – the celebrity-studded brand parties, what the fashion editors are recommending, what the VIP consumers are wearing. It's as if you put all that into a buzz-generating machine and it starts spewing out reams of press writeups and hours of television coverage, a jumble of pictures, soundbites, words, always with the brand prominently placed. If you've done a top-quality job on your cult catalysts, the media frenzy should follow as a natural corollary, measured in column centimeters and television minutes, in readership and viewership.

Simultaneously, on a second front, the talk-of-the-town effect is taking place. Tai-tais are discussing John Galliano's latest creation over lunch and analyzing local celebrity Cecilia or Mi-jung's rendition of it at

Friday night's party. Office ladies are spending their lunchtimes discussing the new Gucci bag and checking out what Kiki or Keiko, the office know-alls, have to say on it. Their bosses are discussing the new watch from Breguet or last night's wow event hosted by Chanel and that amazing fashion show. Youngsters are talking about the look sported by their Canto-pop or Mando-pop or Jap-pop heartthrob. And so it goes, different brands, different segments of consumers, simply talking, buzzing, usually with an appreciative undertone.

That leads us to the final stage, the cult.

THE CULT

Luxury brands have become a cult when people act on the buzz, when they pull out their wallets and buy the stuff. When you see large numbers of people carrying Murakami bags. When Gucci watches start ticking on wrists. When Burberry scarves appear around necks. When you spot too many men with a strap across their heart and the inevitable LV messenger bag straddling their hip. When suddenly everyone is in combat fatigues or candy-striped shirts or skewed necklines or fur-trimmed jackets.

It's out on the street. Your brand and the looks you promote are adopted by the mass of the population. It's the culmination of the process, the sale consummated, the cult created.

Cult tools + Cult catalysts + Buzz = Cult. QED.

No need to wait for three years for this Hermès Birkin look-alike, center top row, sitting happily in broad daylight next to a Kelly copy in Seoul's Itaewon market.

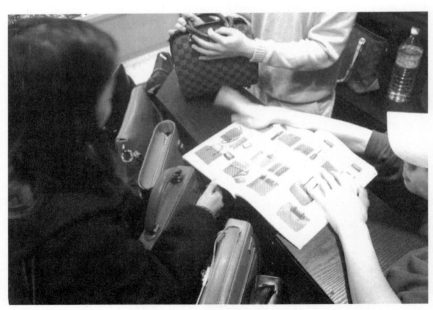

Catalog browsing is a standard technique in fake retailing – you point to the bag on the page, and it appears from thin air in a jiffy.

10

ADVENT OF THE GENUINE FAKES

"To be counterfeited is a symptom of success, certainly. If we weren't copied and counterfeited it would mean that the Prada and Miu Miu labels weren't desirable."

Patrizio Bertelli, CEO Prada[1]

The cult of the luxury brand has unwittingly given birth to an unsavory double: a multibillion-dollar global "fake" industry that, parasite like, lives off the success of brands in the real world.

Counterfeiting of luxury goods has been rampant in Asia since the 1980s, but the structure and dynamics of the fake business have changed dramatically in recent years. Cheap rip-offs still abound, providing a quick fix for the aspirations of the have-nots and the spend-nots, but the worrying trend is the emergence of near-perfect clones – known as "genuine fakes" in the trade – the quality of which is so good that it is finding a willing clientele even among the wealthy. While luxury brands earlier worried about their high-class image being sullied by shoddy imitations, now they are losing *real* sales.

South Korea has the dubious reputation of being the best at faking it – the "made in Korea" label in the counterfeit world is the equivalent of the "made in France" label for the real thing. "French big brands are very afraid of Korea because they can make a very high quality level," says Oh Hyuen-Suk, attachée commerciale at the French Embassy in South Korea.[2] Even the quality-obsessed Japanese consumer is satisfied, making South Korea the largest exporter of fakes to Japan. If further proof of Korean quality is needed, it is this: Employees of luxury houses in Europe are known to favor them too. The Seoul manager of a leading European brand reports:

Every time I have a trip to headquarters in Paris, there will be requests from colleagues to bring them a few fake bags. Chanel, Hermès, and Louis Vuitton are brands most asked for.

China, once known for cheap copies, has made sharp strides in quality and is now more or less at par with South Korea. Chinese imitations pass muster even among Hong Kong's fussy high-society tai-tais, who regularly cross the border into nearby Shenzhen to stock up on excellent replicas of Gucci bags, Rolex watches, and Vuitton wallets. Chinese manufacturers have realized that the devil is in the detail, so they take care of every minute aspect of a bag: the inside lining and pockets, the cloth pouch in which the bag is stored, right down to the paper tag with an "official" serial number and the reassuring announcement that this is an authentic product made in France.

If being copied is a "symptom of success," as Bertelli points out, then the entire counterfeit industry is an ironic snapshot of the successes and failures of brands and products, their desirability quotient reflected perversely in how prolifically they are copied. (In industry circles they say, only half-jokingly, that the one thing a brand manager fears *more* than fakes is *not* seeing his brand being faked.) No surprises, then, that Louis Vuitton's monogram bag rules in the fake world in Asia – of those who bought a counterfeit product, 26 percent purchased LV.[3] Gucci and Burberry follow at 15 and 12 percent respectively, according to a study by Synovate. Unfortunately for Bertelli, Prada, the number two faked brand till the early 2000s, has slipped several notches – only 7 percent had bought it in the same study. Paradoxically, too much success on the fake circuit was the reason for its fall.

In this chapter we look at the extent of the fake trade and how it is practiced, the attitude and behavior of the fake purchasers, and the obstacles that lie ahead in fixing what is essentially daylight robbery. The catch: What do you do when nearly everyone's a culprit?[4]

How Big Is the Fake Market?

The World Customs Organization estimates that the annual sale of *all* counterfeit goods – from pirated CDs to counterfeit medicines – is worth US$540 billion globally. Luxury goods constitute 5 percent of that,[5] covering everything from the omnipresent bags to watches, accessories, perfumes, clothes, and so on – or US$27 billion, worth a quarter of the legitimate luxury industry. Given that fake luxe products sell at a fraction (1–5 percent in Asia, 5–20 percent in Europe/US) of the real price, the sheer *quantity* of fakes sold could be even bigger than the genuine market.

This is reflected in the fact that the number of Asians buying fakes far exceeds those buying genuine luxury brands. The same Synovate study, which covered Hong Kong, South Korea, and Singapore, found that 12 percent of adults had purchased genuine luxury brands, whereas 19 percent had bought a fake.[6] A further 15 percent conveniently "didn't know" whether they had bought a fake, and chances are they're simply too embarrassed to admit it. In effect, up to 34 percent of the population could have bought fake luxury brands.

Thanks to the advent of high-quality fakes, it is not just the poor who are buying them but also the well heeled. The profile of fake purchasers in the Synovate study is startling: 73 percent of them were top executives, professionals, and white-collar workers.[7] Another study conducted in Hong Kong by professors Gerard Prendergast, Leung Hing Chuen, and Ian Phau found that low spenders on fakes were relatively lower-income blue-collar workers with secondary education, whereas the high spenders were white-collar workers with tertiary education earning substantially higher salaries.[8] So much for the moral effect of better education and bigger salaries.

Domestic consumption aside, Asian fake producers export huge quantities. The US ranks as the number one importer of fake luxe goods. The US government places China, Hong Kong, and South Korea as the top three fake exporters into the country,[9] and in the case of Hong Kong the goods have probably been produced in China, as production costs in Hong Kong are uneconomical. Japan is the second biggest importer, followed by Europe. The irony here is that while Western luxury brands – of the genuine kind, that is – are busy conquering Asia, Asia is duplicating them and selling them at a fraction of the price right back to the West.

Furthermore, while Asian tourist-shoppers are flocking to the West to buy genuine luxury brands, there is a reverse flow of Western tourists shopping for fakes in Asia. "Western tourists buy suitcases full of fakes," says a self-confessed addict. "They just shop, shop, shop." These tourists are buying not just for personal consumption but also gifts for family and friends back home, so collectively they constitute another channel of counterfeit exports to the developed world, in this case self-purchased and self-trafficked, one bag at a time.

THE GUILT-FREE TRIP

Why do millions of otherwise honest people buy fakes? Frédéric Hubert – economic attaché at the French Embassy Economic Mission in South Korea, who has been battling counterfeiters on behalf of French luxury brands – explains:

The main problem is cultural. People here don't see buying a counterfeit product as something illegal.[10]

That about sums up the prevailing attitude to fakes in Asia.

The only difference between Asian fake consumers and Western ones is this: The Western ones are conscious that they are doing something wrong but do it anyway (to them, it's the equivalent of a white lie); the Asian consumer does not seem to consider the moral aspect particularly relevant. A study conducted by Gail Tom of the California State University at Sacramento found that American counterfeit purchasers held a neutral attitude toward statements such as "People who buy counterfeit products are committing a crime," "People who sell counterfeit products are committing a crime." What is significant is that they did not disagree.[11] Another study, this one conducted by Gerard Prendergast of the Hong Kong Baptist University, found that Hong Kong's fake shoppers considered moral and ethical issues of little importance.[12]

There is a question of degree, of course. South Korean consumers we interviewed had absolutely no qualms discussing their fake purchases; it was so much a way of life, so much an accepted conclusion that every woman in South Korea owns a few fake pieces, that the very possibility of life without fakes seemed alien. Japanese consumers are at the other end of the spectrum – while the statistics show that Japan imports a significant amount of fakes, we found the average Japanese more interested in the real thing than fakes. They have money, they go to a real store, they buy the genuine article – that's what makes the Japanese the world's biggest luxe consumers.

China is interesting in that it has the entire spectrum from consumers who only buy fakes to others who will not touch them with a barge pole. For starters, there is a huge number of brand-ignorant consumers who don't even know they are buying counterfeit products – they are simply buying an attractive bag with some kind of pattern on it. Then there are legions of fully aware young people, typically starting on their first jobs, who aspire to own imported luxe brands but lack the means. They recognize the social importance of sporting the right logos and promptly buy a few fakes. A year or two into their jobs and some rapid maturing on the *savoir faire* ladder, they realize that counterfeits don't make the mark socially – they are seen as "low class." These people quickly graduate to the real thing and continue their climb up the social scale. Finally, there is the Chinese nouveau riche class, who simply look down on fakes. Their sole purpose is to display wealth and win social kudos. Products are chosen on the basis of high price, the higher the better. In these circles cheap imitations won't do, they don't *cost* enough.

The arrival of "genuine fakes" has triggered a strange new sport among Hong Kong's tai-tais. Nearby Shenzhen has become the equivalent of a tai-tai Disneyland – a couple of girlfriends get together and head off for a day of hands-on entertainment. Shenzhen's Lowu Commercial Center has all the ingredients: the hunt for the best fakes, good-natured bargaining, the manicures and massages, the dim-sum lunches, and by the time you head back home, weighed down by your fake Guccis and Fendis, you have many tales of triumph to narrate to close friends. It's an inexpensive pastime, and the thrill of getting so much for so little money is compelling.

We asked a luxe industry veteran why rich tai-tais buy fakes. Her answer was revealing:

The more wealthy they are, the more stingy they are, let's put it this way. I know some of these women are wealthy, let's not talk Hong Kong wealthy, their husbands are mega, mega Southeast Asian wealthy... they love the buzz of using these handbags, it's fun, it's a kick for them.

The sport is not limited to Hong Kong locals – the large expatriate community indulges in it vigorously. Before trips back home to the US/Europe/Australia they visit Shenzhen, picking up gifts. We heard from a Filipina maid that she has a whole collection of designer-label fakes, thanks to her generous American "Ma'am" who gives her a bag as a present every time she makes a trip to Shenzhen.

Singapore has a strong fondness for fakes, moralistic government notwithstanding. Ditto for Taipei, where even a luxury brand gift is presumed fake until proven genuine. We heard the amusing tale of an office where the female employees have appointed a "fake detector," a colleague with an unusually discerning eye. "Every time someone is gifted a luxury brand item, they take it to her to test its authenticity," says a woman who works there. Malaysia likes fakes as well – at a night market in Kuala Lumpur, our local host proudly vouched for the quality of fake watches on sale: Apparently the local police had destroyed a ton of Rolexes by running a road roller on them, and reportedly many of the watches still kept ticking. Everywhere in Asia, people are faking it with few pangs of conscience.

LOWU TO DONGDAEMUN

There's an elaborate distribution system at work, with thousands of small retailers, cogs in the wheel, putting up little shops in what have become popular fake markets. From Beijing to Shanghai, Hong Kong to Seoul, every city has at least one major location where a feast of fakes is spread out. The sheer scale of operations is mind-boggling: Shenzhen's Lowu Commercial Center is a full-scale mall devoted to fake retailing; Seoul's Dongdaemun area has similar shopping centers where whole floors are earmarked for fakes. It is commonly believed that underground criminal elements control and manage the big picture; to what extent it is hard to say, but well organized it certainly is. We looked at the retail practices in South Korea and China, two of the biggest fake markets in Asia.

Fake retailing in South Korea is a bit like Clinton not inhaling – the merchandise on display is "C grade," with the logos modified sufficiently to be legal under South Korean law, whereas the A-grade goods, spitting images of the real thing, are hidden away discreetly inside the shop. So you go through the game of picking up a C-grade LV handbag – the logo looks like two Vs locked in a vertical embrace – and soon enough you're motioned into the tiny shop and shown the real McCoy, extremely good quality, perfect logo. In China, on the other hand, they put the A-grade goods on display straightaway – the attitude seems to be why waste time with charades, let's call a fake a fake and get on with business, with the police looking conveniently away.

Prices vary depending on the grade, A, B, or C, and hearty bargaining is the norm. Prices are much higher in South Korea compared to China – for similar LV bags, the opening price in Seoul was US$125, whereas in Shenzhen it was US$35. Furthermore, the norm in China is to bring the price down to a third of what is quoted; the norm in South Korea is half. South Koreans are willing to pay high prices for excellent reproductions, sometimes as much as US$100. In China, *that* would be considered a crime. Even a top-of-the-line Hermès reproduction can be brought down to US$50–60 in China.

Shopkeepers extend the reach of their business through the use of Japanese "catalogs," which have become standard equipment in all fake markets. These are fat guides to the world of luxury brand bags, all the styles neatly laid out in rows of tiny pictures labeled with style identification numbers. All you have to do is point to a bag that catches your fancy, and the shopkeeper produces it in seconds. How he manages to provide for such a vast range is amazing – there must be an extraordinary inventory-management system going on in a limited space, and probably a handy backup warehouse around the corner.

When dealing with non-monogram brands like Hermès or Prada, the modus operandi is to withhold the name tags until after the purchase, thus allowing the shopkeepers to stay on the right side of the law a little bit longer. For example, the black Prada rucksacks we saw in Itaewon had the trademark metallic triangle stuck on the bag, cheekily lettered O-R-I-G-I-N-A-L, which the salesgirl hastily assured us would be changed to PRADA as soon as we bought it. An excellent Kelly reproduction had blank metallic tags, while dozens of little "Hermès" name tags sat innocently in a ceramic bowl, ready to be swapped at the word go.

Things get murkier when a few genuine pieces are mixed up with a batch of high-quality reproductions, another standard practice aimed at

Shenzhen: China's Designer-Label Fake Paradise

With Rosie our expert guide leading the way, we make the trip from Hong Kong to Shenzhen in an hour and 15 minutes. The fake-packed Lowu Commercial Center is right next to the train station, a six-story air-conditioned mall humming with shoppers.

You get an Alice in Wonderland feeling walking through a modern mall in broad daylight surrounded by a sea of shops selling illegal copies, all displayed openly. At the first shop we settle into some hearty bargaining, bringing down the US$35 Louis Vuitton monogram handbag to US$12. (The original would cost US$650 in Hong Kong.) It's an A-grade genuine fake, and the salesgirl pulls out a catalog to show us how closely it matches the original style. Then the senior salesman steps in – he yanks out a lighter and holds a flame along the surface of the LV bag, that's his demo proving it is genuine leather, although we panic seeing our selected merchandise about to be set on fire. (Rosie wonders gamely if the flame is fake too.) So now we have a flame-tested leather LV monogram bag, whereas the originals are made in mere canvas.

Impressed, Rosie picks up another LV monogram handbag with double handles, at the same price, and a matching cigarette case for $2.50. On a roll, she goes for a Gucci black-and-white logo-print bag for US$12. We sit down while our purchases are packed, and before we know it we are leafing through a photo album of watches. Oh well, we say yes to a Cartier tank watch for $12, a perfect copy of the real thing. They have us try several Mont Blanc pens priced at $1.25. They write smooth as silk, far smoother than the original in my bag.

All the while we are being threatened with police action – the word has spread that the police are "scheduling" an inspection of the fifth floor, where we are. The two sales-girls and the salesman break into action, picking up all the "logo" items – Gucci, LV, Dior, Fendi – and stuffing them into large plastic garbage bags. The man climbs to the top shelf, pulls out one of the planks of the false ceiling, and deftly tucks away the garbage bags. He's a practiced hand, totally unperturbed, whereas we are growing dis-tinctly jittery. The salesgirl tells us firmly not to worry – she has steel, tempered with a smile, in her voice – the police will catch us, Missy, not you, and besides they are only due at 1 pm.

That gives us 15 unhurried minutes for further fake shopping, and we plump straight for an Hermès Birkin. She produces a light brown one but our heart is set on a red one. The salesgirl vanishes and returns out of breath – she has clearly done a 100-meter dash into some unknown storage facility or a friend's store down the row – hold-

Table 10.2 US$14,125 worth of luxe for US$141.75

	Shenzhen fake price	Hong Kong real price
HANDBAGS		
LV monogram single handle	$12	$650
LV monogram double handle	$12	$650
Gucci black-and-white logo print	$12	$500
Hermès Birkin red leather	$60	$8,500
Tod's red leather tote	$12	$800
OTHER GOODS		
Cartier tank watch	$12	$1,500
Mont Blanc ball pen	$1.25	$125
LV suitcase	$15	$1,250
LV cigarette case	$2.50	$75
LV lipstick case	$3	$75
TOTAL (10 items)	US$141.75	US$14,125

ing a red Birkin. It isn't top quality, but by then we are too far gone into the bargaining and settle at US$60. We push off before the police hit the shop.

Rule number one is to scan the environment before you shop – as soon as we step out, our Birkin neatly packed into an Hermès carton, we are hit by Birkins and Kellys on either side, and experience a severe case of post-purchase dissonance. We have paid too much and there is far better quality available. We see a lovely black "crocodile" Birkin – high-quality cow leather with a crocodile marking on it – and the salesgirl is begging us to take it at $50, cajoling us with, "Missy, just right for high-class lady like you."

Then Rosie goes on a binge, picking up an exquisite soft red leather Tod's bag for $12, an LV suitcase-stroller for $15, and a lipstick case for $3. She's a mean bargainer, she simply says I have no more money, and I still have to buy the train ticket back to Hong Kong. It works.

There are Burberry bags. There are shoes with Ferragamo trimmings. There are Dior sunglasses. There are even "new arrivals" in Paris, not yet in Hong Kong. There's everything a label lover could possibly want.

But we are loaded and we can't physically hold any more.

confusing the police authorities as well as consumers. Department stores in some of the provincial Chinese cities go a step further – they copy the entire retail presentation of the brand, put up a "fake store," and stock it with this dubious mix of real and fake products. Consumers think they are visiting a legitimate store.

By far the most frightening scenario for luxury brands is very high-quality fakes being passed off as the real thing, not in the hinterland of China but in big cities like Tokyo to experienced luxe consumers. Velisarios Kattoulas of the *Far Eastern Economic Review* describes the case of a South Korean counterfeiter with seven factories who is distributing Kelly bags in Japanese stores. The proud counterfeiter says:

We put it on sale in a discount store we work with for about ¥500,000 (US$3,900). We weren't sure what would happen but it sold literally in a day, so ever since we've been selling most of our Kelly bags as original.[13]

Not only is the consumer being duped, the luxury brand is losing a genuine sale.

THE COUNTERFEITERS

Ironically, it is the rise of Asia as a legitimate manufacturing base offering the unbeatable combination of low cost and high quality that has spurred its growth as a counterfeiting center. Since the 1970s, Western companies have steadily handed out manufacturing contracts to Asian countries, often helping set up facilities, training staff, transferring know-how, and supervising production to meet exacting standards. Now that expertise has spilled across the line and is being misused for counterfeit production. The motive: unbelievably high profit margins, in the same league as the drugs trade, estimated to be $10 for every $1 invested.

In some instances, a supplier to one of the famous luxury brands simply runs a few extra shifts a week and sells off this unaccounted-for "excess production" in the local market at highly discounted prices, still making a neat profit. Equally, the counterfeiter may be an ex-supplier, ex-licensee, ex-franchisee, or ex-partner who has the necessary know-how and goes into blatant fake production. A case in point: Guy Laroche, with the assistance of the French Economic Mission in South Korea, won a judicial trial against its former partner turned counterfeiter.[14]

Yet others may have no links to the original brand whatsoever – they are entrepreneurs who choose counterfeiting as their line of work. For them, the starting point is getting a good prototype for copying. Some buy it locally; the Dior store in Shanghai routinely deals with "returned goods" that have been ripped apart and sewn back together by cheeky counterfeiters trying to recoup their prototype investment. Others buy it in Paris, using "organized shopping tours" with the sole purpose of getting prototypes. The French authorities are cracking down on such groups. For example, a group of 13 Hong Kong tourists were handcuffed on *arrival* at Paris airport, detained for 30 hours, subjected to a humiliating strip-search, and put on a plane back home – a bit like the "precrime squad" in *Minority Report*. There was a storm in the Hong Kong press at these strong-arm tactics, but one of the "tourists" admitted that she paid a mere HK$2,000 (US$250) to join the trip and had agreed to buy a minimum of HK$230,000 (US$30,000) worth of luxury goods.[15]

The next requirements are know-how and considerable skill. Counterfeiters employ technicians who have worked at genuine luxury brand manufacturing units – once on board, they train other workers. Some counterfeiters are reportedly hiring Italian technicians as training experts[16] – this could well be the reason behind the sudden rise in quality. Italy incidentally has a super-sized fake industry of its own, the sale of illegal leather goods alone estimated at US$1.5 billion.[17]

Now the manufacturing process has gone global, with say China producing a part of the product and the rest finished off elsewhere. One instance reported in Europe involved the arrest of two Ukrainian mobsters who were behind fake branded perfumes that had been "counterfeited in China, bottled in Australia and assembled in Italy."[18] This sort of complex multijurisdiction case makes the counterfeiters that much harder to catch, prosecute, and convict.

STRONG LAWS, WEAK ENFORCEMENT

Touted as a major tourist attraction, Shanghai's Xiang Yang Market is a sprawling complex with hundreds of stalls bursting with every imaginable fake brand and product. At its entrance is a prominent notice from the Shanghai Administration for Industry and Commerce warning against selling counterfeit goods of some 40 trademarks. Next to it is a police booth where two cops sit idly while business proceeds briskly behind them.

It's not as if the laws aren't in place – while not perfect, legislation in most Asian markets has enough teeth to punish the counterfeiters – it's their lax enforcement that's the real culprit. The policing is a charade and the only conclusion one can come to is that the counterfeiters are "managing" the police rather well – in China, the joke is that the authorities are being taken care of with gifts of *genuine* luxury brands.

Companies have started doing their own policing: hiring investigators and lawyers, collecting evidence, bringing culprits to the attention of the law, and working with local authorities to orchestrate raids. Louis Vuitton alone reportedly carried out 524 raids in China in 2002.[19] "We spend a lot of time and money tracking down these guys," says Tim King of Dunhill. He believes that striking at the root is important – "no point getting the retailers, we have to try and hit the factories."

At the same time, European luxury brands are coming together as a group and collectively lobbying local governments to improve policies, strengthen laws, and enforce them. In a landmark case in 2006, LVMH, Chanel, Prada, Burberry, and Gucci jointly won the first copyright verdict against a landlord at the Silk Street shopping mall in Beijing. The judge ordered the culprit to pay US$13,000 – a paltry sum no doubt, but it's a positive first step nevertheless.

FAKES: A GENUINE DRIVER OF THE CULT?

High consumer demand, high-quality production in huge quantities, high profit margins, widespread distribution, no real penalties, and no trace of a conscience either on the part of the consumer or the counterfeiter – it seems a tough battle for the big brand companies with all the cards stacked against them. Better policing and brands themselves putting up a concerted fight against fakes are certainly yielding results, but we don't expect fakes to disappear any time soon, not as long as human beings lust for luxe and are willing to bend their morals to attain them. However, in the long run we believe a certain uneasy equilibrium will be reached.

Evil as they are, fakes have played a role in spreading the luxury brand cult in Asia. They have acted as a "trial pack," giving a taste of these brands to millions, who slowly but surely over time seek out the real thing.

In the initial stages of luxe fever – the *show off* phase of the Spread of Luxury model – consumers, especially those with high aspirations but insufficient means, resort to fakes. At this stage, the very existence of fakes helps advertise the genuine brand and spreads its usage, albeit fake, among a much wider consumer base, whetting their appetite for luxury. As the market matures and consumers move up the economic ladder, their taste matures too and they start eyeing the real thing. At a certain critical point, pushed along by social pressures and their own desire to upgrade, they cross the line into true luxe. Once they get used to the genuine article, especially the store experience and the service aspects, they are hooked, at least for a while. It is only when consumers reach supreme confidence in their social stature that they flirt with fakes again, but it will be a marginal affair, an occasional one-night stand with a Rolex watch or the thrill of faking it with a Gucci bag that no one can tell from real. As the research findings of Arghavan Nia and Judith Lynne Zaichkowsky demonstrate, the widespread use of fakes does not seem to negatively affect consumers' intention to purchase original luxury brands.[20]

This is exactly the stage at which Japan finds itself today, where fakes are bought and sold, but for the most part consumers stay with the real thing, resulting in a mammoth luxury market. We saw distinct signs of upgrading to the genuine article among consumers we interviewed in South Korea. The same is true for upwardly mobile mainland Chinese consumers, who are even flying abroad to do their luxe shopping. Give China a few more years of rising economic prosperity, and we expect to see increased consumption of genuine luxury goods in the ever-growing upper and middle strata of society. The lower stratum of society will continue to consume fakes, but they too will eventually rise up the economic ladder and graduate to the real thing.

He's quite a mover, our Asian metrosexual man, adopting a "stylish casual" dress code, spending lavishly on designer-label bags, shoes, clothes, jewelry, and watches.

Photo courtesy of *Zip Homme*, Hong Kong.

11

THE FUTURE OF LUXURY

"If the 20th century belonged to America, the 21st surely belongs to Asia."
Suzy Menkes, fashion editor, International Herald Tribune[1]

The grande dame of fashion is right, as always. In fact, with the biggest luxury brand market tucked firmly in its hip pocket, the twenty-first century already belongs to Asia. But what lies ahead is even bigger – so far only a tiny portion of the continent's potential has walked down the designer ramp and millions of Asians are getting ready backstage, steadily acquiring the means and the taste for luxury.

With Asia's inevitable economic rise, democratization of luxe on an unprecedented scale lies ahead. Consider Figure 11.1. Japan is the only country to have decisively made the move into Stage 5, resulting in a large market that, notwithstanding its ups and downs, turns in copious luxe revenues year after year. Hong Kong and Singapore are almost there, but every other Asian country still has plenty of growth to come. Take China. For all its noisy conspicuous consumption, luxury brands have touched less than 1 percent of Chinese so far – the equivalent figure in Japan is 25 percent, in Hong Kong and Singapore 15 percent, in South

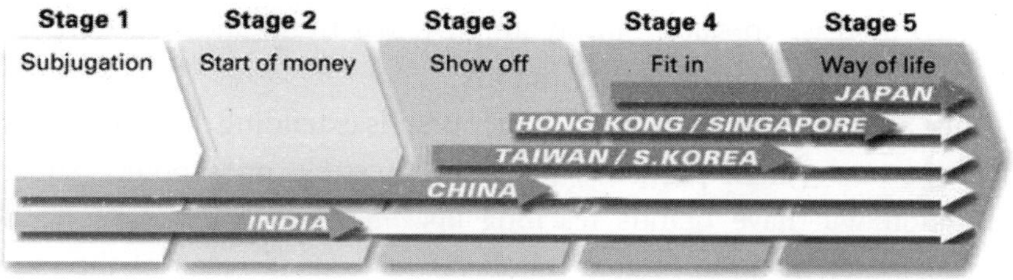

Stage 1	Stage 2	Stage 3	Stage 4	Stage 5
Subjugation	Start of money	Show off	Fit in	Way of life

Figure 11.1 The opportunity ahead: Asian markets will progressively evolve to the next stage

Korea 12 percent. Now factor in China's huge population, ten times that of Japan, and the math shows that it will easily grow to be the biggest luxury market in the world. Then there's India, already following in China's footsteps, plus Thailand, Malaysia, Indonesia, Philippines – Southeast Asian nations that are back on a growth path. Even Vietnam, spurred on by a fast-growing economy, is awakening to luxury, with the likes of Louis Vuitton, Cartier, and Mont Blanc opening stores there. Just catering to the needs of millions more luxe-hungry Asians year on year should keep the industry humming for decades.

Along with this quantitative explosion will come significant qualitative differences. In this chapter we look at five major future trends that will shape the evolution of the luxury cult.

Some Like It Super Haute

We estimate there will be over 50 million luxury brand consumers in Asia by 2010, twice that if you count fake consumption. With the emergence of this large-scale cult, the very definition of luxury will have changed for ever. Ironically, this state of too much luxe in too many hands will engender a reaction in the opposite direction *à la* Simmel, a search for the exclusive, not-for-everybody version, allowing élite customers to distance themselves from the well-heeled mass market. Call it the "super-élitization of luxury," a jab in the eye to the democratization of luxury movement. With increasing numbers of Asians getting promoted to the ranks of the seriously wealthy, the market for extremely high-priced products is already on the rise – for example, Bottega Veneta, known for its very expensive leather-latticed handbags, has seen a sharp increase in sales. Simply amplify that trend and you have the perfect setting for super-luxury brands.

Just as democratization led to luxury brands extending downward with machine-made, mass-produced items at accessible price points, super-élitization will have brands reaching *upward* through exquisite handcrafted pieces made in limited numbers, well out of reach of the mass luxury consumer. Instead of loud logos on canvas bags, these will offer exceptional quality and artistic merit. Joanne Ooi, creative director of Shanghai Tang, sees a trend toward "unprecedented levels of customization" and "hand-made artisanal value" among the "genuinely affluent and genuinely educated."[2] We are already seeing the start of that trend with brands like Louis Vuitton offering very high-priced made-to-order bags in materials such as snakeskin. The Guccissima line from Gucci – embossed logo on leather – is a clear move to its artisanal roots. We also anticipate a revival of haute couture, particularly in markets like India and China where the desire to make grand statements is high.

This is a case of Bourdieu's theory slowly taking effect. As Asia's new money matures, as the numbers of the genuinely affluent expand, status anxiety will give way to confidence, and with it will come a move toward greater individualism. Instead of rushing into the obvious status markers, this set of discerning consumers will show a greater diversity of taste, making choices based on who they are and what they like rather than blindly following the crowd. As this trend spreads it will give rise to a vibrant market with a multitude of niche brands, unique products, and exciting styles. Michael Burke, former head of Christian Dior and now CEO of Fendi, comments on today's exuberant but somewhat indiscriminate way of consuming:

The Asian consumer comes to luxury more recently. Almost anything goes today... as markets evolve, as markets mature, they will become more discriminating and the market will become more segmented.

He sees this discerning consumer buying more "true luxury" as against "psuedo luxury," the former defined by creativity and uniqueness, the latter by a hollow blandness.[3]

Even today, a small section of sophisticated shoppers is showing signs of becoming bored by the sameness of the offering of major brands. They are looking for excitement, the thrill of discovery, something off the beaten path. Bonnie Gokson says:

A lot of people want to go to places where there are nicer little finds. Now it [existing retail] is so predictable... it has lost the spark, it's anaesthetized.[4]

The glitzy retail outlets, the massive flagship stores, the globally standardized image, the same range of products – wonderful factors that drove the democratization of luxury – unfortunately leave the most discerning shoppers cold. While worldwide homogeneity in large-format stores is the diktat today, luxury retailing itself will evolve, finding ways to provide the thrill of discovery in small, intimate settings – a touch of the flea market rendered for the super-élite.

LV Cellphone, Anyone?

"Luxe branding" new product categories has been a key growth strategy, and we see that trend accelerating into hitherto unexplored realms.

Take Louis Vuitton. The original luggage maker has extended its name to a range of handbags, wallets, shoes, ready-to-wear clothes, jewelry and fine watches – and very successfully too. What expertise does a luggage maker have in the specialized field of watch making? Indeed, you might ask what expertise a watch maker has in bag making, considering that watch brands like Cartier are extending into leather bags. The questions are irrelevant in today's world where expertise can be bought pretty much off the shelf. LV, for instance, is using Swiss watch makers who have honed their skills over generations.

Well beyond the bags and shoes, the gorgeous dresses and exquisite jewelry, what luxury brands have really created is a powerful hold over the hearts and minds of people globally, an amorphous property that can now be stretched to encompass a much wider list of products. The real value resides in the brand name itself, its connotations of prestige and luxury easily transferable. It was done often enough in the good old days of Pierre Cardin and Yves Saint Laurent, who happily licensed away their brand to be stamped on hundreds of products. Now luxury brands are intelligently choosing new product categories to brand as against the "anything goes" thinking of the licensing era. The intention is to keep upping the value of the brand with every additional product brought under its purview, zealously guarding against senseless brand erosion. In other words, Louis Vuitton sunglasses priced at US$500 would be a yes. Louis Vuitton frying pans at US$20, something that Cardin allowed, would be a definite no.

"Luxury as a lifestyle" is the guiding principle in picking these new areas. Look back at the history of luxe brand extension and you see it coming in waves, each one breaking into a sumptuous way of life.

Perfumes were an early favorite, usually under license, as were cosmetics and skincare lines. The wave of rejuvenations in the 1990s had brands entering ready-to-wear apparel. With the rise of handbags as major status markers, there was a rush into bags and accessories. Then came a watch-branding wave – ranging from the playful eye-candy sort at a couple of hundred dollars to serious watches to jewelry watches. Now jewelry is under attack – Sagra Maceira de Rosen, former analyst at JP Morgan and now partner at private equity company Hemisphere One, says the fact that it is a massive US$100 billion-dollar market with barely 4 percent so far luxe-branded by the likes of Tiffany, Cartier, and Bulgari makes it a mouthwatering target.[5] Fashion houses like Gucci, Chanel, and Dior have launched fine jewelry lines. They can get pretty fine – a Marc Jacobs-designed Louis Vuitton diamond necklace retails at US$200,000.

What will be the next frontier? We see technology, especially "on-person" technology – mobile phones, Blackberries, iPods, laptops, expensive items that make a personal statement – as new areas for luxe branding. Nokia has already teed off with the Vertu line of premium handsets, using precious metals and prestige marketing to do the job. D&G has teamed up with Motorola, and there's even a Ferrari laptop. More techno innovations keep popping up – your shoe can talk to your iPod thanks to the Nike+iPod sports kit. Will Apple – with design, creativity, and lifestyle already imprinted in its DNA – become a full-fledged luxury brand that one day extends into jewelry and watches? Will Louis Vuitton go techno-luxe, entering the iPod domain, for example? This is entirely in the realm of the possible, a winning combination given Asia's penchant for technology on the one hand and it's great love for luxury brands on the other.

With lifestyles getting ever more luxurious, the possibilities for brand extensions are seemingly endless. Armani is doing flowers. Versace is doing hotels. Esprit is doing hair salons.

RISE OF THE ASIAN METROSEXUAL

If dressing up in a way that doesn't quite fit the macho mold is a defining characteristic of metrosexuality, then the Asian male was halfway there even before the term was invented. He may have gone through a dull patch thanks to the colonial era that imposed Western clothing standards, but the peacock gene is well on the way to being reactivated, especially among young men, spelling a huge opportunity for luxury brands.

To begin with, Asia never quite subscribed to Western notions of manhood – the stereotype of the tall, muscular guy, rough at the edges, the shadow of a two-day beard on his square jaw, chest hair peeping out from an open-collared shirt, remained largely a Western ideal. It's a physical impossibility anyway if you are born shorter, slighter, with hardly any body hair and not much on the chin either, which is the reality for most men from China to Southeast Asia. What is more, the Asian male had a thing for physical adornment all along – he has seen his father and grandfather wear colorful local costumes, and chances are he has donned them himself on special occasions. Jewelry has been an accepted thing – Indian maharajas wore plenty of it, from earrings to elaborate necklaces studded with precious jewels. David Beckham's sarong routine may have been considered gender bending in the West, but it would be just another item of clothing in many parts of Asia. And if a salmon-pink shirt is a must in the Western metrosexual's wardrobe, what do you say about Bollywood stars who sport neon pink and lime green, often on the same shirt?

To this innate propensity, add rising prosperity and the coming of age of Asian metropolises offering the clubbing-gyming-malling-spaing culture, and you have the perfect setting for men taking to metrosexual fashion in a big way. Just how quickly is a surprise – a survey in macho South Korea by advertising agency Cheil found that two out of three men have adopted "androgynous characteristics and lifestyles," judging by their personal care and fashion routines.[6]

Significantly, men are taking charge of their own styling and the results are showing. "In the past, if men wanted to buy a suit, their girlfriends or wives would take the initiative," says Wendy So, editor of Hong Kong men's style magazine *Zip Homme*.[7] With marriage going out of fashion there are more single men around, and they have had to "train themselves" to shop. Left to their own devices, what you see is nothing short of a men's liberation movement, and while they haven't yet reached the male equivalent of the bra-burning stage, they are "becoming more courageous in dressing." The turning point was the dot-com days, when men got official permission to dress creatively. Asian dot-commers didn't just go casual, they went *stylish* casual, and it's a theme that has carried over. Wendy So comments:

Hong Kong men are more "picky" compared to European and American ones. They pay more attention to details... they will really select what makes them "dress" beautifully.

And now men are taking care of their complexions and personal grooming, opening up a huge market for male beauty products and services, estimated to be worth US$19.5 billion by 2008.[8] Men's beauty salons and spas are popping up in every Asian metropolis, offering facials, waxing, slimming treatments, you name it. Cosmetic companies like Clarins, L'Oréal, and Shiseido are launching men's skincare and beauty lines. Even local brands are jumping on the bandwagon. In India, Fair and Lovely, a women's skin-whitening cream company, found to its surprise that 30 percent of its product was being used by men, prompting it to launch Fair and Handsome for men.[9]

"Men are beginning to shop more like women," says Laura Wenke, former senior vice-president, sales and marketing of high-end department store Lane Crawford, which has been seeing a rise in men's contemporary fashion business.[10] They are even showing up at stores on weekday afternoons, just like women do. Ducking the office? Not necessarily. Their work itself has gone a tad metrosexual – it's no longer a staid 9-to-6 job in banking, law, and accounting. Asian men are increasingly venturing into all sorts of creative professions. They are running trendy bars, restaurants, hair salons, and art galleries, being DJs and event managers, jobs that take a round of afternoon shopping in their stride.

Luxury brands are keenly aware of the needs of this new species of men and have definite designs on him. "Men are more free to express themselves," says Michael Burke.[11] This new male may be as interested in clothes as a woman is, but the last thing he wants is to actually dress like one. It's an important distinction, and one that Dior's menswear designer Hedi Slimane apparently brings to the drawing board. "He is a *menswear* designer designing for *men*," explains Burke. Slimane is busy converting Dior's innate creativity and energy into new shapes and silhouettes ("very angular") for men.

Consumer Profile
Conrad Ng: Watch Collector and Luxury Brand Lover

Conrad is representative of the new breed of men in Asia: entrepreneurial and successful on the work front, and not afraid to step out of the confines of the dark-suit-white-shirt-safe-tie routine on the sartorial front. As head of Japan Health Foods, 36-year-old Conrad is rapidly expanding his Hong Kong-based company into new markets in Asia; he is also rapidly expanding his already considerable watch and jewelry collection and, while these are his passion, you won't find him lacking in designer clothes, bags, and shoes.

He has very definite views on what he likes and what he doesn't. "Bulgari used to be my favorite but I stopped buying their watches the day they put their logos on the dial," he says, far preferring the days when "it was so subtle." He still nurtures a soft spot for the brand – when we met at his office he was wearing a chic Bulgari watch-bracelet-ring set, all perfectly matched. And no, the watch did not have that annoying logo on the dial.

Bulgari's loss was Cartier's gain, and Conrad has gone on to buy 30 of its watches, plus several jewelry pieces. For example, he has the "love series" bracelets (once worn, the bracelet can only be opened by a specially designed screwdriver, which is presumably in your lover's hands) in white gold, yellow gold, and pink gold, and as if that wasn't enough, Cartier is making a "one and only one" for him in rose gold with three diamonds on each side. "Very subtle," he assures us.

On his 65-watch collection
"Some of them are actually not very expensive... [he laughs] If you know about watch movements, all Cartier watches are cheap watches.

"The very, very expensive ones? I own 30–40 of them. My most expensive watch is a Breguet. The retail price was HK$700,000 (US$90,000)... [grins] I might sell that one day when I'm short of money." Little chance of that, we suspect, he has been collecting watches for 18 years and hasn't sold one yet.

On his dream watch
"Girard Perregaux 3-bridges tourbillon. It costs HK$1 million (US$128,000)... [he raises his eyebrows] It's one of my dream watches, OK, doesn't mean I have the money to buy it now."

On how he stores his watches

"I divide it into three collections. Very, very expensive ones, I keep at the bank. Very, very cheap ones, I keep on the floor. [We envision him treading gingerly around his apartment, careful not to step on an errant watch] For the moderate ones, I ordered a whole range of boxes from Lane Crawford. I have different boxes, like, this is a Bulgari box, this is a Cartier box... I keep the watches with the bracelets in sets. I have a box for the more sophisticated movements. I also have boxes by theme – rose gold, yellow gold, white gold..."

On how he decides which watch to wear

"After a bath every night, just before I go to bed, I'll pick the watch for tomorrow... and then I'll wear that watch to sleep. This is a very funny habit actually... [he admits with a grin] Sometimes it'll take a long time to decide, and sometimes it's a very short time, it depends. If I have seen a Bulgari advertisement recently, then I say 'Oh! I must wear Bulgari,' so I go to the Bulgari box."

On why he buys Rolex

"People who *know* watches will not buy Rolex... [he wrinkles his nose in disapproval] they are more *mass* production. The reason I bought all my Rolexes was for *flashy* reasons. I bought the pink gold Rolex because I know if I go to China [he makes frequent business trips there] and people want to know my status, then even if I wear my tourbillon they won't know... even if I am wearing a million-dollar watch, they won't know. So for that kind of occasion I need a Rolex."

On designer-brand clothes

"I do buy expensive clothes, but now it is more casual clothing." Earlier he bought designer suits, but he has switched to cheaper local ones. "I buy a lot of Prada. Comme des Garçons is another brand I like, I tend to buy it in Japan."

On shoes

"I'm not a shoe collector, I'm just practical. I buy shoes when they are doing promotions... like at the Gucci sale, I bought five pairs."

On bags

"I have 20–30 handbags. I like LV bags, plain color, not those with logos." He shows us the bag he has brought to work today – it's a "subtle" Louis Vuitton.

The bottom line is this: If men shop like women, the men's market can potentially be as big as the women's – maybe even bigger, given that men tend to have a lot more money on hand.

WESTERN LUXE, MADE IN ASIA

Asked whether LVMH will shift production of luxury goods to low-cost China, Bernard Arnault, chairman of LVMH, famously replied, "No." That stirred a hornet's nest of debate – many people see lowering production costs as a competitive necessity – and even got a stinging retort from David Tang, founder of Shanghai Tang, a Chinoiserie brand now owned by Swiss luxury conglomerate Richemont.

For a product category that has European heritage and craftsmanship at its heart, it is indeed a prickly question. If a Louis Vuitton bag were to be made in China, carefully quality controlled, would it be a lesser bag? If instead of French artisans with generations of experience you had Chinese peasants trained yesterday doing the job, would it still be a genuine French luxury article? What if some of the parts, but not the whole, were made in Asia, would that sully its pristine image? What of consumer perceptions – assuming quality was indistinguishable – would a "made in China" label lower prestige and reverence? These are questions that lead to the ultimate question: What exactly is a luxury brand and when does it cease to be one?

For Asian consumers the answer is relatively clear: They are buying the luxury brand's European mystique and a "made in Europe" label is an important element of that. Will they come around to accepting a "made elsewhere" label? It will take time, but in an increasingly globalized world we believe a change in mindsets will happen. First, we see a perceptual separation of the softer elements – the product design, the brand concept, the marketing program, the quality management – from the actual manufacture; the former tightly associated with the brand, the latter seen as done under the brand's close supervision. Secondly, with improving manufacturing capabilities China's own "brand," currently perceived as cheap, low quality, and mass produced, will go up the ladder. China is building BMWs and flat-screen televisions, it is hosting the Olympics and sending people into space, it is putting up swank skyscrapers and magnetic levitation trains – all of which will eventually seep into a higher perception of Brand China itself. Thirdly, with "made in China" popping up in umpteen product categories, consumers will come to accept it as a matter of fact.

Indeed, for all the fuss, luxury brands have quietly started moving production out of Western Europe. Armani makes 18 percent of its Armani Collezioni line in Eastern Europe. Prada has some of its shoes stitched in Slovenia. Hugo Boss has its US$550 suits made in China. Valentino has its US$1,300 men's suits made in Egypt. Even Celine, part of Arnault's LVMH Group, has its Macadam line of handbags made in China. Here's the twist: Chances are these "made elsewhere" products are likely to be sold in Europe, whereas "made in Europe" products are shipped to Asia. Valentino, for example, rips the "made in Egypt" label from its suits before sending them to European stores – laws don't require a statement of where the product was made – while making suits in Italy for the Japanese market.[12] The Egyptian suits apparently do just fine in Europe, proving that "made in XYZ" is as much a perceptual battle as an actual quality problem. And the final irony is that Asian tourist-shoppers in Europe may well be buying "made in Asia" products.

The production cost differences between Western Europe and developing countries are so large that it is only a matter of time before a majority of production is outsourced. On labor costs alone the difference can be fortyfold – the hourly labor cost in the textile industry in China is 49 cents compared to US$19.82 in France and US$18.63 in Italy.[13] In Egypt it is 88 cents. The writing is on the wall: Outsource to a supplier, or even build your own manufacturing base in China under tight supervision, and you enjoy a significant cost advantage.

At the same time, cost pressures are mounting. Instead of the usual two-pronged spring/summer and fall/winter cycle, the fashion business is now working to faster and faster rhythms, thanks to new competition from the likes of Zara and H&M, which change their offering every month. (The fact that they are significantly lower priced and offer good adaptations of what's in only adds to their lure.) Luxury brands will have no option but to adapt and turn out newer products more often, with the consequent higher costs.

The fact that Asia is the largest luxury goods market adds to the practical need to have a manufacturing base here – it will lead not only to cost savings but also faster time to market.

Patrizio Bertelli, CEO of Prada, would simply prefer to have a "made by Prada" label, wherever country laws permit it. We agree – after all, wherever the physical product is manufactured, the brand is created only in the mind of consumers.

EMERGENCE OF THE ASIAN LUXURY BRAND

Remember that Italy was once the China of Europe. Sure, it had a crafts tradition, and visionaries like Salvatore Ferragamo and Guccio Gucci who started exporting in the 1930s, but for the most part Italy was a manufacturing hub, the country to which production was "outsourced"; as in fact it still is. It is only in the last 30 years that its designers have started hitting the headlines thanks to people like Giorgio Armani and Gianni Versace, and family businesses like Missoni and Fendi that revved up and made an international impact. The Milan fashion show began only in 1975, and has since grown in stature to stand shoulder to shoulder to Paris.

If Italy can go from manufacturing hub to fashion industry capital, can China do the same? Indeed, can Asia produce its own Armani or Versace who can wow at an international level? More importantly, will Asian luxury brands, as and when they emerge, find willing consumers in Asia itself?

In all fairness, Asia already has a smattering of world-class designers, notably from Japan, a country that produced maestros like Yohji Yamamoto, Kenzo, and Issey Miyake in the 1980s. Admittedly, Asia's influence fizzled out after that, except for Vivienne Tam and Shanghai Tang, brands that made an impact in the mid-1990s. What is more, none of the Asian brands has a brand stature or commercial influence on a par with Europe's best.

So what's holding Asia back on the designer front – why can't three billion people produce a fair crop of international-stature luxury brands? We believe the answer lies in the cultural conquest of the mind. Luxury brands are cultural products – they pitch the design sensibilities and artisanal craftwork of a country – and they find customers globally who are willing to use these products in their daily life. Would a French woman wear a cheongsam or a sari on a daily basis? No. But Asians wear

Western clothes every day, and hanker after Louis Vuitton bags and Cartier watches. The world watches Hollywood films and sits up goggle eyed on Oscar night, but how many outside of India care about Bollywood films or the Filmfare Awards?

Asia in particular looks up to the West. Even Yohji Yamamoto, Kenzo, and the like first made their name in Europe before finding acceptance in Asia – they have the recognition of the West, so they are good enough for us, was the unstated thinking. Vivienne Tam couldn't find takers for her designs in Hong Kong – she upped and left for New York, and only when she made it in the West did she find a clientele back home in Asia.

However, with the economic ascendancy of Asia – China and India in particular – its cultural impact will increase too. Major Western designers have drawn inspiration from China and India in recent years. Within China, after the first flush of adulation over everything Western, there is bound to be a resurgence of Chinese pride, a return to the country's cultural roots, albeit interpreted for modern times. In fact, you can already feel the signs – the contemporary Chinese art market, for instance, is simply exploding.

In the meantime, there is a hotbed of designer activity *within* each market and several names have a local following. Every country has a fashion week showcasing local talent, with participation that is enthusiastic if not yet at an international standard. Governments are pitching in with funds and determination to make the fashion industry grow. The Shanghai government is already highlighting the importance of moving up the food chain from being a manufacturer making loose change to a brand making big bucks. In the meantime, brands like Taiwan's Shiatzy Chen and Hong Kong's Blanc de Chine have opened their first stores in Paris and New York respectively.

But ultimately it is Europe's own luxury industry that is going to help give birth to Asia's. Manufacturing is already shifting to Asia, and with it will come know-how and experience. The Western luxe industry is building up retail networks and marketing offices across Asia, transferring retailing skills and marketing savvy to the region. In the meantime, Asian companies have started snapping up Western luxury brands – the French brand Lanvin is owned by Wang Xiao Lan, head of Taiwan's biggest publishing company; Guy Laroche was purchased by Hong Kong manufacturer YGM Trading; and Singapore's Christina Ong has formed a joint venture with Armani to make and sell Armani Exchange products. On the retail front, Hong Kong's Dickson Poon has bought the upscale British department store chain Harvey Nichols.

Put it all together and it is reasonable to expect a few Asian luxury brands in the coming years.

A Sunny Winter's Day in 2011

You step out on the street, joining the lunchtime crowd of fashionably dressed men and women. There's plenty of fur, Fendi, Dior. There are leather jackets, unmistakably Bottega Veneta. Those boots on that slim blonde are definitely the latest from Marc Jacobs. And the bags, almost every man and woman has a designer-label one. It's as if the fall/winter collection has spilt from the runways onto the streets, tossed together and mixed up, the latest Vuitton creation nestling against an Armani jacket, exquisite Chanel jewelry paired with a slinky Gucci dress, a new take on a men's suit by Prada worn with a striking Kenzo scarf. It's done with nonchalance and style.

You walk past a row of artistically designed flagship stores, each rising several floors high into the sky like so many Hermès Ginza buildings transported and lined up, each a living embodiment of the spirit of a brand, with happy shoppers streaming out laden with prominently branded shopping bags. You settle down at a lovely French restaurant overlooking the water, waiting for your client to join you. He strolls in fashionably late, his soft cashmere Hermès overcoat flapping behind him. You shake hands, noting the gleam of a Bulgari bracelet beneath the sleeve of his custom-tailored Zegna suit. He glances at his Breguet tourbillon, apologizing charmingly for his lateness, and then proceeds to make amends by ordering one of the finest meals you've had in a long time.

Paris? Rome? New York? London? Tokyo? It should come as no surprise that the city is Shanghai and your client the latest mainland Chinese technology baron to have entered the Forbes billionaire list at the age of 34.

Welcome to the cult of the luxury brand in twenty-first-century Asia.

NOTES

Introduction: Wear Your Sucess

1　Harper Lee, *To Kill A Mocking Bird* (New York: Warner Books Inc., 1960), p.30.
2　Sheridan Prasso & Diane Brady, "Can the High End Hold Its Own?" *International – Asian Business* (June 30, 2003).
3　Claire Kent, Sarah Macdonald, Mandy Deex, & Michinori Shimizu, "Luxury Goods: Back from Japan," *Morgan Stanley Equity Research – Industry Report* (November 14, 2001), pp.44–5.

1　The Rise of the Luxury Brand Culture

1　Information on the history of European fashion was drawn from the following sources: *The Fashion Book* (London: Phaidon Press, 1998); François Baudot, *A Century of Fashion* (London: Thames & Hudson, 1999); Colin McDowell, *Fashion Today* (London: Phaidon Press, 2000); Valerie Mendes & Amy de la Haye, *20th Century Fashion* (London: Thames & Hudson, 1999).
2　John Andrews, *The Economist: Pocket Asia* (London: Profile Books, 2002), pp. 81, 111, 153, 163.
3　Mendes & de la Haye, *op. cit*, p. 136.
4　*Ibid.*, pp. 78–9.
5　Melanie Flouquet & David Wedick, "LVMH: Wandering in LV Wonderland," JP Morgan, October 11, 2005.
6　Radha Chadha, Store visits, Via Condotti, Rome, June 2002.
7　From store locations on websites of Gucci, Louis Vuitton, Hermès, and Burberry.
8　Mendes & Da la Haye, *op. cit.*, p. 194.
9　"Pierre Cardin: China Could Lead 21st Century Fashion," *People's Daily Online*, May 20, 2002.
10　Gucci Group NV, Annual Report 2001, p. 15.
11　Jacques-Franck Dossin & Luca Cipiccia, "Post Field Trip Report," Goldman Sachs, October 25, 2005, p. 4.
12　Ken Young, "Consumption, Social Differentiation and Self-Definition of the New Rich in Industrializing Southeast Asia," in Michael Pinches (ed.), *Culture and Privilege in Capitalist Asia* (London: Routledge, 1999), pp. 56–85.
13　"Label Love – Regional (Hong Kong, Korea and Singapore): A Study of Luxury Brand Preferences," Synovate, February 2003, p. 10.
14　Chairman's message, LVMH Annual Report 2004, p. 6.
15　*Ibid.*
16　Ian Hawksworth, interview by authors, Hong Kong, February 27, 2003.
17　This section on "Conglomeration of Luxury" references information from the following sources: James B.Twitchell, *Living it Up: Our Love Affair with Luxury* (New York: Columbia University Press, 2002); Patty Huntington, "Power and the Fashion," *South China Morning Post*, July 21, 2001, Features section, pp. 1–3; Alan Ruddock, "Brand New," *HSBC Premier*, Spring 2002, pp. 7–10.
18　*International Directory of Business Biographies*, www.referenceforbusiness.com.
19　"LVMH achieves record results in 2005 – New objective of growth in 2006," company press release, March 2, 2006.
20　Antoine Colonna, Paola Durante, Mark Friedman, Lee Giordano, Nico Lambrechts, Rodolphe Ozun, & Virginia Genereux, "Lap of Luxury: Do Giant Stores Mean Giant Killers?" Merrill Lynch Global Fundamental Equity Research Department, February 20, 2002, p. 81.
21　Sagra Maceira de Rosen, Philip Mitchell, & Asli Tekin, "Gucci: Goodbye to De Sole and Ford," JP Morgan European Equity Research – Research Alert, November 4, 2003.
22　Grant McCracken, *Culture and Consumption: New Approaches to the Symbolic Character of Consumer Goods and Activities* (Bloomington: Indiana University Press, 1988). See chapter 5, "Meaning Manufacture and Movement in the World of Goods," pp. 71–89.
23　Tom Hilditch and Vivienne Chow, "Replay pleas," *South China Morning Post*, July 2, 2002, Features section, p.3.

24   Heike Phillips, "'Designer mask' hoax debunked by Gucci and LV," *South China Morning Post*, March 28, 2003.
25   The Fashion Timeline has been constructed with information from the following sources: *The Fashion Book*, pp. 35, 80, 201, 210, 376, 488; McDowell, *op. cit.*, pp.492–4; Kent *et al.*, *op. cit.*, p. 29; "Plaza 66 – Center of the Center," *Zoom China Plaza 66*, p. 10; "La Maison Hermès in Tokyo," *Discovery*, December 2001, p. 5; *Fruits* (London: Phaidon Press Limited, 2001), inside cover; James Sherwood, "For the Makers of Cool, a Hip vs. Heritage Dilemma," *International Herald Tribune*, October 9, 2002; "Grace Kelly: From Fashion Icon to Princess," *High Society*, British Film Institute Collections and Archives; Mendes & de la Haye, *op. cit.*, p. 126; Lance Morrow, "The Shoes of Imelda Marcos," *Time*, March 31, 1986; *A Century of Fashion*, p.97; www.fashionencyclopedia.com; company websites.

2 Finding Meaning in an LV Bag

1   Thorstein Veblen, *The Theory of the Leisure Class* (New York: Random House, 2001), p. 123.
2   Tim Lim, "A User's Guide to Fashion," *Post Magazine*, April 20, 2003, p. 25.
3   Serge Brunschwig, phone interview by the authors, Paris, April 24, 2003.
4   Federation of the Swiss Watch Industry FH, "World Distribution of Swiss Watch Exports," 2005.
5   Hong Kong Trade Development Council website, "Trade Fair at a Glance, Mobile Leisure – Hong Kong International Auto, Boat & Leisure Show," April 8–11, 2006.
6   Caroline Roberts, interview by Radha Chadha, Hong Kong, October 7, 2002.
7   John Andrews, *The Economist: Pocket Asia* (London: Profile Books, 2002).
8   Veblen, *op. cit.*, p. 29.
9   "World Wealth Report 2006," Merrill Lynch/Capgemini, p. 5.
10   *Ibid.*, p. 31.
11   Forbes China Rich List, 2002.
12   "World Wealth Report 2002," Merrill Lynch/Capgemini, p.8.
13   Datamonitor Global Wealth Model, phone interview with Alan Shields of Datamonitor, Australia, with Radha Chadha, February 24, 2006.
14   Datamonitor Global Wealth Management Model 2002, given by Simon Pearse, by email April 30, 2003.
15   Michael Burke, interview by the authors, Hong Kong, July 21, 2003.
16   Ian Hawksworth, interview by the authors, Hong Kong, February 27, 2003.
17   "Not in the Bag", *South China Morning Post*, December 10, 2005, p. C8.
18   "Hong Kong's Li Ka-shing Tops Forbes HK/Macau/Taiwan Richest Businessmen List," Yahoo! Business News, February 17, 2006.
19   James B. Twitchell, *Lead Us Into Temptation: The Triumph of American Materialism* (New York: Columbia University Press, 1999), pp. 204–5.
20   www.thislittlepiggywenttoprada.com; VOGUE.COM, Daily News, October 24, 2005.
21   Tom Doctoroff, *Billions: Selling to the New Chinese Consumer* (New York: Palgrave Macmillan, 2005), p. 28.
22   Nicole Fall, interview by Radha Chadha, Tokyo, November 19, 2002.
23   Jean Nicol, interview by Radha Chadha, Hong Kong, March 25, 2003.
24   Michael Pinches, "Cultural Relations, Class and the New Rich of Asia" in Michael Pinches (ed.), *Culture and Privilege in Capitalist Asia* (London and New York: Routledge, 1999) pp. 1–55.
25   *Ibid.*
26   Abhijit Majumder, "Ambani Towers as MTV Youth Icon," Times News Network, September 4, 2003. Additional information from Forbes India's Richest List.
27   Originally from Geert Hofstede, *Culture and Organizations* (London: McGraw-Hill, 1991) p. 129, reprinted in Harry C. Triandis, *Individualism and Collectivism* (Boulder: Westview Press, 1995).
28   Triandis, *op. cit.*
29   David Yau-fai Ho, "On the Concept of Face," *American Journal of Sociology*, Vol. 81, No. 4, January 1976, pp. 867–84.

3 Japan: An Insatiable Yen for Luxury

1   Claire Kent, Sarah Macdonald, Mandy Deex, & Michinori Shimizu, "Luxury Goods: Back from Japan," Morgan Stanley Equity Research – Industry Report, November 14, 2001, p. 14.
2   Melanie Flouquet & David Wedick, "European Luxury Goods. Looking Ahead: A Review of our Luxury Goods Universe," JP Morgan European Equity Research, January 10, 2006, p. 3.
3   Hata, Kyojiro, *Louis Vuitton Japan: The Building of Luxury* (New York: Assouline Publishing, 2004), p. 111.

4 "Chanel Opts for Absolute Luxury in Tokyo Store," *AFP*, December 1, 2004, www.expatica.com.
5 James Brook, "Roppongi Hills on the Cutting Edge of Tokyo," *New York Times*, January 7, 2004, as it appears on HoustonChronicle.com; and www. roppongihills.com, English and Japanese versions.
6 Kent *et al.*, *op. cit.*, p. 19.
7 "Sogo: Not Quite so Gone," *Japan Consuming*, Vol. 4, No.3, March 2003, p. 1.
8 Kent *et al.*, *op. cit.*, p. 20.
9 Alex Kerr, *Dogs and Demons: The Fall of Modern Japan* (London: Penguin, 2001), pp. 285–6.
10 *Ibid.*, p. 291.
11 Harry C. Triandis, *Individualism and Collectivism* (Boulder: Westview Press, 1995), p. 54. Yuhei Komoda's story originally from D. E. Sanger, "Student's Killing Displays Dark Side of Japan's Schools," *New York Times*, October 15, 1993.
12 Edward T. Hall, *Beyond Culture* (Garden City, New York: Anchor Books, 1977), pp. 63–4.
13 Originally from E. Hamaguchi, "A Contextual Model of the Japanese: Toward a Methodological Innovation in Japan Studies," *Journal of Japanese Studies*, Vol. II, 1985, pp. 289–321, as quoted in Shuzo Abe, Richard P. Bagozzi & Pradip Sadrangani, "An Investigation of Construct Validity and Generalizability of the Self Concept: Self-Consciousness in Japan and the United States," *Journal of International Consumer Marketing*, Vol. 8, No. 3/4, 1996, p. 97.
14 Keiichiro Nakagawa & Henry Rosovsky, "The Case of the Dying Kimono: The Influence of Changing Fashions on the Development of the Japanese Woolen Industry," in Mary Ellen Roach-Higgins, Joanne B. Eicher & Kim K. P. Johnson (eds), *Dress and Identity* (New York: Fairchild Publications, 1995), pp. 19–39.
15 Keiko Tanaka, "Japanese Women's Magazines: The Language of Aspiration" in Dolores Martinez (ed.), *The World's of Japanese Popular Culture: Gender, Shifting Boundaries and Global Culture* (Cambridge: Cambridge University Press, 1998), pp. 110–32.
16 Stephanie Assmann, "Japanese Women's Magazines: Inspiration and Commodity," *Electronic Journal of Contemporary Japanese Studies*, Discussion Paper 6, October 2003.
17 Ian Bickley, interview by Radha Chadha, Tokyo, November 19, 2002.
18 Ambar Brahmachary, interview by Radha Chadha, Tokyo, November 19, 2002.
19 Mark Blair, interview by Radha Chadha, Tokyo, November 18, 2002.
20 Bertrand de Streel, interview by Radha Chadha, Tokyo, November 19, 2002.
21 Masahiro Yamada, *Parasito Shinguru no Jidai* (The Age of the Parasite Singles) (Tokyo:Chikuma Shinsho, 1999).
22 Hiroyuki Takahashi & Jeannette Voss, "Parasite Singles: A Uniquely Japanese Phenomenon?" Japan Economic Institute Report, No. 31A, August 11, 2000, p. 3.
23 "Japanese Women Progress, but Hardly at All," *Japan Consuming*, Vol. 3, No. 10, October 2002, p. 11.
24 Yuko Naito, "More and More Men Are Getting Left on the Shelf," *Japan Times*, May 25, 2000.
25 Yukari Kagami, interview by Radha Chadha, Tokyo, November 22, 2002.
26 Hiroshi Ogawa, interview by Radha Chadha, Hong Kong, December 5, 2002.
27 "Louis Vuitton: A Fabulous 150-year Voyage," *LVMH, The Magazine*, September 15, 2004.
28 Serge Brunschwig, phone interview by the authors, Paris, April 24, 2003.
29 Hata, *op. cit.*
30 John Clammer, "Aesthetics of the Self: Shopping and Social Being in Contemporary Urban Japan," in Rob Shields (ed.), *Lifestyle Shopping: The Subject of Consumption* (London and New York: Routledge, 1992), pp. 195–215.
31 Kent *et al.*, *op. cit.*
32 Michael Causton, interview by Radha Chadha, Tokyo, November 21, 2002.
33 Suzy Wetlaufer, "The Perfect Paradox of Star Brands: An interview with Bernard Arnault of LVMH," *Harvard Business Review*, October 2001, pp. 116–23.
34 Hata, *op. cit.*, p 68.

4 Hong Kong and Taiwan: Yin and Yang of Luxury

1 Pierre Bourdieu, *Distinction: A Social Critique of the Judgement of Taste* (London and New York: Routledge & Kegan Paul, 1986).
2 David Evans, "Lai See – Seventh Heaven," *South China Morning Post*, April 30, 2002, Business 2 section, p. 3.
3 Store locators at www.gucci.com and www.hermes.com.
4 "Label Love – Regional (Hong Kong, Korea and Singapore): A Study of Luxury Brand Preferences," Synovate, February 2003, p. 19.
5 Kate Whitehead & Nury Vittachi, *After Suzi: Sex in South China* (Hong Kong: Chameleon, 1997), p. 107.

6   Taking sales within the country: Hong Kong's 7 million people support an imported luxury market of US$3.5 billion (a luxe per capita of US$500), while Japan's 127 million population supports a US$18.4 billion luxe market (a luxe per capita of US$145).

7   "A Statistical Review of Hong Kong Tourism 2001," Hong Kong Tourism Board, May 2002, pp. 31, 47.

8   Hong Kong Tourism Board research figures, and David O'Rear, "Shopping Spree," *The Bulletin*, Hong Kong General Chamber of Commerce, August 2004.

9   Paulene Hsia, interview by the authors, Hong Kong, May 21, 2003.

10   Ian Hawksworth, interview by the authors, Hong Kong, February 27, 2002.

11   Tom Hilditch, "Branded by their Bags," *South China Morning Post*, January 23, 2003, Features section, p. 6.

12   Shirley Lau, "Label Guide Targets Tongue-Twisted Tai-Tais," *South China Morning Post*, April 22, 2002.

13   James B. Twitchell, *Living it Up: Our Love Affair with Luxury* (New York: Columbia University Press, 2002).

14   Gordon Mathews, "Cultural Identity and Consumption in Post-Colonial Hong Kong," in Gordon Mathews & Tai-lok Lui (eds), *Consuming Hong Kong* (Hong Kong: Hong Kong University Press, 2001).

15   "Remembering Tiananmen," *South China Morning Post*, June 5, 2003.

16   May Sin-mi Hon, "Amid an Identity Crisis, Support for Taiwan Independence Is Up," *South China Morning Post*, January 8, 2003.

17   May Chan, "Local students Apathetic Towards China," *South China Morning Post*, October 2, 2003.

18   Jean Nicol, "Shopping for a new identity?" *South China Morning Post*, March 7, 2003.

19   Caroline Roberts, interview by Radha Chadha, Hong Kong, October 7, 2002.

20   Bonnie Gokson, phone interview by the authors, Hong Kong, May 23, 2003.

21   Jason Wordie, "Why Hong Kong Never Really Bade Darewell to its Concubines," *South China Morning Post*, June 29, 2003.

22   Nancy Valiente, interview by Radha Chadha, April 12, 2003.

23   Lawrence Elms, interview by Radha Chadha, Taipei, February 20, 2003.

24   Eva Chang, interview by Radha Chadha, Taipei, February 19, 2003.

25   Sophie Jiang, interviewed on behalf of the authors, January 2006.

5   China: From Mao Suits to Armani

1   Annie Wang, "People's Republic of Desire," *South China Morning Post*, May 14, 2003.

2   Mark O'Neill, "China's Richest Get Gloriously Rich," *South China Morning Post*, October 12, 2005.

3   Melanie Flouquet & David Wedick, "Luxury Goods: Reporting Back from China," JP Morgan, October 5, 2004.

4   "China: The New Lap of Luxury," Ernst and Young, September 2005.

5   "French Hope to Tap Luxury Market," Industry Updates, China Daily Information Company, November 2, 2005.

6   Hiroshi Ogawa, interview by Radha Chadha, Hong Kong, December 5, 2002.

7   Serge Brunschwig, phone interview by the authors, Paris, April 24, 2003.

8   Lynn Pan, interview by Radha Chadha, Shanghai, October 14, 2002.

9   Traditional full-length Chinese robe worn by men.

10   Pierre Bourdieu, *Distinction: A Social Critique of the Judgement of Taste* (London and New York: Routledge & Kegan Paul, 1986).

11   Hannah Beech, "Wretched Excess," *Time Asia*, Vol. 160, no. 11, September 23, 2002.

12   Rupert Hoogewerf, "2002 China Rich List," *Forbes Global*, November 11, 2002, pp. 56–7.

13   Yu Lei, interview by Radha Chadha, Shanghai, October 16, 2002.

14   Gu Ming, interview by Radha Chadha, Shanghai, October 14, 2002.

15   Charlotte Windle, "China Luxury Industry Prepares for Boom," BBC News, September 27, 2005.

16   Hung Huang, "Safety in Shopping," *Newsweek*, October 28, 2002.

17   There are many studies on *guanxi*, including Gan Wang, "Cultivating Friendship through Bowling in Shenzhen," in Deborah S. Davis (ed.), *The Consumer Revolution in Urban China* (Berkeley: University of California Press, 2000), pp. 250–67; David Wank, "Bureaucratic Patronage and Private Busiess: Changing Networks of Power in Urban China," in Andrew G. Walder (ed.), *The Waning of the Communist State: Economic Origins of Political Decline in China and Hungary* (Berkeley: University of California Press, 1995); Alan Smart, "Gifts, Bribes and Guanxi: A Reconsideration of Bourdieu's Social Capital," *Cultural Anthropology*, Vol. 8, No. 3, 1993, pp. 388–408.

18   James McGregor, *One Billion Customers: Lessons from the Front Lines of Doing Business in China* (London: Nicholas Brealey Pubishing, 2005), p. 97.

19   "Asia   and   the Pacific Regional   Highlights   –   Corruptions Perceptions Index   (CPI) 2005,"

Transparency International press release.

20 Kelvin Chan, "Asian Graft Worsens but HK Earns Second-Cleanest Mark," *South China Morning Post*, March 13, 2003.

21 "Foreign Investment Jumps by 54pc," *South China Morning Post*, March 14, 2003, p. A6.

22 Shanghai Foreign Investment Service Center website, www.sfisc.com/en/jjfz.asp.

23 Pamela Yatsko, *New Shanghai: The Rocky Rebirth of China's Legendary City* (Singapore: John Wiley & Sons, 2001), p. 187.

24 Peung Vongs, "China's New Concubines: The Kept Can be Keepers, Too," Pacific News Service, AsianConnections.com, January 22, 2004.

25 Allen T. Cheng, "Sex, Lies and Videotape", *South China Morning Post*, July 26, 2003.

26 Enoch Yiu, "Booming Shanghai Slowly but Surely Catching in the Pay Stakes," *South China Morning Post*, November 11, 2002.

27 Mark O'Neill, "Chinese Tourists Set to Rise as EU Prepares to Ease Visa Restrictions," *South China Morning Post*, January 26, 2003.

28 Jacques-Franck Dossin, Aaron Fischer, Luca Cippiccia, & Esther Silli, "Luxury Goods: Analysis of Chinese Demand Potential," Goldman Sachs, December 20, 2004.

29 Maggie Sun, interview by Radha Chadha, Shanghai, October 16, 2002.

30 "Asia Pacific Market and Mediafact," Zenith Optimedia, 2002, p. 44.

31 Gu Ming, interview by Radha Chadha, Shanghai, October 14, 2002.

32 Didi Kirsten-Tatlow, "Style Trial – China's Dolls Get in Vogue," *South China Morning Post*, 21 August 2005.

33 "Happy Graduation! From Madame Figaro," *Madame Figaro Newsletter*, Summer 2002.

34 "Xiao Kang: Dreams of Prosperity, Special Report on China," Jones Lang LaSalle, Q4 2005.

35 Eva Yu, interview by Radha Chadha, Shanghai, October 16, 2002.

36 Ben Simpfendorfer, "China Perspectives," JP Morgan, June 2004.

37 Tim King, interview by the authors, Hong Kong, February 27, 2003.

38 Cathy Holcombe, "Results Hide Huaneng's Links," *South China Morning Post*, April 12, 2002.

39 "Princelings March into the Corridors of Power," *South China Morning Post*, March 3, 2003.

40 Henri Li, interview by Radha Chadha, Beijing, October 17, 2002.

41 Richard Lee, interview by Radha Chadha, September 5, 2005.

42 Jeff Smith & Jean Wylie, "China Youth Define 'Cool'," *China Business Review*, Jul–Aug 2004.

43 Maris Gillette, "What's in a Dress? Brides in the Hui Quarter of Xi'an," in Deborah S. Davis (ed.), *The Consumer Revolution in Urban China* (Berkeley: University of California Press, 2000), pp. 81–106.

6 South Korea: Indebted to Luxury

1   Hyon-Ju Cho, interview by Radha Chadha, Soeul, December 12, 2002

2   Kim Hae-noon, "As Rich Prosper, Many More Are Left Back," *Korea Times*, December 2002.

3   Kim Wan-soon, "Shop Till You Drop," *Korea Times*, July 4, 2001.

4   Young-Chull Kim, interview by Radha Chadha, Seoul, December 13, 2002.

5   Sarah Kim, interview by Radha Chadha, Seoul, December 12, 2002.

6   Jihao Jang, "Economic Crisis and its Consequences," in Don Chull Shin, Conrad P. Rutkowski, & Chong-Min Park (eds), *The Quality of Life in Korea* (Dordrecht: Kluwer, 2003) pp. 51–70.

7   H.S. Jun, interview by Radha Chadha, Seoul, December 12, 2002.

8   Kim Hae-noon, *op. cit.*

9   "Label Love – Regional (Hong Kong, Korea and Singapore): A Study of Luxury Brand Preference," Synovate, February 2003, p. 20.

10 Gary Cross, *An All-Consuming Century* (New York: Columbia University Press, 2002); Juliet B. Schor, *The Overspent American: Why We Want What We Don't Need* (New York: Perennial, 1999); Daniel Horowitz, *The Morality of Spending: Attitudes Toward the Consumer Society in America, 1875–1940* (Ivan R. Dee, 1992); Thomas Princen, Michael F. Maniates, & Ken Conca (eds), *Confronting Consumption* (MIT Press, 2002); Goldian Vandenbroek & E.F Schumacher (eds), *Less Is More: The Art of Voluntary Poverty: An Anthology of Ancient and Modern Voices Raised in Praise of Simplicity* (Inner Traditions, 1996); Robert H. Frank, *Luxury Fever: Why Money Fails to Satisfy in an Era of Excess* (Princeton University Press, 2000); Juliet B. Schor, *OverWorked American: The Unexpected Decline of Leisure* (New York: Basic Books, 1993).

11 John de Graaf, David Wann, & Thomas H. Naylor, *Affluenza: The All-Consuming Epidemic* (San Francisco: Berrett-Koehler, 2002).

12 Laura C. Nelson, *Measured Excess: Status, Gender, and Consumer Nationalism in South Korea* (New York: Columbia University Press, 2000), p. 163.

13 Charles Scanlon, "The Price of Beauty in South Korea," BBC News, South Korea, February 3, 2005.

14 Amy White, "Man-made Faces Front Korean Campaigns," *Media*, March 11, 2005.

15 "Cheeky Fencer Loses Face," *Olympic Briefs, South China Morning Post*, January 22, 2006.
16 Sarah Kim, interview by Radha Chadha, Seoul, December 12, 2002.
17 "Korea's Credit-Card Push Backfires," *South China Morning Post*, December 8, 2002, Sunday Money section, p. 12.
18 "Firms Rue Days of Credit-Card Boom," *South China Morning Post*, May 24, 2003.
19 Cho Haejoang, "Living with Conflicting Subjectivities," in Laurel Kendall (ed.), *Under Construction: The Gendering of Modernity, Class, and Consumption in the Republic of Korea* (Honolulu: University of Hawaii Press, 2002), pp. 175–6.
20 Andrei Lankov, "Hwasin 1st Department Store," *Korea Times*, November 22, 2002.
21 Carter J. Eckert, "The South Korean Bourgeosie: A Class in Search of Hegemony," in Hagen Koo (ed.), *State and Society in Contemporary Korea* (Ithaca: Cornell University Press, 1993), p. 122.
22 Nelson, *op. cit.*, pp. 14–17.
23 H.S. Jun, interview by Radha Chadha, Seoul, December 12, 2002.
24 Park Moo-jong, "Moral Re-armament," *Korea Times*, November 2, 2003.
25 Cho Haejoang, *op. cit.*, p. 173.
26 *Ibid.*, p. 185.
27 Park Moo-jong, *op. cit.*
28 "Xiao Kang: Dreams of Prosperity, Special Report on China's Retail Future," Jones Lang LaSalle, Q4 2005.

7 Single-Season Sisters: Singapore, Malaysia, Thailand, Indonesia, and the Philippines

1 *The World Factbook 2006*, Central Intelligence Agency, https://www.cia.gov/cia/publications/factbook/index.html; Mangai Balasegaram, "Analysis: South-East Asia's Chinese," BBC News, August 29, 2001; authors' analysis of luxury market size.
2 "Label Love – Regional (Hong Kong, Korea, and Singapore): A Study of Luxury Brand Preferences," Synovate, February 2003, p. 5, 16.
3 "MasterCard MasterIndex and Insights Reports," A/P Region Reports, Insights 4Q, 2005, www.mastercard-masterindex.com.
4 Carolyn Hong, "Malaysia's Super Malls," *Straits Times*, February 13, 2006.
5 *Tourism Highlights 2005 Edition*, Madrid: World Tourism Organization.
6 Matt Armitage, "Gulf State of Mind," *South China Morning Post*, October 25, 2005.
7 "MasterCard MasterIndex and Insights Reports," *op. cit.*
8 World Tourism Organization *op. cit.*
9 Marion Hume, "Meet Me at the Mall," *Time*, Style & design supplement, Spring 2006.

8 India: The Next China?

1 Melanie Rickey, "Louis Vuitton New Delhi," Fashionwindows.com, April 7, 2003.
2 Carol Matlock & Manjeet Kriplani, "Bagging Some Big New Markets," *BusinessWeek*, March 22, 2004.
3 Xavier Bertrand, interview with Radha Chadha, September 2005.
4 "Luxury Goods and the Indian Consumer," FICCI Survey, January 2006.
5 Vijay Murjani, phone interview with Radha Chadha, October 2005.
6 Shobha De, interview by Radha Chadha, Munbai, September 21, 2005.
7 Rajesh K. Shukla, S.K. Dwivedi, Asha Sharma, & Sunil Jain, "The Great Indian Middle Class: Results from the NCAER Market Information Survey of Households," National Council of Applied Economic Research and Business Standard, 2004.
8 *Ibid.*
9 "Now 50,000 Indians in $1 mn-plus league," *Economic Times*, June 12, 2003; *World Wealth Report 2006*, Merrill Lynch/Capgemini, p. 31.
10 Forbes.com, Forbes World's Richest People 2004 and 2006 lists.
11 Gurcharan Das, *India Unbound: From Independence to the Global Information Age* (New Delhi: Penguin Books, 2002), p. 262.
12 Anuradha Mahindra, interview with Radha Chadha, September 2005.
13 Prasanna Bhaskar, interview with Radha Chadha, September 2005.
14 Forbes Ranks India's 40 Richest, Press Release, December 10, 2004, New York. www.forbesinc.com/newsroom/ releases/editorial/FG122004.doc.
15 Ashish Choradia, interview with Radha Chadha, September 2005.
16 Kamal Bharucha, interview with Radha Chadha, September 2005.
17 Ruchika Mehta, interview with Radha Chadha, September 2005.

18 Zainab Nedou, interview with Radha Chadha,New Delhi, September 24, 2005.
19 Radhika Bhalla, "Desi College Students Get that Heady IIM Feel," *Economic Times*, New Delhi, December 8, 2005.
20 Anuj Chopra, "Indian Graduates Are Top of the Class for Multinationals," *South China Morning Post*, April 24, 2006.
21 Alex Curuvilla, interview with Radha Chadha, Mumbai, September 20, 2005.
22 "India Diamond Mart Growth Is the Highest, says DTC," *Business Standard*, November 9, 2005, http://www.ibef.org/artdisplay.aspx?cat_id=441&art_id=8282.
23 "Retail Real Estate: Malls in India," *Images Retail*, 2005, www.imagesretail.com.
24 Shirin Batliwala, interview with Radha Chadha, Mumbai, September 19, 2005.
25 Martine Beaumont, interview with Radha Chadha, New Delhi, September 22, 2005.
26 Vinita Saxena, tour/interview with Radha Chadha, September 2005.
27 http://www.msnbc.msn.com/id/5297284/.
28 Anand Giridharadas, "Cool Begins to Catch up to India," *International Herald Tribune*, March 1, 2006.
29 Vishal Chawla, interview with Radha Chadha, New Delhi, September 24, 2005.
30 Shankar Aiyar, "Black Money Boom," *India Today*, December 19, 2005, p. 25.
31 *Ibid.*
32 N.R. Narayana Murthy, "Can India Be Free of Corruption?" *India Today*, January 23, 2006.
33 Nasreen Kabir & Jonathan Torgovnik, *Bollywood Dreams: An Exploration of the Motion Picture Industry and Its Culture in India* (Phaidon Press, 2003).
34 Anuj Kumar, "The Changed Trousseau," *The Hindu*, October 26, 2004, http://www.thehindu.com/thehindu/mp/2004/10/26/stories/2004102600520300.htm.
35 Anuj Kumar, "The Goose Is Yet to Turn Golden!" *The Hindu*, December 31, 2005. http://www.thehindu.com/thehindu/mp/2005/12/31/stories/2005123103510300.htm.
36 Arshiya Kapadia, "Fashion Panorama – Taking a Look at the History of Fashion in Hindi Cinema Down the Years," http://www.3to6.com/final_style/fedages_90.htm.
37 "Luxury Goods and the Indian Consumer," FICCI Survey, January 2006.
38 Madhurima Nandy, "*Vogue* Coming, *GQ* May Follow," Hindustan Times: Luxury Conference, January 14, 2006.
39 http://www.forbes.com/lists/2005/77/VX6G.html.

9 How the Cult Is Created

1 Jim Frederick, "Move Over, Andy Warhol," *Time*, May 26, 2003, pp. 42–4.
2 Serge Brunschwig, phone interview by the authors, Paris, April 24, 2003.
3 Georg Simmel, "Fashion," *American Journal of Sociology*, Vol. 62, No. 6, May, 1957, pp. 541–58.
4 Herbert Blumer, "Fashion: From Class Differntiation to Collective Selection," in Mary Ellen Roach-Higgins, Joanne B. Eicher, & Kim K.P. Johnson (eds), *Dress and Identity* (New York: Fairchild Publications, 1995), pp. 378–92.
5 Malcolm Gladwell, *The Tipping Point* (London: Abacus, 2000).
6 Melanie Flouquet & Philip Mitchell, "Bulgari: Watch the Growth," JP Morgan Equity Research – Company Report, October 18, 2002, p. 23.
7 Ian Hawksworth, interview by the authors, Hong Kong, February 27, 2003.
8 Wendy So, interview by Radha Chadha, Hong Kong, July 15, 2003.
9 "Cartier: High Jewellery" (advertisement), *South China Morning Post*, April 29, 2002, p. 5.
10 Gu Ming, interview by Radha Chadha, Shanghai, October 14, 2002.
11 Conrad Ng, interview by Radha Chadha, Hong Kong, June 9, 2003.
12 Ian Hawksworth, interview by the authors, Hong Kong, February 27, 2003.
13 Bonnie Gokson, phone interview by the authors, Hong Kong, May 23, 2003.
14 "Dress Like Beckham," *Ming Pao Weekly*, June 7, 2003, p. 58.
15 Bonnie Gokson, phone interview by the authors, Hong Kong, May 23, 2003.
16 Niki Law & P. Ramakrishnan, "Scarlet Dream Machine Leaves HK's Elite Green with Envy," *South China Morning Post*, July 26, 2003, City section, p. C1.
17 Kate Hippensteen, *Ganguro Girls: The Japanese "Black Face"* (Koeln: Koenemann, 2001), p. 7.
18 Kim Ju-young, "Getting the Goods, Real or Counterfeit," *Korea Times*, March 12, 2003.

10 Advent of the Genuine Fakes

1 Stacy Meichtry, "Special Courts to Put Fashion Fakes on Trial," *International Herald Tribune*, July 25, 2002.

2 Oh Hyuen-Suk, interview by Radha Chadha, Seoul, December 12, 2002.

3 "Label love – Regional (Hong Kong, Korea and Singapore): A Study of Luxury Brand Preferences," Synovate, February 2003, p. 25.

4 A word on terminology: Some of the academic literature distinguishes between counterfeit, pirated, and imitation brands on the basis of intention to deceive consumers. A counterfeit is made with the specific intention to deceive consumers into believing it is the original. A pirated version makes no bones about being a copy and the consumer is aware (from price and location cues) about its non-genuine status, hence they are also known as non-deceptive counterfeits. An imitation is also non-deceptive – it imitates the original but makes some small changes in logo (for example LW instead of LV) or design details that in certain Asian countries allow it to be legal, or at least on the fringe of legality. We have avoided this hair-splitting by simply calling them all fakes – the word commonly used by Asian consumers – and when we do use these terms, we do so interchangeably, as the intention to deceive is largely irrelevant as far as Asian luxe fake shoppers go. They know exactly what they are buying.

5 Alessandra Galloni, "Faked Out: As Luxury Industry Goes Global, Knock-Off Merchants Follow," *Wall Street Journal*, January 31, 2006, p. A1.

6 "Label love," *op. cit.*

7 *Ibid.*

8 Gerard Prendergast, Leung Hing Chuen, & Ian Phau, "Understanding Consumer Demand for Non-Deceptive Pirated Brands," *Marketing Intelligence and Planning*, Vol. 20, No. 7, 2002,pp. 405–16.

9 "Korea Third Largest Counterfeit Exporter, Handbags Top US Seizures," www.wgsn.com, January 25, 2002.

10 Frédéric Hubert, interview by Radha Chadha, Seoul, December 12, 2002.

11 Gail Tom, Barbara Garibaldi, Yvette Zeng, & Julie Pilcher, "Consumer Demand for Counterfeit Goods," *Psychology and Marketing*, Vol. 15, No. 5, August 1998, pp. 405–21.

12 Prendergast *et al.*, *op. cit.*

13 Velisarios Kattoulas, "Bags of Trouble," *Far Eastern Economic Review*, March 21, 2002, pp. 52–5.

14 Frédéric Hubert, interview by Radha Chadha, Seoul, December 12, 2002.

15 Stella Lee, "Strip-Searched and Handcuffed: Tourists Tell of Paris Nightmare," *South China Morning Post*, January 21, 2003, p. 3.

16 Kattoulas, *op. cit.*

17 "Fakes Threaten Fabric of Italian Society," ICC Commercial Crime Services, December 11, 2000.

18 Meichtry, *op. cit.*

19 Fionnuala McHugh, "Show of Confidence," *South China Morning Post*, July 3, 2003, City section, p. C5.

20 Arghavan Nia & Zaichkowsky, Judith Lynne, "Do Counterfeits Devalue the Ownership of Luxury Brands?" *Journal of Product and Brand Management*, Vol. 9, No. 7, 2000, pp. 485–97.

11 The Future of Luxury

1 Karl Treacy, "Luxury Lightens Up: At the IHT Conference," Fashionwindows.com, December 8, 2002.

2 Joanne Ooi, phone interview by Radha Chadha, February 17, 2006.

3 Michael Burke, interview by the authors, Hong Kong, July 21, 2003.

4 Bonnie Gokson, interiview by Radha Chadha, Hong Kong, May 23, 2003.

5 Sagra Maceira de Rosen, phone interview by Radha Chadha, London, July 9, 2003.

6 Ling Liu, "Mirror Mirror," *Time*, October 31, 2005.

7 Wendy So, interview by Radha Chadha, Hong Kong, July 15, 2003.

8 Ling Liu, *op. cit.*

9 Geethika Sasan Bhandari, "Out of the Closet," *India Today International*, December 5, 2005.

10 Laura Wenke, interview by the authors, Hong Kong, May 16, 2003.

11 Michael Burke, interview by the authors, Hong Kong, July 21, 2003.

12 Alessandro Galloni, Cecilie Rohwedder, & Teri Agins, "More Fashion Houses Drop 'Made In Italy' for 'Made Elsewhere'," *Asian Wall Street Journal*, September 28, 2005.

13 *Ibid.*

ACKNOWLEDGMENTS

This book has made us realize how much kindness there is out there. Researching ten diverse countries across Asia and pulling together a story that has never been told before has required inputs from hundreds of people. From company heads who explained their vision for Asia, to women who took us through their wardrobes, to people who helped with research and organization – everywhere, we have found enthusiastic support. Our heartfelt thanks to each one of you for your generosity.

This marathon wouldn't have been possible without the encouragement of many special people. To Nick Brealey, our publisher, whose astute guidance and firm handling was just what we needed. To Sally Lansdell who polished the rough edges and edited the book with much TLC. To Neil Herndon for commenting on early drafts and believing in us. To Paulene Hsia for introducing us to the academic resources at the Hong Kong Polytechnic University. To Pin Lee who helped research and shape the material on Southeast Asia. To Dr. Kaori O'Connor whose belief in the project kept us going through some rough times. To Jennifer Crewe for her guidance and gracefulness. To fellow Bauhinians – Julia Courtenay-Tanner, Marie Webster, Leong Kwong Yee, Helena Hu, Vicki Button, Janette King, Angela Leung – whose love and level-headed advice was invaluable. To Jane Camens who taught us how to "just write."

To Christina Tang who calmly organized dozens of photos, charts, permissions, and got the manuscript just so. To Carmen Law and Vienna Tsang who tirelessly supported this endeavor from day one. To Elizabeth Chung, Jessie King, Gloria Wong, Jessie Lee, Kareem Jalal, and Forest Au for getting the innumerable elements of the book together. To Marlyn for a perpetual supply of tea and sympathy.

To some very special women who opened up doors for us in many countries: Caroline Roberts, Prasanna Bhaskar, May Kim, Korakot Srivikorn, and Devyani Raman.

Those who generously supplied photographs have been credited where appropriate in the text.

Above all, our thanks to the people we interviewed, whose experiences, feelings, thoughts, and ideas have been the primary source for this book. They have ranged from global heads of major luxury brands to country managers, from functional heads – retail, operations, sales, marketing, public relations – to store managers and salesgirls. Equally, we have spoken with a cross-section of experts from associated areas – shopping malls and department stores, agents and distributors, fashion and lifestyle media, advertising agencies and consumer research companies, luxury equity analysts and retail consultants, and, of course, consumers. These are some of the people we'd like to acknowledge:

Indira Anggraini, Om Arora, Keiko Bang, Richa Bansal, Shirin Batliwala, Martine Beaumont, Douglas Benjamin, Xavier Bertrand, Kamal Bharucha, Ian Bickley, Sanjeev Bijli, Mark Blair, Zhang Bo, Anne-Cannelle Boyer, Ambar Brahmachary, Serge Brunschwig, Michael Burke, Michael Causton, Mickey Chak, Hazel Chan, Lawrence Chan, Eva Chang, Srivikorn Charn, Vishal Chawla, Richard Chen, Ginny Cheng, Peter Cheung, Hyon-Ju Cho, Iris Cho, Mi-Jung Cho, Hye-Jeong Choi, Ashish Chordia, Yolanda Choy, Antoine Colonna, Wisnu Darmawan, Shobha Dé, Sagra Maceira de Rosen, Bertrand de Streel, Hugues de Vautibault, Neil Ducray, Michele du Lac, Jean-Michel Dumont, Lawrence Elms,Nicole Fall, Jeffrey Fang, Melanie Flouquet, Philippe Fortunato, Hubert Frederic, Clarissa Fu, Nandini Ghosal, Kitty Go, Kenneth Goh, Bonnie Gokson, Danielle Han, Ian Hawksworth, Andrew Ho, Sandra Hu, Sophie Jiang, HS Jun, Hee Jung Jung, Yukari Kagami, Victoria Kalb, William Kee, Claire Kent, Sarosh Khatib, Mathew Kichodhan, Hea Sung Kim, Sarah Kim, Young Chull Kim, Cicilia King, Tim King, Sumiko Kokubu, Julia Kuo, Jackson Kwok, Lars Larsen, Tansy Lau, Sandra Law, David Lee, Janet Lee, Kam Lee, Michael Lee, Richard Lee, Yu Lei, Henri Li, Justin Lin, Alan Liu, Tricia Liu, Adrienne Ma, Marina Mahathir, Anuradha Mahindra, Deli Makmur, Cathleen Maleenont, Suparna Malhotra, Stephanie Means, Ruchika Mehta, Choi Min, Gu Ming, Kiki Moran, Superna Motwane,Vijay Murjani, Chanda Narang, Zainab Nedou, Jean Nicol, Conrad Ng, William Ng, Kamal Oberoi, Hiroshi Ogawa, Hyeun-Suk Oh, Bee Bee Ong, Joanne Ooi, Lynn Pan, Dong-Min Park, Simon Pearse, Marielou Phillips, Mark Prendergrast, Shen Qing, Vicky Ross, Yogesh Samat, Kanan Sangani, Dian Sastrowardoyo, Vinita Saxena, Frank Schurman, Jaideep Sengupta, Alan Shields, Ambika Shrivastava, Janet Shuen, Pranay Sinha, Wendy So, Anjali Sondhi, Cha Hee Sook, Yuki Srikarnchana, Maggie Sun, Yuko Suzuki, Alistair Tan, Alex Tang, Jill Telford, Gaynor Thomas, Roger Tredre, Siri Udomritthiruj, Henny Udy, Neeraj Vadera, Jenny Wang, Laura Wenke, Adrian Wong, Beryl Wong, Evangeline Wong, Hazel Wong, Marvin Wong, Hae-Ryung Woo, Bao Yifeng, Christina Yu, Eva Yu.

INDEX